MW01058202

TURNING POINTS WITH GOD

TURNING POINTS WITH GOD

365 Daily Devotions

DAVID JEREMIAH

Tyndale House Publishers, Inc.
Carol Stream, Illinois

Visit Tyndale online at www.tyndale.com.

TYNDALE and Tyndale's quill logo are registered trademarks of Tyndale House Publishers, Inc.

Turning Points with God: 365 Daily Devotions

Copyright © 2014 by David Jeremiah. All rights reserved.

Previously published in 2010 as *Pathways: Your Daily Walk with God* by Turning Point Ministries. First printing by Tyndale House Publishers, Inc., in 2014.

Cover pattern copyright © Pulvas/iStockphoto. All rights reserved.

Interior pattern copyright © vectorkat/Shutterstock. All rights reserved.

Author photograph taken by Alan Weissman, copyright © 2013. All rights reserved.

Designed by Ron Kaufmann

Published in association with Yates & Yates (www.yates2.com).

ISBN 978-1-4143-8048-3

Printed in China

20	19	18	17	16	15	14
7	6	5	4	3	2	1

Teach me, O LORD, the way of Your statutes,
And I shall keep it to the end. . . .
Make me walk in the path of Your commandments,
For I delight in it.

PSALM 119:33, 35

He leads me in the paths of righteousness
For His name's sake.

PSALM 23:3

If you have the capability of watching television with connection to cable stations, you have probably found that at any time of the day there are more than a dozen different types of exercise and diet plans claiming to provide the user with a "new you" and a "better life." While it cannot be ignored that most of us would be better off if we exercised more and ate extra servings of fruits and vegetables each day, a change in that part of our lifestyle would not ultimately affect our eternal rewards or resting place.

The path that many have chosen to follow is often not the path leading to God. As believers, we must use care to get on the path that leads only to God. Once we become believers in Christ, we need to keep our eyes on Him, not looking to the right or left, but looking only to Him for our daily walk.

Some people look at the pathway that leads to God and reject it, thinking the pathway is too narrow, but those who trust in God know that the path is safe and secure because our Savior is leading the way. In Micah 6:8 we read, "He has shown you, O man, what is good; and what does the LORD require of you but to do justly, to love mercy, and to walk humbly with your God?"

In *Turning Points with God: 365 Daily Devotions*, there is a devotional with a Scripture reference for each day of the year, leading you to the path filled with mercy and truth. As we seek God and His Word, He is faithful to meet us, guide us, and direct our footsteps in "the paths of righteousness" (Psalm 23:3).

All the paths of the LORD are mercy and truth,
To such as keep His covenant and His testimonies.

PSALM 25:10

David Jeremiah
Fall 2014

JANUARY

All the promises of God in Him are Yes, and in Him Amen,
to the glory of God through us.

2 CORINTHIANS 1:20

Today's a day like any other—the sun comes up and goes down, and time clicks along at its usual speed. But with our calendars and in our minds, today marks a new beginning, a chance to press the restart button of life. In His grace, God gives us a new day every twenty-four hours and a new year every 365 days. He's the Lord of new beginnings and the King of fresh hope.

Think of it this way. Without Christ, we're like passengers on a doomed ship, sailing into the night, fearing the storms ahead and hoping there's enough entertainment on board to distract us from our forebodings. But with Him in our hearts, we're sailing under a heavenly flag with the Captain of our salvation at the helm. We know this will be a good voyage—a great year—even if there are choppy waters along the way.

We can face the future without fear, for "all the promises of God in Him are Yes, and in Him Amen, to the glory of God." This is the *year* that the Lord has made! We will rejoice and be glad in it (Psalm 118:24).

To Thee our prayers addressing, still ask Thee
for Thy blessing: Grant us a joyful year.
PAUL EBER, THE LUTHERAN HYMNAL

> The Helper, the Holy Spirit, whom the Father will
> send in My name, He will teach you all things.
>
> JOHN 14:26

It has become increasingly difficult in this day and age for us to hear our own thoughts and feelings. In order to keep up with life, it seems we must travel at the speed of society, never stopping to take a deep breath and listen to the Holy Spirit's leading. As frustrating as this may be, it is not a new challenge.

When Jesus walked the earth, He was constantly surrounded by a multitude of people; but He knew that the most important relationship He could invest in was with His Father, for it was His Father's voice that would lead and guide Him. Therefore, He spent a large amount of time in prayer and conversation with God.

A woman was once asked how she knew the voice of the Spirit. She answered, "How do you know your husband's step and your child's cry from the steps and cries of all others?" For her, the voice of the Spirit was as familiar as the unique sounds of her husband and child.

In order for us to be sensitive to the Spirit's leading, we must spend time getting to know His voice, because the more intimately we know Him, the easier it will be to hear His voice above all others.

Father, quiet my heart and mind so I may hear
the leading of Your Spirit in my life.

January 3

WHO'S SERVING WHOM?

No one can serve two masters; for either he will hate the
one and love the other, or else he will be loyal to the one and
despise the other. You cannot serve God and mammon.

MATTHEW 6:24

Pretend you are given a bank account that receives a fresh deposit
of $86,400 every day. You are free to spend the money any way
you want, but the unspent balance is not carried forward to the next
day. Regardless of what you've spent by the end of the day, the balance is reset daily at $86,400. What would you do with such a bank
account?

Now consider the fact that each dollar represents the number
of seconds in one day: 24 hours per day x 60 minutes per hour x
60 seconds per minute = 86,400 seconds. Once they are "spent," they
disappear, and the balance is reset at 12:00:01 a.m. every day. Some
people become slaves of what they have; they live frantic lives, trying
to spend time, talent, and treasure before they lose those things. In
so doing, they become servants of things that are supposed to serve
them. Jesus said we cannot serve both God and money (things of this
world). And the only way to keep our priorities straight is to have a
wise, godly plan: today I'm going to glorify God this way with my time,
talent, and treasure. Do you have such a plan?

To have a plan and not follow it is the same as having no plan
at all.

We view all of life as a sacred trust to be used wisely.
MORAVIAN COVENANT FOR CHRISTIAN LIVING

4 | TURNING POINTS WITH GOD

January 4

IT TAKES A LIFETIME

Solid food belongs to those who are of full age . . .
those who by reason of use have their senses exercised
to discern both good and evil.

HEBREWS 5:14

It has been said that the new birth takes but a moment; spiritual maturity takes a lifetime.

Nowhere is this more clearly demonstrated than in the Parable of the Sower, in which Jesus warns His disciples about the many different ways God's Word will be received. He says that when some people receive the Word, it is snatched away by the devil as soon as it enters their hearts. Others receive the Word with joy but fall away during a time of temptation. Still others hear the Word yet remain entangled in the cares of the world, making it impossible for them to bring any spiritual fruit to maturity. Finally, Jesus tells of the ones who, "having heard the word with a noble and good heart, keep it and bear fruit with patience" (Luke 8:11-15).

Spiritual maturity is the result of a continual process of growth that takes time and patience. If we remain rooted in the Word and nourished through prayer and fellowship with the Lord, we will surely see our faith grow as never before.

Christians should move on to spiritual maturity. We must feast on the meat of God's Word and put into practice the lessons we have learned. It's the only way to grow up.

HADDON W. ROBINSON

REMEMBERING AND RESPONDING

> I will delight myself in Your statutes; I will not forget Your word.
>
> PSALM 119:16

Which is easier—to make your bed in the morning or leave it unmade? To volunteer for a community project or to watch TV all weekend? To vacuum, wash, and wax your car or to leave it dirty? The easiest choices reflect the Second Law of Thermodynamics: all work processes tend toward a greater state of disorder over time without fresh injections of new energy.

This law applies both physically and spiritually. Leave your car parked in a field, and it will rust and fall apart. The same will happen in your spiritual life. Forget to maintain the spiritual disciplines you have learned, and in time, your life will take on increasing signs of disorder. That's what happened to the Israelites when they returned to Jerusalem from captivity. They started out obeying God, but in time they lost their energy. They stopped giving Him the first and best from their lives, and the prophet Malachi called them to account (Malachi 3:7-9). If you can see disorder creeping into your life, make sure you are still giving your first and best to God.

Remembering and responding to God's will takes new energy every day. That's just the way it is this side of heaven.

People need to be reminded more often
than they need to be instructed.
SAMUEL JOHNSON

January 6

$5.50

Take careful heed to yourselves, that you love the LORD your God.

JOSHUA 23:11

When James E. Carter was pastor of University Baptist Church of Fort Worth, he shared an experience from younger days that he called "the greatest tithing testimony I ever observed." He said that one day as he waited to see the manager of a grocery store, a widow came in to cash her old-age-assistance check for $55. The grocer asked how the woman wanted it, and she replied, "It doesn't make any difference, just so I have a five-dollar bill and a fifty-cent piece."

As the owner gave her the money, Carter noticed that she tucked the coin into the bill, folded it up, and placed it in a corner of her purse. "This is my tithe," she explained. "I put it separate so I won't spend it." It was a scene Carter never forgot, and it later influenced his own faithfulness in the area of tithes and offerings.

That elderly woman didn't have much, yet she honored God with her substance and with the first part of all her income. Stewardship is not merely a matter of obligation; it's a matter of love. When you love someone, you want to express your gratitude and affection.

Our stewardship should be faithfully accomplished and lovingly practiced. Are we as wise as that wise, old widow?

You have to start tithing when you have little
if you are going to tithe when you have much.

JAMES E. CARTER

Your word I have hidden in my heart.

PSALM 119:11

Michael Billester visited eastern Poland during the late 1930s and gave a Bible to one of the villagers while there. The villager read it, was converted, and passed the book to two hundred others, who were all saved by reading it. When Billester returned in 1940, the group gathered for a worship service, and he suggested they all recite a few Bible verses they had memorized. A man stood up and said, "Perhaps we have misunderstood. Did you mean verses or chapters?" Billester was astonished to learn that the people had memorized whole chapters of the Bible. In fact, together, the two hundred villagers knew almost the entire Bible by heart.

We need to view committing Scripture to memory to be as important as the Polish villagers did. Value its power and effectiveness in our lives as much as Jesus did when He used it to defend Himself against Satan's temptations.

Remember the true purpose for memorizing Scripture—"that you may be able to stand against the wiles of the devil" (Ephesians 6:11)—and make it a priority to spend some time etching the Word of God into your heart and mind.

Nobody ever outgrows Scripture; the Book widens and deepens with our years.

CHARLES HADDON SPURGEON

EYES ON THE PLATE

Jesus sat opposite the treasury and saw how
the people put money into the treasury.

MARK 12:41

How would you feel if your pastor followed the ushers down the aisle one Sunday, inspecting what you put into the offering plate? In a sense, that's exactly what Jesus did in Mark 12. He watched carefully as the people brought their money to the Temple and offered it to the Lord. After all, it was His Father's house, and He had good reason to inspect what was taking place.

We think that what we do with our money is our business; but it's God's business, and He doesn't apologize for watching with intense interest to see what we do with our income.

Notice, however, that Jesus wasn't impressed with the *amounts* given that day but rather with the *heart attitudes* of the givers. The least giver of all, the widow who had only two mites, was the largest giver in Jesus' book, "for they all put in out of their abundance, but she out of her poverty" (Mark 12:44).

Remember, Jesus is watching, and the Lord is interested in how we manage our money. After all, we're simply His stewards.

――――――― ༺☙༻ ―――――――

The most obvious lesson in Christ's teaching is that there is no happiness in having or getting anything, but only in giving.

HENRY DRUMMOND

GOD'S GREAT SECRET

This is the victory that has overcome the world—our faith.

1 JOHN 5:4

The British preacher Charles Spurgeon had a magazine entitled *The Sword and the Trowel* that was popular throughout England in the late 1800s. In one issue, Spurgeon wrote an editorial in which he compared life with a maze, indicating that life is confusing, but there is a key. Spurgeon wrote, "God himself has spoken the great secret. It is one word, 'FAITH'—faith in Jesus for pardon, faith in the Father for providential provision, faith in the Holy Spirit for all grace. In ordinary pathways men walk by sight; but in the way of life, if we would prosper, we must walk by faith. God is unseen, but He is ever near to those who trust Him. His promises are sure, and He is ever ready to fulfill them. He hears and answers the prayers of believing souls. There is reality in His presence, and true support in His comforts."

If you've entrusted God with your eternal soul, don't you think you should trust Him with your daily needs and burdens? Shouldn't you trust Him enough to give your offerings? Enough to claim the daily strength He offers?

Yes, yes, and yes again! Faith is God's secret for the Christian, and you can trust Him today.

Follow the clue of faith without leaning to your own understanding, and you shall thread the maze of life.

CHARLES HADDON SPURGEON

> [John the Baptist] said: "I am 'the voice of one
> crying in the wilderness: "Make straight the way
> of the LORD,"' as the prophet Isaiah said."
>
> JOHN 1:23

God said, "I AM WHO I AM" (Exodus 3:14). Abraham said, in effect, "I am old" (Genesis 17:17). Jacob said, "I am Esau your firstborn" (Genesis 27:19). Moses said, "I am not eloquent" (Exodus 4:10). Gideon said, "I am the least in my father's house" (Judges 6:15). Ruth said, "I am a foreigner" (Ruth 2:10). Nehemiah said, "I am doing a great work" (Nehemiah 6:3). Jesus said, "I am the door, the light, the bread, the good shepherd" (John 10:9; 8:12; 6:35; 10:14). Paul said he was the chief of sinners (1 Timothy 1:15).

How would you answer the question "Who are you?" When John the Baptist was asked that question, he spoke without hesitation: "I am the voice." John was not confused, and he did not stutter. He knew exactly who he was and what he was called to do. He was called to be "the voice"—to announce the coming of the Kingdom of God and of the Messiah of Israel. It didn't bother John that he wasn't the Messiah. The only thing that would have bothered him was not to speak clearly. John was a satisfied man, confident and content in his knowledge of himself.

Can you say the same about yourself? Take a moment and fill in the blank: "I am _____." Then decide, "How happy am I with my answer?" If you're not sure about either, ask God for His insight.

Self is the opaque veil that hides the face of God from us.

A. W. TOZER

January 11
AN UNNATURAL CHOICE

> You love righteousness and hate wickedness;
> therefore God, Your God, has anointed You with the
> oil of gladness more than Your companions.
>
> PSALM 45:7

People who live exclusively in one culture live much of their lives subconsciously. That is, they are so used to the ways and traditions of their homeland that they don't have to think before acting. But when they go to another culture to visit or to live, every choice is a conscious one, because everything is new. They have left their natural state and are living in an unnatural one.

Jesus' "culture" was one of intimate fellowship with the Holy Spirit. From eternity past He had lived with the Father and the Spirit in heaven, and when He came to earth, that relationship continued. He was human and had to submit to the Spirit, but He had no sinful nature that battled against the Spirit. Not so with us. Our sinful, fleshly nature is not naturally at home with the Spirit. So, moment by moment, we have to choose to obey Paul's command to "be filled with the Spirit" (Ephesians 5:18). Jesus is our example, but the choice is ours.

Choose today to be filled with the Spirit. It is a humanly unnatural choice, but one that your new, Christlike nature will gladly agree with.

God commands us to be filled with the Spirit; and if we are
not filled, it is because we are living beneath our privileges.

D. L. MOODY

January 12
THE KOHINOOR DIAMOND

> When they had eaten breakfast, Jesus said to Simon Peter,
> "Simon, son of Jonah, do you love Me more than these?"
> He said to Him, "Yes, Lord; You know that I love You."

JOHN 21:15

Queen Victoria received the stunning Kohinoor diamond as a gift from a maharajah when he was a boy. Later, as a grown man, this maharajah visited Queen Victoria again and asked for the stone. Taking the diamond and kneeling, the maharajah gave it to the queen again, saying, "Your Majesty, I gave you this jewel when I was a child, too young to know what I was doing. I want to give it to you again in the fullness of my strength, with all my heart and affection and gratitude, now and forever, fully realizing all that I do."

Many Christians gave their hearts to Jesus as children, but how wonderful to come with greater knowledge and maturity and to say, "I know I'm Yours, but I want to be Yours with all my heart and affection, fully realizing all that I do."

Sometimes we need to renew our vows to Him, just as Peter did following the Resurrection. Sacrificing for God is worth it, and a renewed commitment is like a fresh start with a tried-and-true Friend.

Are you His in the totality of your life?

Ah, yield Him all; in Him confide
Where but with Him doth peace abide?
GERHARD TERSTEEGEN

WHAT I WOULDN'T GIVE

A day in Your courts is better than a thousand.
I would rather be a doorkeeper in the house of my
God than dwell in the tents of wickedness.

PSALM 84:10

You know it when it happens. It might be someone you feel could mentor you in your vocation. Or it might be a new friend with whom you establish an immediate connection. Or it might be the love of your life. Regardless of when and how, there are times when you think, "I'd give up next week for the chance to spend one more day with this person!"

The author of Psalm 84 felt that way, only he was ready to give up more than a week: he was ready to give up a thousand days for one day in God's presence. A young Jewish man, Andrew, and his friend followed Jesus as soon as they met Him, and they spent the rest of the day hanging out with Him (John 1:35-40). That's how most people today feel when they meet Jesus—they just can't get enough of Him. A lot of people who are not followers of Christ would probably become Christians if they could just make contact with His irresistible presence. Many have given up a lot to spend as much time with Him as they can.

It's also easy to take His presence for granted, to forget what a pure pleasure Jesus can be, one-on-one. If it's been awhile since you gave up something to be with Him, consider doing so soon.

The Christian tastes God in all his or her pleasures.

J. I. PACKER

January 14

THE FOUR LEPERS

> We are not doing right. This day is a day of
> good news, and we remain silent.
>
> 2 KINGS 7:9

The lepers in 2 Kings 7 were trapped between the Syrian army and the town of Samaria, which was under siege and slowly starving. During the night, the Lord created a cacophony of sounds, like the onrush of a mighty army. Jolted awake, the Syrians fled in confusion, leaving their plunder behind.

When the lepers ambled into the Syrian camp, they were amazed to find it deserted with all the food and treasures there for the taking. But while ransacking the booty, a thought struck them: *We are not doing right. This is a day of good news, and we remain silent.* Running to the city gates, they shared their message and told the good news—the enemy had been defeated, food was available, and the nightmare had ended in victory.

The lesson is hard to miss. In a desperate world, we have Good News! How can we then remain silent? Today someone needs the gospel that we've discovered for ourselves, and now is the time for sharing. Someone today is waiting to see or hear Jesus through you.

The devil loves "curing" a small fault by giving you a great one.

C. S. LEWIS

WHEN OPPORTUNITY KNOCKS

As we have opportunity, let us do good to all,
especially to . . . the household of faith.

GALATIANS 6:10

Merriam-Webster.com defines *opportunity* as "a favorable combination of circumstances, time, and place." But Thomas Edison said, "Opportunity is missed by most because it is dressed in overalls and looks like work." Francis Bacon wrote, "A wise man will make more opportunities than he finds." And writer Thomas Peters warned, "If a window of opportunity appears, don't pull down the shade."

The Bible also talks about opportunities, but with a difference. While the world looks for opportunities for success, the Christian looks for opportunities for servanthood.

We don't know how much time we have left on earth, so it's important to do what we can for the Lord at every opportunity. Is there someone you can help today? Is there a friend needing a favor, a call, a note, or a financial gift? Is there a little extra money in your purse that could advance the Kingdom? Is there a neighbor who needs a plate of cookies or a word of counsel?

Unexpected windows of opportunity will appear today, giving you the chance to serve and to give. Look for those occasions, and don't pull down the shade.

Opportunity rarely knocks on your door. Knock rather on opportunity's door if you ardently wish to enter.

B. C. FORBES

[Jesus said,] "Believe also in Me.... Keep my commandments."

JOHN 14:1, 15

One day a struggling Christian visited his minister. "I've read books on discipleship," said the visitor, "taken theology courses by correspondence, and stayed up late doing assignments for my Bible study group. But I'm confused. Can you tell me how to be a victorious Christian?"

Pulling a hymnal from its shelf, the pastor opened to these words: "Trust and obey, for there's no other way to be happy in Jesus, but to trust and obey."

That's it in a nutshell. Sometimes the Christian life isn't easy, but it's always simple. We walk by faith and live in obedience. Godliness is the simplicity of taking God at face value, doing what He says, and watching Him bless our lives.

Sometimes in trusting and obeying, we find ourselves wanting to do God's part as well as our own. Perhaps you have a problem that seems to have no answer—maybe a wayward child. You can do your part to pray, love, and communicate. But then you must trust God to do His part to convict, convert, and change.

Every problem is an opportunity to trust; every situation is an opportunity to obey. And when it comes down to it, every part of our Christian life falls into those two categories: trust and obey!

For the favor He shows, for the joy He bestows,
Are for them who will trust and obey.

JOHN H. SAMMIS

SMOKE SIGNAL

Now no chastening seems to be joyful for the present, but
painful; nevertheless, afterward it yields the peaceable fruit
of righteousness to those who have been trained by it.

HEBREWS 12:11

A story is told of a shipwreck survivor who washed up on a deserted island. After he had been there a few days, he built himself a hut and prayed to God for rescue. Each day he anxiously looked out over the horizon as he waited for God's deliverance in the form of a passing ship. One day, after returning from a hunt for food, he discovered that his hut had been consumed in flames. He was devastated and believed it to be the worst thing that could have happened to him on the island; everything he had was gone. The next day, however, a ship arrived and the captain said, "We saw your smoke signal."

Sometimes, when it seems our whole world is crumbling, it is difficult to believe that God is at work on our behalf. But just when we think all is lost, God unfolds His plan and teaches us that He had it under control the whole time.

Friends, God's ways are not our ways. His thoughts are unlike our thoughts. His plans are so much bigger than we could ever imagine or dream. Let Him work in His unique way, and watch as His beautiful plan is revealed in your life.

*Keep praying, but be thankful that God's
answers are wiser than your prayers!*
WILLIAM CULBERTSON

January 18
IN DUE SEASON

> Let us not grow weary while doing good, for in due
> season we shall reap if we do not lose heart.
>
> GALATIANS 6:9

Seeds can remain dormant for years until conditions are right for growth. For example, while excavating the palace of Herod the Great, archaeologists at Masada found seeds that had hibernated for two thousand years. In 2005, one of the seeds—a Judean date palm—was planted, and it germinated. It's the creative genius of God that designed this latent potential into such a small seed.

As we go through life, we're to sow the seeds of the gospel, but it may take a while for them to germinate. William Carey was seven years in India before seeing his first convert. It took seven years in Burma before Adoniram Judson saw his first conversion. Robert Morrison toiled for seven years before the first Chinese national was brought to Christ. Robert Moffat waited seven years to see evidence of the moving of the Holy Spirit on his mission field in Africa.

It might take seven years or seventy—but there's power in the gospel seed, and our job is to plant. So don't lose heart. "He who continually goes forth weeping, bearing seed for sowing, shall doubtless come again with rejoicing, bringing his sheaves with him" (Psalm 126:6).

---

*How rich his reward who has waited patiently
till the seed should spring and grow up!*

A. J. GORDON

January 19
FAILURE AND FAITH

Moses said to God, "Who am I that I should go to Pharaoh,
and that I should bring the children of Israel out of Egypt?"

EXODUS 3:11

When it comes to heroes revered by three world religions, no individual shines brighter than Moses. The deliverer of the Hebrews from Egypt is mentioned more times in the New Testament than any other Old Testament figure and is the most prominent prophetic figure in the Muslim Koran. What is it about Moses that makes him a hero to so many?

The juxtaposition of failure and faith is probably at the heart of Moses' mystique. We can identify with Moses' failure as a young man guilty of manslaughter. And we can also identify with his fears and doubts when God called him to be the deliverer of his Jewish people. But beyond identifying with Moses' humanity, we revere his faith: he was brave, faithful, outspoken, compassionate, and loyal. And he kept his eye on the eternal prize. Moses was all we know we are and all we know we want to be. He was a failure, but he was also faithful. And God honored his faithfulness instead of rejecting him for his failure. If you have failed, don't give up. God used Moses, and He wants to use you.

The worst failure is failing to act on (have faith in) that which you know to be true.

You don't drown by falling in the water;
you drown by staying there.
EDWIN LOUIS COLE

Brethren, I do not count myself to have apprehended; but
one thing I do, forgetting those things which are behind
and reaching forward to those things which are ahead.

PHILIPPIANS 3:13

The British equivalent of the American phrase to "eat crow" is to "eat humble pie." In the Middle Ages, servants in the lord's hall of a castle would be fed a pie made from the inner organs of a deer— the deer's *umbles*. This lower-class meal supposedly served as the inspiration for eating "humble pie." Whether eating crow or humble pie, either is an exercise in humiliation.

The apostle Paul found himself in a humiliating situation when he embraced as his own Savior and Lord the very Jesus he had established a reputation for persecuting. *Humiliation* is akin to being humbled, and Paul was certainly humbled by his experience with Jesus on the Damascus road (Acts 9). Everything he had been advancing toward in Judaism he had to forget. Embracing Jesus as the Jewish Messiah meant he had to say, "I'm sorry. I was wrong." Looking back, Paul saw the error of his ways. Looking forward, he saw the expectation of His praise.

If you need to say "I'm sorry" to God or to another person, don't put it off. It could be the dividing point between the past and the future.

The self-righteous never apologize.
LEONARD RAVENHILL

January 21

SPEAKING OUT

[Jesus] said to those who sold doves, "Take these things away!
Do not make My Father's house a house of merchandise!"

JOHN 2:16

"Cheap grace is the mortal enemy of our church." Those are the opening words of *The Cost of Discipleship*, written by German pastor-theologian Dietrich Bonhoeffer. Many know him as the author of this and other books, but not all know that he was executed by hanging in 1945 for the part he played in resisting Adolf Hitler's Nazi government in Germany. As a Christian, he spoke out for what he knew to be true, though it cost him his life.

We could call Dietrich Bonhoeffer a modern Christian activist—and we could call Jesus of Nazareth the first one in history. When Jesus saw that the Temple in Jerusalem had been turned into a marketplace where unscrupulous vendors were profiting from the guilty consciences of worshipers, His righteous anger took over. Driving them out, He cleansed His Father's house and incurred the wrath of those who valued their own interests above God's (John 2:13-22).

The day may come when you are faced with something you know is not right. The temptation is just to pass by, to look the other way. But if you don't speak up for God, who will? Be thankful that Jesus was willing to speak up for righteousness even though it cost Him His life.

It costs to follow Jesus Christ, but it costs even more not to.

UNKNOWN

> Do not be conformed to this world, but be transformed
> by the renewing of your mind, that you may prove what
> is that good and acceptable and perfect will of God.
>
> ROMANS 12:2

"It's the real thing." "Just do it." "Keeps going and going and going." The right words have the ability to stick like glue in our memory. In the Christian world, a phrase written by Englishman J. B. Phillips in his translation of Romans 12:2 has attained the same legendary status: "Don't let the world around you squeeze you into its own mold."

That's a beautiful word picture of the pressure the world system puts on those who live in it. That happened to Lot, the nephew of Abraham. The two men's flocks were overgrazing the land, and their owners decided to separate. Lot looked around and chose ready access to the enticements of the wicked city of Sodom, while Abraham went in the opposite direction (Genesis 13:5-13). That decision led to a future of futility for Lot and almost cost him his life on more than one occasion. Have recent decisions you've made conformed you more to the values of God's Kingdom or to those of the world?

Being conformed is good (Romans 8:29) as long as the mold is a godly one.

Unless there is within us that which is above us,
we shall soon yield to that which is about us.

P. T. FORSYTH

January 23

YOU CHOOSE FIRST

Remember the words of the Lord Jesus, that He said,
"It is more blessed to give than to receive."

ACTS 20:35

Many large law firms and individual attorneys try to take on a certain amount of *pro bono* work each year. Work done *pro* (Latin, "for") *bono* (Latin, "the good") is accomplished without charge for clients who are unable to afford an attorney. It is legal work done "for the common good," given away by the attorney at no charge to the client. From Jesus' perspective, *pro bono* work of any sort— legal or other kinds—is a blessed event since "it is more blessed to give than to receive."

When Abraham and Lot decided to go their separate ways in the land of Canaan, Abraham took the initiative and told his nephew, "Choose whatever portion of land you want, and I'll take what remains." Lot chose the best for himself—the well-watered plains of the Jordan River Valley—while Abraham moved farther into arid Canaan. But because Abraham placed a priority on giving instead of receiving, God blessed him in many ways. Lot, on the other hand, created a legacy of worldliness and sin for himself and his family (Genesis 13). Whenever you have the opportunity, give! It is an act God promises to bless.

Giving is a God kind of choice. Whenever we choose to act like God, blessings will follow.

When it comes to giving, some people stop at nothing.

UNKNOWN

Whatever your hand finds to do, do it with your might.

ECCLESIASTES 9:10

A humorous sermon illustration gives an example of the wrong attitude toward work:

Manager: "I'm sorry I can't hire you, but there isn't enough work to keep you busy."

Applicant: "You'd be surprised how little it takes."[1]

This is clearly an exaggeration in order to make a point, but some people truly have this mentality toward work. They don't take pride in the performance of their responsibilities; rather, they take pride in their professions. According to the Bible, however, this is backward thinking. Even servants should do their best, not caring about their lowly positions but working with integrity for their real Master, who is God (Colossians 3:23).

It is difficult not to get caught up in the pursuit of power and position. After all, in the eyes of the world, these are highly prized and sought-after treasures. But when we lock eyes with Jesus and turn a deaf ear to the praises of men, the only thing that truly matters is doing everything with the motivation of pleasing and honoring Him. It is from God that the gift of work comes, so it is to Him that our efforts should be aimed.

Do everything in its own time. Do everything in earnest;
if it is worth doing, then do it with all your might.

ROBERT MURRAY M'CHEYNE

---

[1] *Pulpit Helps*, Sept. 1990 (Chattanooga: Pulpit Helps).

GOOD, BETTER, BEST

Better is a little with the fear of the LORD,

than great treasure with trouble.

PROVERBS 15:16

Have you studied the "Better" verses in the book of Proverbs? There are more than twenty of them—"Better is a dinner of herbs where love is, than a fatted calf with hatred." "Better is a little with righteousness, than vast revenues without justice." "Better is a dry morsel with quietness, than a house full of feasting with strife" (Proverbs 15:17; 16:8; 17:1).

It's not that the "fatted calf," "vast revenues," and the "house full of feasting" are all wrong. It's just that they're inferior. In our materialistic age, we forget that true wealth is gauged by our enjoyment of what we have, not by our longing for more. It's measured by its worth to God's Kingdom.

In *Strengthening Your Grip*, Charles Swindoll points out that money can buy medicine but not health. It can purchase a house but not a home. It can buy companionship but not friends. It can provide a bed but not sleep.

Keep God first in your life and in your finances. Thank Him for the things you have, but remember: "Better is the poor who walks in his integrity than one perverse in his ways, though he be rich" (Proverbs 28:6). It is God who "gives us richly all things to enjoy" (1 Timothy 6:17)—and that's the best thing of all.

Money can buy the good life, but not eternal life.

CHARLES SWINDOLL

> Peter and John answered and said to them, "Whether it is right in
> the sight of God to listen to you more than to God, you judge. For
> we cannot but speak the things which we have seen and heard."

ACTS 4:19-20

During periods of history such as the Reformation and the Crusades, it was not unusual for some who professed to be true Christians to take this attitude when persecuted for their faith: "Recant now, repent later!" In other words, deny Christ today in order to stay alive—then ask God's forgiveness later.

Peter denied Christ when he was accused of being one of His disciples, but he didn't do it hypocritically. Yes, he feared for his life. But there is no evidence that his perspective was so crass as to casually deny Jesus and then ask His forgiveness later. No, Peter was caught in an unplanned and unprepared-for moment of sheer terror—one that would haunt him forever. But Jesus forgave Peter a few days after His resurrection and commissioned him to take care of His sheep (John 21:15-19). Looking back, Peter saw fear; looking forward, he saw faith. If you have failed Christ along the way, remember that He died to forgive the past and to empower the future.

Failures forgiven become a formidable foundation for future faith.

I think that if God forgives us we must forgive ourselves.

C. S. LEWIS

BE A PHILIPPIAN

> My God shall supply all your need according
> to His riches in glory by Christ Jesus.
>
> **PHILIPPIANS 4:19**

Hermeneutics is the science of interpretation, especially of sacred or other literary texts. The English word comes from the Greek word *hermeneuo*, "to translate" or "interpret." A key principle of hermeneutics is that interpretation must be done in context. For example, verses in the Bible must be interpreted in context to avoid misunderstanding.

Taken out of context, Philippians 4:19 can appear to be an absolute promise of God to supply every Christian's financial needs. But Paul wrote these words to the church at Philippi, which had given sacrificially to him while he was in jail. The promise of God's generous financial blessing was made to those who themselves had given generously and sacrificially. It is a perfect illustration of reaping what is sown (Galatians 6:7). The Philippians understood the principle that all we have comes from God, and they used what was theirs to bless others. God, in turn, Paul promised, would bless them and meet their needs. So if you have needs, be a Philippian. Develop a lifestyle of blessing others, and then look expectantly for God to bless you.

Let your life be a living verse to be interpreted in a context of generosity.

It is in giving that we receive.

FRANCIS OF ASSISI

ADVANCING THE CAUSE

Go home to your friends, and tell them what
great things the Lord has done for you.

MARK 5:19

The thirty-four-year-old general was striking and handsome, with blue eyes and reddish hair. Major General George McClellan gave the impression of strength and vigor, and as one historian said, "Dashing about on a magnificent horse, he seemed omnipresent" on the battlefield. He had a brilliant mind, and when Abraham Lincoln told him that the supreme command of the army was on his shoulders, he responded, "I can do it all." But he actually did very little; for all his organization and personal charisma, he seemed unable to advance his forces or to attack. Finally Lincoln gave up on him, saying, "If General McClellan does not want to use the army, I would like to borrow it for a while."

Many Christians are well equipped, well trained, and well financed. No generation of believers has ever been more affluent or had more tools, more plans, or more programs. But are we really attacking the enemy and advancing the cause? Are we winning our friends to Christ? Are we witnessing for Him?

God has placed us where we are in order to reach those around us and tell them what He has done in our lives.

---

*I tell you when the Spirit of God is on us for service, resting
upon us, we are anointed, and then we can do great things.*

D. L. MOODY

COMMON BLESSINGS
AND BURDENS

He makes His sun rise on the evil and on the good,

and sends rain on the just and on the unjust.

MATTHEW 5:45

In Matthew 5:45, Jesus speaks of God's fairness and graciousness. Every morning the sun gives another day's life to all humanity, whether evil or good. Refreshing showers fall on the lawns of committed Christians and of their pagan neighbors. While some blessings are reserved only for the children of God, others are common to the entire world.

In the same way, some burdens are borne by believers, such as persecution or sorrow over lost souls. But other burdens are shared by all humanity, and being a Christian doesn't make us immune from trials. Even seasoned Christians need to remember this, or else we'll find ourselves thinking, *If God loves me so, why am I in such painful straits? Why don't other people have these problems?*

Sorrow is universal, but for the believer, it is redemptive, because God turns it to good. Dr. F. B. Meyer wrote, "In suffering and sorrow God touches the minor chords, develops the passive virtues, and opens to view the treasures of darkness, the constellations of promise, the rainbow of hope, the silver light of the covenant."

Trust Him today, and rejoice in His mercies whether it's sunny or raining.

Let us believe that God's love and wisdom
are doing the very best for us.

F. B. MEYER

> Most of the brethren in the Lord, having become confident by
> my chains, are much more bold to speak the word without fear.

PHILIPPIANS 1:14

When the great preacher Harry Ironside complimented the cook at a conference center on her biscuits, she gave him a valuable lesson: "The flour itself doesn't taste good, neither does the baking powder nor the shortening nor the other ingredients. However, when I mix them all together and put them in the oven, they come out just right."

The same can be said for many of the circumstances in which we find ourselves in life. Limitations, pain, shortages, injustice, failure—none of those "ingredients" are palatable by themselves. But in every case, when the circumstances of life are mixed together by God's providence, something good results. When the apostle Paul found himself imprisoned for preaching the gospel, it had to be distasteful! Yet the result was that his brethren were emboldened to preach the gospel even more. It is the believer's responsibility to focus not on the "ingredients" but on the entire "recipe" to see what God is preparing.

If your circumstances are not palatable at the moment, step back and see if you can't find a reason to rejoice in the end result.

The whole point of the letter to the Philippians
is: I rejoice, now you do the same!

J. A. BENGEL

INSURANCE OR ASSURANCE?

You shall rejoice in every good thing which the LORD
your God has given to you and your house, you and
the Levite and the stranger who is among you.

DEUTERONOMY 26:11

Taken as a whole, no group of Christians lives such a prosperous existence as the church in America. Yes, individual believers experience personal setbacks and occasional sufferings, as do believers in other lands. For the most part, however, there is a cushion of affluence and provision in the West that lessens the pain of our temporary sufferings.

But do affluence and prosperity make us better believers? In explaining why the church was growing so much more rapidly in Africa than in America, one African bishop said, "In America you have blessed insurance. In Africa all we have is blessed assurance!" In other words, the less people have, the more they tend to see their need for God. The converse is also true: the more people have materially, the less they tend to see their need for God. We ought to be on our knees thanking God for all our many blessings. But while we're there, we ought to ask Him not to let our blessings obscure our vision of and dependence on the "Blesser."

If you have more of God's provisions than you have of God Himself, it may be time for an assurance check.

---

*Wherever riches have increased, the essence of
religion has decreased in the same proportion.*

JOHN WESLEY

FEBRUARY

IMAGE MAKEOVER

> Whom [God] foreknew, He also predestined to be
> conformed to the image of His Son, that He might
> be the firstborn among many brethren.
>
> ROMANS 8:29

There is a growing epidemic in Western cultures: dissatisfaction with one's body image. Men and women are reporting that they are not happy with how they look. Painful attempts at finding a solution run the gamut from daily workouts in the gym to eating disorders and plastic surgery. Even then, the goal for too many remains elusive.

We're not happy with our physical image, but God is not happy with our spiritual image. Fortunately, He has a solution: He has chosen us to be eternally conformed to the image of His own Son, Jesus Christ. But just as "no pain, no gain" applies to diet and exercise, it applies in the spiritual realm as well. Here is God's principle for reshaping our spiritual image: He will not spare present pain if it means eternal profit. The Old Testament patriarch Jacob, long a deceiver, is a good example. God used Jacob's uncle Laban, who was himself a shady dealer, to teach Jacob some hard lessons (Genesis 29–30). If you're experiencing pain, see if you can find the eternal profit that it is designed to produce.

Based on how long each will last, which of our images—body or soul—should get most of our attention?

Pain can either make us better or bitter.

TIM HANSEL

February 2
CURING ME-FIRST-ISM

[An elder must not be] a novice, lest being puffed up with
pride he fall into the same condemnation as the devil.

1 TIMOTHY 3:6

The late theologian Francis Schaeffer wrote that when we violate one of the Ten Commandments, we actually violate two. Violating any other commandment means first violating the tenth: "You shall not covet." To want another god, another day to work, to fail to honor our parents, to steal from another person . . . all are expressions of covetousness—the desire to take for ourselves.

Pride is likely another type of "root" sin, since it appears from Scripture that it was the first sin ever committed. Before the creation of man, when Satan was the "son of the morning" (Isaiah 14:12), he rose up in pride against God and declared he would "be like the Most High" and "exalt [his] throne above the stars of God" (Isaiah 14:13-14). Pride is the motivation that tempts us to put ourselves at the center of the universe, to make ourselves more important than anyone else. Pride leads to conflict and condemnation with us, just as it did with Satan. When you encounter conflict in your path, check first to see if pride is involved.

Repenting of pride—"me-first-ism"—releases us to heal conflicts by becoming servants to others.

It is . . . pride that feedeth at the root of all the rest of our sins.
RICHARD BAXTER

Do not rejoice in this, that the spirits are subject to you, but
rather rejoice because your names are written in heaven.

LUKE 10:20

We know about the twelve apostles, but Jesus had seventy other disciples who walked with Him and whom He sent on a ministry tour in Luke 10. In verse 17, these seventy returned with joy, saying, "Lord, even the demons are subject to us in Your name." Jesus acknowledged their success but gave a gentle warning. Their joy should be based on more than their perceived success; it should rest in the simple fact that their names were written in the Lamb's Book of Life.

Ministry is a difficult task, the results of which are not always immediate or obvious. If we base our morale on visible success, we may become proud of our accomplishments or discouraged over momentary setbacks or prolonged struggles. Whatever we're doing for the Lord, however great or small, the Lord expects us to be faithful regardless of the setting and outcome—and to rejoice in one thing above all: our names are written in heaven!

*All believers are through grace . . . enrolled among His family;
now this is a matter of joy, greater joy than casting out devils.*

MATTHEW HENRY

> [Jesus] replied, "If you have faith as small as a mustard
> seed, you can say to this mulberry tree, 'Be uprooted
> and planted in the sea,' and it will obey you."

LUKE 17:6, NIV

Many Christians know that George Müller cared for more than ten thousand orphans in his lifetime in England and was a man of astounding faith. But not all know that he was not always such a faithful man. His early life in Prussia was marked by lying, gambling, drinking, and imprisonment for fraud. At age fifteen he gave his attention to cards and drinking with friends while his mother lay dying.

This is the same George Müller who, later in life, would sit his orphans down at a table with empty bowls and thank God for the food He was going to provide. And God always did. George Müller's life goes to show that faith is a learned discipline. Faith does not come naturally, but supernaturally. The natural man believes when he sees, but the supernatural man sees when he believes. And Jesus taught that it does not take as much faith to see as we might think—faith as small as a tiny seed can see mountains moved.

If you are lacking great faith today, exercise the faith you have, and then ask God for more. Faith, fruit, more faith, more fruit—believing God is a self-perpetuating experience.

───────── ⟐ ─────────

Faith is not belief without proof, but trust without reservation.
D. ELTON TRUEBLOOD

February 5

STRENGTH BY FAITH

When we were still without strength, in due
time Christ died for the ungodly.

ROMANS 5:6

Imagine the foolishness of a politician or social reformer going to a cemetery to preach his message: "Be better, be just, be tolerant, be committed, be stronger," he would call out. The response he got would be the same as when the living are exhorted to live strong lives without the empowerment of God. Physically dead people have no strength by which to act, nor do those without the Holy Spirit.

When Peter and John went to the Temple in Jerusalem one afternoon, they encountered a man crippled from birth begging for money outside the Temple gate. He was totally without strength in his legs—he was carried there daily by his friends. Peter and John had no money to give him, so they gave him what he needed more: strength and an opportunity to praise God. The man's healing and his exuberant praise paint a beautiful picture of what Christ has done for us. When we lacked spiritual strength because of our sin, Jesus died for us, removing the sin and giving us new strength in the Spirit. All we needed to do was believe in Him.

You do not need your own strength to receive God's strength. You need only do what the crippled man did: believe God's message and rejoice.

We have no power from God unless we live in the
persuasion that we have none of our own.

JOHN OWEN

TRUE AND TRUTH

Jesus said to [Thomas], "I am the way, the truth, and the
life. No one comes to the Father except through Me."

JOHN 14:6

Dr. Albert Mohler Jr., president of the Southern Baptist Theological Seminary, offers these thoughts on truth in our day: according to postmodern theory, truth is not universal, is not objective or
absolute. Every culture establishes its own truth. All truth is socially
constructed. Truth is made, not found. The role of the intellectual is to
deconstruct truth claims in order to liberate the society.

Pontius Pilate had a postmodern mind-set—he asked Jesus,
"What is truth?" (John 18:38). Just a few hours earlier, Jesus answered
that question when talking to His Father in heaven: "Your word is
truth" (John 17:17). Jesus might have been thinking of the words of
the psalmist in Psalm 119:160: "The entirety of Your word is truth."
Instead of turning to God for truth, postmodernists make it up as they
go along—what's true today may not be true tomorrow. But our God
never changes (James 1:17). What was true yesterday is true today
and will be forever (Hebrews 13:8). Don't wonder what is true—turn
to the One who is true and the truth.

Knowing Jesus means you can spend your time living the truth,
not looking for it.

Let us rejoice in the truth, wherever we find its lamp burning.
ALBERT SCHWEITZER

HONEST BONES

In all things [show] yourself to be a pattern of good works;
in doctrine showing integrity, reverence, incorruptibility.

TITUS 2:7

Rachel Rohanna, a high school freshman in Pennsylvania, won a regional golf tournament by having the lowest score—even after being assessed a two-stroke penalty for hitting the wrong ball. Once she discovered she had mistakenly hit another player's ball, she called a penalty on herself and informed the tournament officials. Her grandfather, a teaching pro, later said, "I know Rachel. She plays fair."

In the game of golf, players keep their own scores. That means integrity—a self-imposed honor code—is the rule of the day. How nice it would be if integrity were the rule of the day at every level of life. It should be, but unfortunately it is not. Honesty, sincerity, integrity—these should be traits of the person who traffics in truth as a follower of Jesus Christ. When Jesus first met Nathanael, He said of him, "There's a real Israelite, not a false bone in his body" (John 1:47, *The Message*). What a wonderful assessment of someone's character! Make it your mission in life to have people say of you, "I know you—you always play fair."

Being an honest person means you never have to remember who you were or what you said when you were with someone.

---

*Character is always lost when a high ideal is sacrificed
on the altar of conformity and popularity.*
CHARLES HADDON SPURGEON

STORMS OF OBEDIENCE

[After preaching the gospel, they returned,] strengthening
the souls of the disciples, exhorting them to continue
in the faith, and saying, "We must through many
tribulations enter the kingdom of God."

ACTS 14:22

One of the unanswered questions in the book of Acts is why young John Mark deserted Paul and Barnabas on their first missionary journey (Acts 13:13). Could it have been because of their trials on the island of Cyprus? A sorcerer named Elymas tried to prevent Paul and Barnabas from preaching to the Roman official (Acts 13:8). Maybe John Mark wondered if their mission was truly in the will of God.

It's natural to think that obedience leads to tranquillity. But just the opposite is often true: obedience to God can result in trials. Storms often come because we have been obedient, not disobedient. That was certainly true of those in the New Testament. The four Gospels and Acts recount that those who were wholly committed to fulfilling God's calling encountered one attack and obstacle after another. Every follower of Jesus should get this matter settled up front: the deeper we go into the Kingdom of God, the more likely we are to meet with resistance.

If you are obeying God and are in a storm at the same time, you are following in the footsteps of the heroes of faith.

*I find that doing the will of God leaves me with
no time for disputing about His plans.*
GEORGE MACDONALD

February 9

GOD'S RESTORATION PROJECT

He is faithful ... to cleanse us from all unrighteousness.

1 JOHN 1:9

According to *Christian History and Biography*, visitors to the Sistine Chapel once saw Michelangelo's beautiful frescoes marred by muted colors and dark shadows. Many people assumed the artist had painted them that way on purpose. The real culprits, however, were grime and pollution.

A major restoration project in the 1980s showed what a thorough cleaning can do. Using computer technology and chemical solvents, experts repaired damaged sections and wiped away accumulated grime. The result was a brilliant, colorful room that reveals Michelangelo's genius and leaves us breathless with his vivid images.

Some people have been caked with grime so long they think that's the way they're supposed to be. They need a thorough cleansing. Those dysfunctional attitudes, destructive habits, harsh words, self-defeating actions, and secret sins—they can all be wiped away by the blood of Jesus Christ.

He forgives thoroughly and He forgives eternally; and if He forgives like that, shouldn't we be merciful and forgiving to others? Do you need His forgiveness for yourself? Do you need to forgive someone else?

Wipe away the grime, and see the beauty of the Master Artist.

---

*Cleansed and made holy, humble and
lowly, right in the sight of God.*
ELISHA HOFFMAN

BAREFOOT CHRISTIANS

[Stand,] having shod your feet with the
preparation of the gospel of peace.

EPHESIANS 6:15

Soldiers in antiquity sometimes faced a frightening prospect. Their enemies would set spikes into the ground that would slice open a soldier's foot like a razor. Roman forces, therefore, wore sturdy boots called *caligae*, which were less likely to be punctured.

It won't do to be a barefoot Christian. We must be shod with the preparation of the gospel of peace. Our feet, in the Scriptures, are symbols of going. Both Isaiah and Paul speak of the beautiful feet of those bearing good tidings. Jesus told us to go into all the world with the good news of Jesus Christ.

There is a certain safety when we're shod with evangelistic zeal. When we're determined to share Christ, our feet are, as it were, protected from many of the spikes the devil plants in our pathway. Every problem becomes a pulpit, and every sorrow becomes a sermon. Whatever the devil throws at us becomes an occasion to witness for Christ. Paul told the Philippians, "The things which happened to me have actually turned out for the furtherance of the gospel" (Philippians 1:12).

Don't go barefoot into battle. Fit your feet with the gospel of peace.

The Gospel of peace . . . brings the joyful tidings of
peace betwixt God and man by the blood of Jesus; and
this is so welcome to the trembling conscience.
WILLIAM GURNALL, THE CHRISTIAN IN COMPLETE ARMOR

OUR NEED, GOD'S CHOICE

Immediately [Jesus] talked with them and said to
them, "Be of good cheer! It is I; do not be afraid."

MARK 6:50

Two artists were asked to create original paintings that represented their ideas of peace. One artist painted a beautiful mountain scene: gorgeous colors, deer in the meadow, a bubbling stream—the absence of conflict. The other artist painted a dark picture of a violent storm that was sending the ocean waves crashing against the face of a cliff. But there, tucked into a nook in the cliff, was a bird resting quietly, its face buried beneath its wing, totally at rest in the midst of the storm.

There are two ways God can answer our prayers when we seek peace. He can remove the storms, as in the first painting, or He can give us peace in the midst of the storms, as in the second. Twice in His relationship with His disciples, Jesus gave them peace during storms. Once, He calmed the storm (Mark 4:35-41), and once He came to them in the midst of the waves (Mark 6:45-52). We are free to ask Him to remove the storms of life, but we grow deeper when He leaves us in them and gives us His peace to make it through.

If you are seeking peace right now, you can have it. But it's best to let God decide how to give it to you.

Stayed upon Jehovah, hearts are fully blest;
finding, as He promised, perfect peace and rest.
FRANCES RIDLEY HAVERGAL

> If a man is overtaken in any trespass, you who are
> spiritual restore such a one in a spirit of gentleness,
> considering yourself lest you also be tempted.

GALATIANS 6:1

Have you criticized anyone recently? Complained about another's actions, attitudes, or words? In *Edges of His Ways*, Amy Carmichael suggests filtering our words through three sieves: "Is it true? Is it kind? Is it necessary? All of us who have tried to remember these three sieves, and have used them, know what a help they are. We are sorry when we ever forget them."

Paul's advice in Galatians 6:1 goes even further. Instead of simply refraining from criticism, we should seek to restore the other person; and Paul, too, gives us three sieves: Are we spiritual ("you who are spiritual")? Are we gentle ("in a spirit of gentleness")? Are we careful ("considering yourself lest you also be tempted")?

Suppose someone at church has done something unwise. Instead of spreading the news, why not prayerfully ask God to speak to that person. Then, if you feel led, approach that person with concern and gentleness. If you're harsh, you'll drive him or her away, but gentleness is like salve on a wound.

James promised: "He who turns a sinner from the error of his way will save a soul from death and cover a multitude of sins" (James 5:20).

My Lord, my Savior, pour Thy love through me.
AMY CARMICHAEL

MIRACLE OF MULTIPLICATION

He took the seven loaves and the fish and gave
thanks, broke them and gave them to His disciples;
and the disciples gave to the multitude.

MATTHEW 15:36

Many people are familiar with the Seven Wonders of the Ancient World (the Great Pyramid of Giza, Babylon's hanging gardens, and others). Did you know that many refer to compound interest as the eighth wonder of the world? Compounding occurs when the interest on our savings also begins to earn interest, and money seems to multiply miraculously.

Well, money doesn't multiply miraculously, but some things do. For instance, when Jesus took a few loaves of bread and fish from a young boy and fed thousands of people, that was miraculous multiplication. And when He takes our small but faithful contribution to His Kingdom and causes much fruit to be borne, that's miraculous multiplication as well. We never know when the smallest act on our part will be exactly what the Lord needs to bring about a significant result. A word of witness for Christ might change a life or—in time—the world.

You might be the venue for a miracle of multiplication today if you will just give Jesus what you have.

Take my life and let it be consecrated, Lord, to Thee. . . . Take
my hands and let them move at the impulse of Thy love.

FRANCES RIDLEY HAVERGAL

HOSEA AND GOMER

> Go, take yourself a wife of harlotry and children of harlotry, for the
> land has committed great harlotry by departing from the LORD.
>
> HOSEA 1:2

Church history is filled with examples of couples who served the cause of Christ together: Martin and Katharine Luther, Jonathan and Sarah Edwards, Jim and Elisabeth Elliot, Adoniram and Ann Judson. Each of these couples demonstrated what should characterize every marriage that is centered on Christ: sacrifice and commitment.

No story illustrates sacrifice for and commitment to the will of God more than that of Hosea and Gomer in the Old Testament. The northern kingdom of Israel was in a state of moral and spiritual degeneracy. In order for God to demonstrate His love for Israel, He told His prophet Hosea to take for a bride the morally and spiritually degenerate Gomer. Her adultery was a picture of Israel; Hosea's sacrifice and commitment to her, a picture of God's love. Hosea's actions were aimed at Gomer's reform and restitution, just as God's actions in judging Israel were intended to produce Israel's reform and restitution.

Are you and your spouse willing to sacrifice your comfort to serve God in whatever He calls you to do?

No sacrifice can be too great for me to make
for Him who gave His life for me.

C. T. STUDD

February 15

HIGH THINKING

As the heavens are higher than the earth, so are My ways
higher than your ways, and My thoughts than your thoughts.

ISAIAH 55:9

There's only one source for negative thinking, unhealthy emotions, anxious thoughts, impure minds, and fretful spirits—low thinking. We naturally see things from our own perspective. God looks at things differently, and His Word is the codification of His insight. As we trust His promises and see life through the lens of Scripture, we become high thinkers.

When the King James Version was released in 1611, the translators attached an "Address to the Reader," which said, in condensed form, that Scripture "is a whole paradise of trees of life, which bring forth fruit every month . . . and the leaves for medicine. . . . A shower of heavenly bread . . . a whole cellar full of oil vessels; whereby all our necessities may be provided for. It is a [pantry] of wholesome food, against [moldy] traditions; a Physician's shop against poisoned heresies; a [code] of profitable laws, against rebellious spirits; a treasury of most costly jewels against beggarly rudiments . . . a foundation of most pure water springing up unto everlasting life."

When your thoughts are negative, unhealthy, anxious, impure, or fretful, turn to God's thoughts, and let His Word dwell in you richly.

*Look up and not down; look forward and not
back; look out and not in; and lend a hand.*

EDWARD EVERETT HALE

BLESSINGS ABOUNDING

"Try Me now in this," says the LORD of hosts, "if I will not open
for you the windows of heaven and pour out for you such
blessing that there will not be room enough to receive it."

MALACHI 3:10

One day a young man appeared at the door of a missionary's home
in Africa, holding a fish on a string. When the missionary questioned him about it, he said, "You taught us to tithe, so here is my
tithe."

The missionary took the fish gratefully, but before the young man
could leave, the missionary asked him, "Where are the other fish? If
this is a tithe, shouldn't there be nine other fish on this string?"

"I'm going to catch them right now!" the young man replied.

This young man lived in expectancy! He knew that God was waiting to bless him. He planned on it, he acted on it, and he spoke of it
with boldness, confidence, and faith.

In today's passage, God speaks through Malachi, challenging us
to test His faithfulness. When we follow God's plan for giving and
return to Him what rightfully belongs to Him in the first place by
tithing faithfully, He will amaze us. Give God a gift that is beyond your
comfort zone, and see His blessings abound today.

---

*Blessed be to God for the day of rest and religious
occupation wherein earthly things assume their true size.*
WILLIAM WILBERFORCE

CLEOPAS

Their eyes were opened and they knew Him; and He vanished
from their sight. And they said to one another, "Did not our
heart burn within us while He talked with us on the road?"

Cleopas and his friend trudged back to Emmaus on Sunday afternoon, confused over reports that their friend Jesus of Nazareth
was alive. Problem was, He was dead, and they knew it. Being pre-
occupied, they scarcely noticed footsteps behind them as a stranger
caught up and came alongside them. Soon the stranger was explaining to them from the Old Testament how logical it was that the Messiah should die and rise three days later. Old Testament prophecy
presented the resurrection of Christ as both a physical reality and a
theological necessity: sane, logical, wonderful, and real!

Arriving home, Cleopas invited the stranger to supper, and as
the man broke and distributed the bread, suddenly their eyes were
opened and they saw *Him* (Luke 24:31-32).

Remember as you walk in the park, drive along the road, sit on
the patio, or gather at the table, that Jesus is alive. He is with you, and
His Word is sane, logical, wonderful, and real.

Turn your eyes upon Jesus, look full in His wonderful face.
And the things of earth will grow strangely
dim, in the light of His glory and grace.

HELEN HOWARTH LEMMEL

> You will keep him in perfect peace, whose mind
> is stayed on You, because he trusts in You.
>
> ISAIAH 26:3

In his book *Truman*, David McCullough shares this story:

> As President [Truman] felt more than ever a need to see and
> make contact with what he called the everyday American.
> And he always felt better for it. On a recent evening in
> Washington, on one of his walks, he had decided to take a
> look at the mechanism that raised and lowered the middle
> span of the Memorial Bridge over the Potomac. Descending
> some iron steps, he came upon the bridge tender, eating his
> evening supper out of a tin bucket. Showing no surprise that
> the President of the United States had climbed down the
> catwalk and suddenly appeared before him, the man said,
> "You know, Mr. President, I was just thinking about you." It
> was a greeting Truman adored and never forgot.[2]

If the Lord Jesus showed up at your workplace today, could you
say, "You know, Lord, I was just thinking about You"? Where is your
mind today? Every temptation comes to us via our thoughts. Reinforce
your mind with God's Word, and keep your mind stayed on Him.

*Our defeat or victory begins with what we think,
and if we guard our thoughts, we shall not have
much trouble anywhere else along the line.*

VANCE HAVNER

[2] David McCullough, *Truman* (New York: Simon & Schuster, 1992), 623.

February 19
TRUSTING IN ADVANCE

> [Abraham was] fully convinced that what [God]
> had promised He was also able to perform.
>
> ROMANS 4:21

Phillip Yancey wrote, "Faith is trusting in advance what will only make sense in reverse." That reminds us of Paul's analogy, likening faith to a shield that deflects the arrows of the enemy (Ephesians 6:16). Our difficulties are darts Satan throws to cause us depression and defeat. Nothing is more stressful than disunity at church, broken relationships at work, disagreement among friends, or division in the home. We can't make sense of these things when they occur, but we can trust God with the outcome.

Faith lifts us up as we determine to trust God despite the circumstances, being fully convinced that He is able to do what He has said. He has promised to work all things together for good, to hear and answer our prayers, to guard our hearts and minds with His peace, to never leave or forsake us, and to restore our souls (Romans 8:28; John 15:7; Philippians 4:7; Hebrews 13:5; Psalm 23:3).

Faith is trusting God because of His promises. Life in a Christian environment isn't easy, but you can stand up to Satan's attacks when you know who you're fighting against. You can deflect his darts with the shield of faith.

---

*When [God] finds a soul penetrated with a living
faith, He pours into it His graces and favors
plentifully; there they flow like a torrent.*

BROTHER LAWRENCE

TRUST HIS TIMETABLE

> After fourteen years I went up again to Jerusalem
> with Barnabas, and also took Titus with me.
>
> GALATIANS 2:1

A computer-savvy high school graduate volunteers for the US Army to work with computers and earn educational benefits that will allow him to attend college after his discharge. But he is dismayed to learn that before ever touching a keyboard, he'll have to go through basic training—mud, guns, marching, little sleep, being yelled at by drill sergeants—to learn to be a soldier first. He agrees because he knows it is the path to his ultimate goal.

Sometimes when we pray and ask the Lord to help us achieve a goal in life, we become impatient with the seemingly circuitous route God takes to get us there. Take the apostle Paul, for instance. After coming to know Christ (Acts 9), it was fourteen years before he ever went back to Jerusalem to meet the elders of the founding church of Christianity. There is no indication from Scripture that Paul was impatient with that fact. But given his can-do attitude, Paul might have wondered, *Why the delay? What is God doing?* If you are asking God for help with something right now, be willing to trust His timetable.

There is no need to arrive anywhere before God wants you to be there.

---

*Faith is the art of holding on to things in spite
of your changing moods and circumstances.*

C. S. LEWIS

MAN'S CHIEF END

> If anyone suffers as a Christian, let him not be
> ashamed, but let him glorify God in this matter.
>
> 1 PETER 4:16

In 1643, the English Parliament asked leaders of the Church of England along with other theologians to meet at Westminster Abbey to provide guidance on spiritual and ecclesiastical affairs. Over the course of several years, three documents emerged: the *Westminster Confession of Faith*, the *Larger Catechism*, and the *Shorter Catechism*. The most famous part of the documents is question one of the *Shorter Catechism*: "Q. What is the chief end of man? A. Man's chief end is to glorify God, and to enjoy him forever."

Joseph was one of the most blessed and prosperous individuals in the Old Testament because he seemed to understand the point of that first question. He was willing to let God be God in his life and to respond positively and faithfully to everything God did. Even when Joseph was thrown into prison unjustly, he was used by God (Genesis 39:19-23). Is there any situation in your life in which you are not responding positively and faithfully to God—not glorifying Him?

There can be no enjoyment of God without first glorifying God.

The word of God, which is contained in the Scriptures
of the Old and New Testaments, is the only rule to
direct us how we may glorify and enjoy him.

QUESTION 2, WESTMINSTER SHORTER CATECHISM

A MAN OF SORROWS

Jesus wept.

JOHN 11:35

Someone once said, "You may soon forget those with whom you have laughed, but you will never forget those with whom you have wept."

When we are experiencing sorrow, one of the greatest comforts is knowing that someone else has gone through a similar trial and has felt the sadness we feel. In such dark times of life, we tend to cling to those friends who have been where we are. Jesus is one such friend. He experienced the death of a very close friend, watched as some of His disciples openly betrayed Him, and kept silent as He was unjustly beaten and hung on a cross. Needless to say, He was "a Man of sorrows and acquainted with grief" and can therefore relate to us on a very personal level when we are experiencing pain and grief (Isaiah 53:3).

If you are in a time of sadness and sorrow and feel that no one understands you, remember that Jesus understands because He has experienced pain too. You can trust that He has been wherever you are and will walk with you through your darkest hour.

The blood of Christ stands not simply for the sting of sin on God but the scourge of God on sin, not simply for God's sorrow over sin but for God's wrath on sin.

P. T. FORSYTH

February 23

THE PARALYTIC

When Jesus saw their faith, He said to the
paralytic, "Son, your sins are forgiven you."

MARK 2:5

A man went to the dentist, suffering from a bad toothache. The
dentist, in his examination, realized that the source of the problem was deeper than the tooth and sent the man to a cardiologist,
where he was treated for heart disease.

In the story in Mark 2, four friends carried a paralytic on a
stretcher to Jesus. Unable to get through the crowds, these men lowered their buddy through the roof, and the man descended right in
front of Jesus. Looking at him, the Lord detected a heart problem. This
man needed forgiveness. Perhaps he had caused an accident that had
hurt others and left himself paralyzed. His condition may have even
been the result of his own folly and sinfulness.

Jesus banished his sins forever, then proceeded to heal him
completely.

Our problems and needs run deeper than we sometimes know,
but when we walk with the great Physician, He diagnoses accurately
and heals completely.

When a spiritual cure is wrought by the Great Physician,
praise is one of the surest signs of renewed health.

CHARLES HADDON SPURGEON

MOUNTAIN CLIMBING

> An undisciplined, self-willed life is puny; an
> obedient, God-willed life is spacious.
>
> PROVERBS 15:32, *THE MESSAGE*

Pemba Dorje Sherpa, from Nepal, climbed Mount Everest from base camp to the summit in a time of eight hours and ten minutes on May 21, 2004, the fastest ever ascent of the world's tallest mountain. Most people have never climbed to the summit of Mount Everest, let alone set a world record doing it. It takes a lot of determination, hard work, and self-discipline to accomplish that kind of feat. What does the character trait of self-discipline mean to the Christian lifestyle?

We live in a world that is filled with many choices, many emotions, and many appetites that would pull us down and away from the peak of God's best. Biblically, self-discipline manifests itself through our obedience to Him and is important in any endeavor of life. It's best defined as the ability to regulate one's conduct by principle and sound judgment rather than by impulse, desire, or social custom. We'd much rather please ourselves. But just as we need to practice self-control in our bodies through exercise, nutritious eating, and a healthy lifestyle, we need to discipline our minds to do what's right. With God's help, you can climb every mountain you face.

*Heavenly Father, give me the strength to be self-disciplined
in my continuous pursuit of a relationship with You!*

REACH THE HEART

Honor your father and mother ... that it may be well
with you and you may live long on the earth.

EPHESIANS 6:2-3

Why is it so important for children to honor and obey their parents? It's not because we need well-behaved children, nor is it simply because we are adults and they are minors. God commands children to obey their mothers and fathers because it is training for the respect and obedience needed for a healthy relationship with the Lord. And when children understand that in being obedient to their parents they are obeying Christ, then their hearts are impacted forever. Becoming acquainted with submission to a loving authority and obedience to a caring parent makes it easier for children to have a genuine desire to love, serve, and obey God.

Every word of the Bible was written for a specific purpose, and the command to "honor your father and mother" is no exception. Jesus set the standard for obedience when He walked the earth. Not only did He put Himself under the authority and leadership of His earthly mother and father, but He also obeyed His true Father even unto death to pay the price for our sins. Let us follow in His example by honoring our parents and teaching our children to do the same.

---

*Obedience is the gateway through which knowledge,
yes, and love, too, enter the mind of the child.*

ANNE SULLIVAN

February 26
COME TO CALVARY

> Much more then, having now been justified by His
> blood, we shall be saved from wrath through Him.

ROMANS 5:9

Calvary is a reminder to each and every one of us that our sin—our falling short of God's glory, our active or passive rebellion from the beginning with Adam to this very day—is what nailed Jesus Christ to the cross. How easily we forget; how easily we fall back into the very kinds of sins from which we have been redeemed and, in a sense, crucify Him afresh in our hearts.

If we have come to the cross for salvation, if we have accepted the Lord into our lives and into our hearts, we can leave our sin at the cross because the price has been paid, once and for all. Horatio Spafford stated it clearly: "My sin, not in part but the whole, is nailed to the cross, and I bear it no more."

The mercy of God is wide enough for us all. It is everlasting, and it goes deep enough to cover every sin that we have ever committed. We can be released from the guilt of sin because the payment has been made and we have been forgiven.

Come to Calvary to remember, and leave redeemed.

Come to Calvary's holy mountain. . . . Here a pure
and healing fountain flows to you, to me, to all.

JAMES MONTGOMERY

SORT OF SORRY

> Godly sorrow produces repentance leading to salvation, not
> to be regretted; but the sorrow of the world produces death.
>
> 2 CORINTHIANS 7:10

Like a young child, the fledgling church at Corinth was doing a lot of things wrong. There were divisions, church members were suing one another, and they were misusing spiritual gifts. But the most egregious of their errors was tolerating a sexually immoral brother in the church. Paul told them in 1 Corinthians 5 in no uncertain terms not only that the sin was wrong but also that they were wrong to tolerate it.

He writes the church again in 2 Corinthians 7 to commend them for their repentance—for dealing with the problem. And he draws an important distinction between repentance and regret. Regret often means, "I'm sorry for all this trouble," while repentance always means, "I'm sorry for my sin, and I purpose to turn from that path and follow God in obedience and holiness." Regret says, "I'm sorry I got caught." Repentance says, "I'm sorry I sinned." If you have sinned and are vacillating between regret and repentance, read Paul's full explanation and choose wisely.

The wrong path never turns into the right path. The only way to get off the wrong path is to go back to where you got on and take the right path.

To do so no more is the truest repentance.

MARTIN LUTHER

UNDER THE SPOUT

[God] gives more grace.

JAMES 4:6

Have you ever wondered how you can be a recipient of God's grace? Years ago I heard a preacher who explained it this way: God has a grace pipe up in heaven, and out through that grace pipe all His grace comes down to earth. All we have to do as His people is stand at the spout. You've just got to find where the grace is coming from, get under the spout, and stay there so God can pour His grace right down on your life.

God told Moses that he had found grace in His sight. Let's take a moment to examine the life of Moses and to learn from his example. First of all, Moses was a man of God (Ezra 3:2). He followed the commands of the Lord and led the children of Israel to the Promised Land. Second, he was a servant of God (Deuteronomy 34:5). Moses gave up his rights as an Egyptian prince and chose to spend his life under the rule of the Almighty. And last, he was a friend of God (Exodus 33:11). How else does one build a friendship except through close communication and intimate conversation? Moses worshiped God.

So how can you experience more grace? Stand under the spout, allowing God to pour Himself into your life and your soul so that He takes control—then you can be God's person, His servant, His friend.

Grace is but glory begun, and glory is but grace perfected.
JONATHAN EDWARDS

MARCH

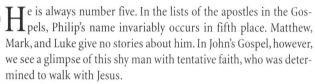

March 1

PHILIP

Philip said to him, "Come and see."

JOHN 1:46

He is always number five. In the lists of the apostles in the Gospels, Philip's name invariably occurs in fifth place. Matthew, Mark, and Luke give no stories about him. In John's Gospel, however, we see a glimpse of this shy man with tentative faith, who was determined to walk with Jesus.

In John 6, Philip seemed anxious about where they would get enough money to feed the crowds, and later, before the Passover Feast in the upper room, he wanted more information, asking Jesus, "Show us the Father" (John 14:8). But Philip had a true missionary spirit and was always directing people to the Savior. He brought Nathanael to Christ in John 1, and some Greek pilgrims in John 12.

According to the ancient historian Eusebius, Philip eventually became a great evangelist in Asia and was buried in Hierapolis after a lifetime of inviting people to come and see Jesus.

We may be shy, may struggle with our faith, and may feel we need more information before we can be truly effective. But we can always say, as Philip did, "We have found Him of whom Moses in the law, and also the prophets, wrote—Jesus of Nazareth. . . . Come and see" (John 1:45-46).

*The first impulse of a born-again Christian
is to win somebody to Jesus.*

W. A. CRISWELL

DIZZYING HEIGHTS

Holy, holy, holy, Lord God Almighty, who
was and is and is to come!

REVELATION 4:8

Have you visited the Grand Canyon? When you stand on the rim, peering down into that immense chasm with its vast width and dizzying depths, it's easy to be awestruck. There's an overwhelming sense of majesty and downright terror that you feel while standing on the edge—especially if you're afraid of heights. The fear of God is like that. It isn't an unhealthy fear but an overwhelming sense of the sheer greatness of God Himself.

Touring the Grand Canyon doesn't diminish our sense of awe; it increases it. In the same way, having a personal relationship with God through Jesus Christ doesn't lessen our fear of God; it enhances it.

The angels in heaven are in God's direct presence, and their song reflects their worship: "Worthy is the Lamb who was slain to receive power and riches and wisdom, and strength and honor and glory and blessing!" (Revelation 5:12).

Familiarity with the Lord never leads to careless devotion. We never "get used to" Him. The closer we draw to our Lord, the greater He becomes in our eyes. And that's good, because "the fear of the LORD is the beginning of wisdom" (Psalm 111:10).

In glory He is incomprehensible, in greatness unfathomable,
in height inconceivable, in power incomparable, in wisdom
unrivaled, in goodness inimitable, in kindness unutterable.

THEOPHILUS OF ANTIOCH

March 3

WHEN ALL ELSE FAILS

> Your faith should not be in the wisdom of
> men but in the power of God.
>
> 1 CORINTHIANS 2:5

Who hasn't had this thought flash on Christmas Eve or the night before a child's birthday: *When all else fails, read the directions?* It was bad enough when figuring things out involved mostly nuts and bolts and a couple of simple tools. Now we have endless levels of digital commands to figure out when it comes to electronic gadgets. It seems the more complicated things get, the more determined we become to figure them out by ourselves.

And that holds true for our spiritual lives as well. The more difficult our circumstances, the more determined we are to figure things out on our own without having to call upon God. What we fail to realize is that such times are part of our training, that God allows us to get to the end of our ability just so we will learn to call upon Him. That was certainly part of the original disciples' training—like the time they fished all night with no "luck" until they listened to Jesus' advice and saw their boat filled with fish.

If you are nearing the end of your rope, maybe it's time to call on the Lord. There is great victory in realizing the limits of your own ability—and the limitlessness of His.

One of the best ways to get back on your feet is to first get on your knees.

UNKNOWN

66 | TURNING POINTS WITH GOD

STILL, SMALL VOICE

> His sheep follow him because they know his voice.
>
> JOHN 10:4, NIV

In the classic film *Field of Dreams*, the main character, Ray Kinsella, hears a small voice say, "If you build it, he will come." He interprets this to mean he needs to build a baseball diamond in the middle of his cornfield. He could ignore the voice and go on with his less-than-fulfilling life; instead, he chooses to listen and follow each prompting to see where it leads. For a while, it seems he will never find the meaning of the repetitious phrase. But at the end of the movie, the reason for the baseball field is revealed: to restore Ray's broken relationship with his deceased father. Because he listened to the quiet voice that only he could hear, he found peace and fulfillment for his life.

This may sound like a familiar plot: Noah heard the same kind of voice when he was instructed to build the ark, and each step of the way he trusted that God had a purpose for it.

When God speaks to you in a still, small voice, listen carefully. He is unfolding a plan for your life. If you trust Him each step of the way, you will ultimately find peace and fulfillment as you follow Him.

Keep the posture of an upright man . . . cheerfully and patiently awaiting the directing voice; and it will not be long ere God shall say to you . . . "Go forward."

CHARLES HADDON SPURGEON

Love one another; as I have loved you,
that you also love one another.

JOHN 13:34

A little girl used her mother's expensive gold wrapping paper to wrap a present. But money was tight, and the mother was upset that her daughter had wasted the paper. Nevertheless, the girl brought the gift to her mother and said, "This is for you." Though embarrassed by her earlier reaction, the mother became upset again when she saw the box was empty. "Don't you know that when you give someone a present, there's supposed to be something inside?" With tears in her eyes the girl said, "Oh, Mama, it's not empty! I blew kisses into it until it was full." Crushed, the mother fell to her knees, wrapped her arms around her daughter, and begged for her forgiveness. From that moment on, the mother kept the gold box by her bed to remember the unconditional love of her child.

God has given us an infinite amount of His unconditional love. Just as the gold box was a reminder of a child's love for her mother, the Word of God reminds us that our Savior loved us even unto death. Let us never forget this truth and always strive to love as God loves.

Though we cannot think alike, may we not love alike?

JOHN WESLEY

PATIENCE WITH PRODIGALS

> Father, I have sinned against heaven and in your sight,
> and am no longer worthy to be called your son.

LUKE 15:21

A mother and father wrote to Billy Graham with this question (paraphrased): "Our son left home several years ago because we didn't approve of his lifestyle. We've had no contact with him until he called recently and said he'd like to come home for Thanksgiving. We want to see him, but as far as we can tell nothing has changed in his life. What advice would you give us?"

Billy Graham answered: "Did the prodigal son's father know whether or not his son had changed his way of living when he welcomed him home?" (Luke 15:20). The obvious answer is no. Dr. Graham went on to counsel the parents not to blow out the flame that was flickering in their son's soul, be it ever so faint. Just as the Prodigal Son in Luke 15 had to swallow his pride, so did the son of these parents. And that's a step in the right direction. If there is a prodigal in your family, wait patiently while God works in his or her life to produce genuine repentance. Be ready to fuel the flame of repentance with love and forgiveness when you see it flickering with life.

The smallest step in the right direction is a step toward God. If God's arms are open, so should ours be.

The glory of Christianity is to conquer by forgiveness.

WILLIAM BLAKE

FOLLOWING JUST ONE

Jesus said to him, "If I will that he remain till
I come, what is that to you? You follow Me."

JOHN 21:22

There is a disconnect between the results of national polls concerning religion and religious reality. For instance, according
to one poll, upwards of 90 percent of Americans claim to believe in
God, and a large majority of those claim to be Christians. If that's
true, where are all these followers of Christ? It would seem that many
people believe it's possible to follow Christ and follow other religions
or the ways of the world at the same time.

Jesus made it clear in His teachings that His "religion" is an
exclusive one: "I am the way, the truth, and the life. No one comes
to the Father except through Me" (John 14:6). In a modern, pluralistic culture, that doesn't sit well. And it didn't sit well with Peter, who
was momentarily confused about "followership." To Peter, Jesus said
(paraphrase), "Don't worry about what others are doing. *You follow
Me.*" When someone asks you what you are, religiously speaking, do
you say, "I'm a (name of your denomination)"? Or do you say, "I'm a
follower of Jesus Christ—a Christian"?

In an age that values tolerance and rejects absolutes, it will never
be popular to say, "I follow only One."

Christianity can be condensed into four words:
admit, submit, commit, and transmit.

SAMUEL WILBERFORCE

THE GOOD AND BAD OF AVERAGE

We dare not class ourselves or compare ourselves
with those who commend themselves.

2 CORINTHIANS 10:12

Everyone learns in school to compute the average of a group of numbers: add the numbers together, then divide the sum by the number of numbers added. Sometimes being average is desirable: having an average body temperature of 98.6 degrees is a good thing. But being an average weight in a culture where obesity is on the rise is a warning signal.

One place where average is definitely not acceptable is in spiritual maturity. If all the subjects in a study are totally depraved to begin with (Romans 3:10-18), then an average level of maturity is not likely to be the result you're looking for. Scripture says we have one model to strive for on the path of spiritual maturity—and it is not average. Rather, perfection is the goal (Matthew 5:48). While attaining perfection this side of heaven will not happen, our attitude should be the same as Paul's: striving to live without offense toward God or others. When searching for a model in this life, choose Christ. It is His likeness you have been called to reach (Romans 8:29).

Body temperature is best when it is average, but spiritual temperature is best when it's off the chart.

*The farther a man knows himself to be from
perfection, the nearer he is to it.*

GERARD GROOTE

March 9

EYES TO SEE, EARS TO HEAR

Open my eyes, that I may see wondrous things from Your law.

PSALM 119:18

A well-known Old Testament scholar spent the summer in Jeru-salem as part of a team of scholars working on a new transla-tion of the Bible. When he returned to the classroom in September, he told his students it had been a carnal, spiritually dry summer. His students were shocked. Hadn't the professor been studying God's Word all day? He replied, "It became a project instead of a passion. We became so familiar with the intricacies of the text that we stopped seeing its grandeur."

Is it possible to study the Bible in a carnal fashion? Apparently so. Maybe when you read the professor's testimony, you said to yourself, "That's happened to me." You don't have to be a scholar or translator to lose sight of the inestimable privilege of reading God's Word. It can happen when you become so faithful with your quiet time that it becomes a routine—something to check off your to-do list for the day. The nation of Israel once had eyes to see and ears to hear God, but she grew carnal. As a result, she failed to hear and see the living Word of God standing in her midst. Don't let that happen to you.

Pray today and ask God to open your eyes and show you fresh and wonderful things from His Word.

Take away, O Lord, the veil of my heart
while I read the Scriptures.

LANCELOT ANDREWS

March 10

WITHOUT EXCUSE

The heavens declare the glory of God; and the
firmament shows His handiwork.

PSALM 19:1

After orbiting the earth, Russian cosmonaut Yuri Gagarin is reported to have said, "I looked and looked, but I didn't see God." For many, that was ultimate proof: if God was thought to live in heaven, and a scientist like Gagarin didn't see Him, He must not exist.

But the Bible says that God has "at various times and in various ways" spoken (revealed Himself) to humanity and "has in these last days spoken to us by His Son" (Hebrews 1:1-2). The fact that God didn't reveal Himself to a Russian cosmonaut in space means nothing. Jesus has not revealed Himself physically to humanity on earth in the twenty-first century, but He did in the first century. Likewise, we have no burning bushes today as Moses had in the fourteenth century BC. But God has revealed Himself to all of humanity in one way or another so that, as Paul wrote, we are "without excuse" (Romans 1:20).

Don't fail to believe in God through His Son, Jesus Christ, because you have not seen Him in the way you desire or expect. Rather, embrace the revelation God has given through the living and written Word, lest you be found without excuse.

Open my eyes, that I may see glimpses of truth Thou hast for me. . . .
Open my ears, that I may hear voices of truth Thou sendest clear.
CLARA H. SCOTT

March 11

THE ROAD TO CALVARY: HUMILITY

[Jesus] poured water into a basin and began to wash the disciples'
feet, and to wipe them with the towel with which He was girded.

JOHN 13:5

Your boss has assigned you a task: come up with a creative solution to a problem that has been costing the company money. You
tackle work at night and on weekends, doing the needed research.
Your boss is enthusiastic about your proposal. Later, in a company-
wide meeting, the president gives your boss credit for the solution.
Over time, you find it increasingly difficult to continue serving your
boss faithfully.

Serving people who have wounded us is a challenge. Jesus overcame that challenge on the night He was arrested, accused, and
sentenced to die. He had gathered with His disciples to celebrate
the Passover, when He took a towel and a basin of water and began
to wash their feet. In that group of twelve was Judas, a thief and a
generally disagreeable sort, whom Jesus knew was about to betray
Him (John 13:1-6). Judas left the meeting early to arrange the betrayal
of Jesus, but not before Jesus washed his feet, along with those of the
faithful eleven who remained.

The next time God asks you to serve someone you would rather
not, remember how, on the road to Calvary, Jesus washed the feet of
an unlovely man.

It is a contradiction to be a true Christian and not humble.
RICHARD BAXTER

WHO DO YOU KNOW?

[Jesus] is also able to save to the uttermost those who come to God
through Him, since He always lives to make intercession for them.

HEBREWS 7:25

When we retrieve the daily mail from the mailbox, we scan the
pieces, looking for a handwritten envelope and a familiar name
in the return address. When we call a stranger to ask for business or a
favor, we try to mention the good name of a mutual acquaintance. In
the world of business and interpersonal relations, it's most often not
what we know, but *who* we know, that counts.

And that could not be more true when it comes to knowing God.
What chance would mere mortals have in connecting with God—
receiving His favor or His forgiveness—if we did not know someone
"on the inside"? And it turns out, we do—if we know Jesus Christ.
The Bible tells us that Christ came from God (John 8:42) and has
returned to God (John 14:1-4), where He "lives to make intercession"
for us (Hebrews 7:25). When Satan comes to accuse us before God
(Job 1:9-11), Jesus speaks up immediately and tells the Father, "It's
okay—they are ours. Their sin is covered by My blood."

Do you know Jesus? Do you rely upon His standing with the
Father? Do you approach the Father in Jesus' name? Who we know
will make the difference for all eternity.

Every discussion where [God's] name is not heard is pointless.
BERNARD OF CLAIRVAUX

SIGNS OF CHRIST'S LIFE

> I have been crucified with Christ; it is no longer
> I who live, but Christ lives in me.

GALATIANS 2:20

When we go to the doctor and our vital signs are checked, we don't command our body to have a pulse, to perform respiration by breathing, or to have a 98.6° temperature. The signs of good health in the human body are natural manifestations of a body that is alive and well.

The same is true of the signs of spiritual health. True manifestations of spiritual vitality are not so much about what we do but about what Christ does in and through us. As the apostle Paul wrote, the lives we now live in Christ are not our lives but Christ's life in us. Indeed, one of the purposes of Christ saving and indwelling numerous individuals on earth is that all of us together might do greater works than He could have done as one person (John 14:12). Do we not have the freedom to yield to the presence of Christ (His Spirit) in us or to resist His work? Yes, and we can even perform good works in our own strength. But only what is done by faith will last and be acknowledged (1 Corinthians 3:11-15).

Whatever you are doing for Christ, make sure your signs of life are signs of *His* life in you.

Whatever you are doing, in company or alone, do it all to the glory of God. Otherwise, it is unacceptable to God.

RICHARD BAXTER

MAKE CHANGES, NOT EXCUSES

My son, do not despise the chastening of the
LORD, nor detest His correction.

PROVERBS 3:11

In 1983, as a thirteen-year-old, Tommy Moe was offered an endorsement to ski competitively. But he was caught sneaking out of camp to smoke marijuana and was banned from competitions. Tommy's father, an Alaskan construction worker, ordered him to come home. After Tommy had spent the Arctic summer laboring twelve to sixteen hours a day, his father asked him if he'd rather be a construction worker or part of the ski team training in Argentina. "It humbled me up pretty fast," Tommy said. And it showed. At age fifteen, Tommy was invited to the US National Alpine Championships in Colorado, and at the 1994 Olympics, he took gold in the men's downhill.

How do you respond to your heavenly Father's correction? God may correct us through a friend, a boss, a coach, a pastor—or He may put the need for self-correction in our own hearts. Just think what would have happened to the gospel message if the apostle Paul had not responded to Christ's confrontation on the Damascus road (Acts 9). When God shows you that change is needed in your life, don't make excuses. Instead, make the change.

An excuse is nothing more than an argument disguised as a reason.

———— ◦◦◦ ————

*You must learn to discipline yourself
for the purpose of godliness.*

JAY ADAMS

HOW CRISES CLARIFY

> I want you to know, brethren, that the things which happened to
> me have actually turned out for the furtherance of the gospel.

PHILIPPIANS 1:12

When new Christians begin memorizing Bible verses, Philippians 4:4 is almost always included: "Rejoice in the Lord always. Again I will say, rejoice!" But when those young Christians discover that Paul wrote that verse while confined to prison, shackled in chains, the words suddenly take on a whole new meaning: rejoice always, even when your faith might cost you your life!

Crises have a way of forcing us to clarify what we actually believe. Paul was excited when his faith landed him in prison, because he discovered that the gospel was being preached even more. In other words, his crisis was not a crisis of faith; it was a crisis *because* of his faith. And it was a crisis that resulted in his faith being strengthened, not weakened. When Peter was charged with being friends with Christ, he denied that the relationship existed (Matthew 26:69-75). The shame he felt caused him to clarify his faith, and it never failed him again.

The next time you face a crisis, your faith will be clarified one way or the other—either strong or weak. Plan now to be pleased with what that crisis reveals.

The purest suffering produces the purest understanding.

JOHN OF THE CROSS

March 16

PARENTAL PREFERENCE

My son, do not forget my law, but let your heart
keep my commands; for length of days and
long life and peace they will add to you.

PROVERBS 3:1-2

Because Harold Wilke was born without arms, he learned at an early age to trust his mother. Harold recalls sitting on the bedroom floor while trying to put on a shirt and having a very difficult time. "I was grunting and sweating, and my mother just stood there and watched. Obviously, I now realize that her arms must have been rigidly at her side; every instinct in her had wanted to reach out and do it for me." A well-meaning friend observed the situation and questioned his mom, "'Ida, why don't you help that child?' My mother responded through gritted teeth, 'I am helping him.'"

Sometimes our heavenly Father deals with us in a similar way. Perhaps He has said no to one of your most heartfelt requests or allowed you to go through a painful situation. As the ultimate parent, God's answers always have a loving purpose. He gives us only what's good for us. He tries to prepare us to have faith and to go out on our own to face challenges. Trust Him today.

Heavenly Father, I'm so thankful to have You watch over me.

March 17

LIGHT OF THE WORLD

You were once darkness, but now you are light
in the Lord. Walk as children of light.

EPHESIANS 5:8

Today, March 17, is the day tradition says was the death date
(AD 461 or 493) of Patrick, patron saint of Ireland. Born in
Britain, Patrick was captured by Irish raiders as a teenager and
forced into slavery in Ireland until he escaped six years later. After
returning to his family in Britain, he supposedly had a vision of a
man who gave him a letter, calling him to return to Ireland with the
gospel.

And return he did. Though there is scant historical documenta-
tion about Patrick's ministry in Ireland, the abundance of traditions
(not to mention his sainthood) speaks of the brightness and consistency of the spiritual light he took into a dark land. Today is a good
day to remember that, like Patrick, every Christian is called by God to
go into the world and be "the light of the world" (Matthew 5:14)—a
light that should not be hidden but should shine brightly. What is the
light? It is the good works of love and service we perform in the name
of Christ that cause men to glorify God in heaven (Matthew 5:16).

Light has one purpose: to illuminate the darkness. If we never
penetrate the dark corners of this world with our presence, how will
they be illumined?

The gospel is light, but only the Spirit can give sight.

A. W. TOZER

A TASTY PRESERVATIVE

You are the salt of the earth; but if the salt loses
its flavor, how shall it be seasoned?

MATTHEW 5:13

In ancient cultures, salt was so valuable that it was often used as a medium of exchange. It not only added flavor to food but also was valued as a preservative. Animal flesh was dried and salted in order to keep from spoiling—to preserve its life-giving nutrients until it was consumed.

When Jesus told His disciples that they were the "salt of the earth," they would have immediately recognized the metaphor. But they probably had to think about its implications. The flavor they were to add to the world speaks of the abundant life Jesus came to give (John 10:10). But their role as a preservative required deeper understanding. Without the spiritual presence of God in this world, darkness would quickly overtake everything. When the church is taken up from the earth in the future, evil will have its way (2 Thessalonians 2:1-12). But as long as Christians are on earth, the Holy Spirit is working through them to convict the world of sin, righteousness, and judgment (John 16:8-11).

By living for Christ today, you add abundant flavor to this world and hold back the darkness so that more might believe.

---

*We are the salt of the earth . . . not the sugar. Our ministry
is to truly cleanse and not just to change the taste.*

VANCE HAVNER

March 19
MOMENTS OF GRACE:
THE ALABASTER JAR

She broke the flask and poured it on His head.

MARK 14:3

"She has done a beautiful thing to me," said Jesus about the woman with the alabaster jar (Mark 14:6, NIV). Notice the preposition: "She has done a beautiful thing *to* me."

We're eager to do things *for* Jesus, to rush about in ministry—singing in the choir, visiting, caring for others, evangelizing, leading studies, entertaining, going to meetings, and meeting the needs of others—that's good and pleasing to God.

But one thing is even better—doing something beautiful *to* Jesus, honoring Him with the alabaster box of praise in response to His grace in our lives.

The phrase "sacrifice of praise" occurs three times in the Bible—twice in Jeremiah (17:26 and 33:11) and once in Hebrews 13:15, which says, "Let us continually offer the sacrifice of praise to God, that is, the fruit of our lips, giving thanks to His name."

When you praise Him though you don't feel like it, and when you rejoice in your heart despite the hardships you're facing—that's the alabaster box of praise. Every moment is a moment of grace in our lives, and every day is the right time to praise God.

Then let us gladly bring our sacrifice of praise;
let us give thanks, and sing, and glory in His grace.
CHARLES WESLEY

IDLE TALES?

Their words seemed to them like idle tales, and they did
not believe them. But Peter arose and ran to the tomb.

LUKE 24:11-12

Luke is considered a historian of first rank, whose verifiable accuracy put him head and shoulders above his secular peers. His two works, the Gospel of Luke and the Acts of the Apostles, boldly assert that Jesus of Nazareth rose physically from the tomb on Easter.

Luke didn't expect us to take this on "blind faith." He opened his Gospel by telling us that he had carefully investigated everything from the beginning so we'd know the certainty of the things we've been taught (Luke 1:3-4). And he began his book of Acts by telling us that after the Resurrection, Jesus showed Himself alive "by many infallible proofs" (Acts 1:3).

Scientist Henry Morris said, "The bodily resurrection of Jesus Christ from the dead is the crowning proof of Christianity. If the resurrection did not take place, then Christianity is a false religion. If it did take place, then Christ is God and the Christian faith is absolute truth."

Our faith is warm and personal, but it is based on cold, hard facts—not on idle tales.

---

*For a very simple reason: I am not able to explain away
an event in history—the resurrection of Jesus Christ.*

JOSH McDOWELL, WHEN ASKED WHY HE
COULD NOT REFUTE CHRISTIANITY

NO ALTERNATIVE

Who is a God like You, pardoning iniquity?

MICAH 7:18

A publication from TransWorld Radio told the story of a Cuban drug trafficker named Miguel. On one occasion when he was evaluating a piece of land for a potential crop, an old lady who lived on the plantation gave him a New Testament. He began reading about the Lord Jesus.

Some time later, Miguel suffered an accident and lost a lot of blood. Being in pain that evening, he turned on the radio to distract his thoughts. There he heard a preacher talking about our guilt and God's forgiveness. Miguel later said, "I felt I had no alternative but to accept Jesus into my life. I felt the peace of heaven, and I was happy for the first time."

Following his recovery, Miguel cut down his plants, burned his laboratory, and got rid of everything related to drug trafficking. He shared Christ with his workers, and every single one of them received Jesus Christ as Lord and Savior. "From our little band of cocaine farmers," Miguel wrote, "have come twelve pastors."

It's terrible to live a guilty life. Christ can wash away our sins, free us from regret, and give new meaning to life. Don't wallow in your guilt any longer. You can feel the peace of heaven and be happy in Him.

There's no alternative.

Gone, gone, gone, gone—yes, my sins are gone!

HELEN GRIGGS

THE LORD REIGNS

Let the heavens rejoice, and let the earth be glad; and
let them say among the nations, "The LORD reigns."

1 CHRONICLES 16:31

Five times the Bible declares, "The Lord reigns!" When we really believe that, our thinking changes about every situation in life. Take the way people treat us, for example. It's easy to fly off the handle, harbor bitterness, and let resentment eat away at our souls. Humanly speaking, such reactions may seem justified, for people can do terrible things to us.

But when we recognize the absolute rule of God over even the smallest matters, we can trust Him to use even those injuries for glorious good. Think of Joseph, who forgave his brothers for their horrible mistreatment (Genesis 45). He understood they meant it for evil, but God meant it for good (Genesis 50:19-20).

Think of the hymnist Fanny Crosby. Once, when asked about the doctor who may have caused her blindness in infancy, she said, "If I could meet him, I would tell him that he unwittingly did me the greatest favor in the world.... How in the world could I have lived such a helpful life as I have lived had I not been blind?"

Because God reigns, we can forgive others and trust Him with the hurts.

*The sin of unforgiveness is a cancer that destroys
relationships, eats away at one's own psyche, and,
worst of all, shuts us off from God's grace.*
ROBERTSON McQUILKIN

SATISFIED

"My people shall be satisfied with My goodness," says the LORD.

JEREMIAH 31:14

In his final days, just before slipping into unconsciousness, Memphis pastor Adrian Rogers told friends by his bed, "I am at perfect peace."

Few people leave behind "last words" now because of medication to lessen suffering and pain. But in the times before the widespread use of anesthesia, people actually planned their dying sayings in advance.

Hymnist John Newton said as he was dying, "I am satisfied with the Lord's will." The "Sweet Singer of Methodism," Charles Wesley, said on his deathbed: "I shall be satisfied with Thy likeness— satisfied, satisfied!"

Sir David Brewster, inventor of the kaleidoscope, said as he passed into heaven: "I will see Jesus. . . . Oh . . . I feel so safe and satisfied!" John Calvin said as he was dying, "I am abundantly satisfied."

It isn't just the dying who are satisfied, of course; it should be the living, too! As Clara Williams's old hymn says,

Hallelujah! I have found Him
Whom my soul so long has craved!
Jesus satisfies my longings,
Through His blood I now am saved.

We love the truth as it is in Jesus; and
nothing but that will satisfy us.
CHARLES HADDON SPURGEON

SERVE AS JESUS SERVED

> Put on tender mercies, kindness, humility,
> meekness, longsuffering.
>
> COLOSSIANS 3:12

If you want to know exactly how to serve as Jesus served, all you have to do is look at the passage of Scripture found in Philippians 2:6-8.

There are six steps to Jesus' service to sinful humankind:

He made Himself of no reputation.
He took the form of a bondservant.
He came in the likeness of man.
He humbled Himself.
He became obedient to the point of death ...
Even the death of the cross.

Jesus understood something that we, as Christians, ought to take to heart regarding service to our Lord: when God is given all the glory and honor and we remain hidden in the background, more lives are led to Christ, and the Kingdom of Heaven is enriched and enlarged. The One who deserves unending recognition for what He did never even asks for a thank-you. He simply wants people to love His Father and accept His forgiveness. Strive to serve like Jesus: with meekness, humility, and love.

In Christian service, the branches that bear
the most fruit hang the lowest.
ANONYMOUS

March 25

A WORLD OF DIFFERENCE

> Now hope does not disappoint, because the love of God has been
> poured out in our hearts by the Holy Spirit who was given to us.

ROMANS 5:5

A schoolteacher once asked her class, "What's the difference between the North and the South Poles?" One boy replied, "All the difference in the world." Well, that also answers the question "What's the difference between a victorious Christian and a defeated Christian?" In Romans 5, Paul reminds us of our benefits in Christ and describes three special gifts that should produce a constant stream of thanksgiving in our hearts.

First, we have a hope that doesn't disappoint. Our hope in Christ isn't mere wishes and wannabees. It's sure and certain, sealed with the reality of Christ's resurrection. It cannot disappoint us.

Second, we have love poured into our hearts. The Greek verb conveys the idea of "gushing." We're like children at the base of a waterfall, trying to catch the flow in our little cups.

Third, we have the Holy Spirit. Jesus Himself lives within us by His indwelling Spirit.

Whatever your circumstances, remember those three facts, and they will make a world of difference in your attitude today.

Inspire us, heavenly Father, to make Thy will our will,
not in sullen submission, but gladly and gratefully.
MICHAEL GUIDO

MAKE YOUR SERVICE COUNT

If anyone serves, they should do it with the strength God provides,
so that in all things God may be praised through Jesus Christ.

1 PETER 4:11, NIV

USMC First Sergeant David Bishop (retired) entered the military with the motivation to serve his country and fulfill his patriotic duty. When it was time for retirement, Dave decided to pledge his service to a different authority and serve his country with a new motivation. He would visit new recruits, 250 at a time, and present the gospel to them, making sure his continued service to the country would count for eternity. To this day, he visits new recruits with the motivation of winning their hearts for Christ.

If you are a child of God, you have been given marching orders from the Lord to serve with the motivation of sharing the good news of the gospel. Are you following those orders, or have you gone AWOL (absent without leave)?

Through Jesus' death on the cross, He left us His perfect example of serving to save souls. The King of kings offered His life so we could spend eternity with Him. If you have lost your vision for the unsaved souls of this world, ask God to open your eyes and your heart to the ways you can serve in an effort to save.

Lord, point out to me the lost souls that need
saving, and show me how I can serve them.

BE FRIENDLY

A man who has friends must himself be friendly.

PROVERBS 18:24

Comedian Milton Berle once quipped, "You know you're getting older when it takes more time to recover than it did to tire out."

As we age, our energy doesn't seem to go as far. But we *do* grow in wisdom, love, and maturity. Our goal should be to expand our circle of influence, to reach out to more people, and to share Christ with our generation and the next.

In other words, our address books shouldn't shrink with age. Sometimes it's easy to bury our old friends without making new ones, but how wonderful to let the joy of Jesus shine through us, whatever our age. How wonderful to make new friends as long as we live.

One man smelled good whenever and wherever he was. His very body seemed to exude a pleasant fragrance. His secret was working in a perfume factory, where he breathed the aromas every day. He became a walking perfumery.

That should happen to Christians. We're different ages and we all have diverse personalities, but at any age we should be so permeated by the joy of the Lord that we can't help but share it with all we meet.

[The apostle Paul's] friends came in all ages and backgrounds, and he seems to have taken great care to cultivate them.

GORDON MacDONALD

GRACE AT GUNPOINT

The name of the LORD is a strong tower; the
righteous run to it and are safe.

PROVERBS 18:10

Steve and Anne Seaberry were taken by surprise when awakened
by armed robbers in the middle of the night. They watched in dis-
belief as everything they owned—including their wedding rings—
was packed into their own car. As the thieves were preparing to leave,
they pointed a cocked gun at the homeowners. But when Steve and
Anne began repeating aloud the name of Jesus, the bullet immediately fell to the floor, and they were left unharmed. They credit God's
sufficient grace for this miraculous event.

God doesn't promise to always intervene on our behalf, but if He
does, nothing is too hard for Him. We live in a world where danger is
about us on every side. And wise is the Christian who prays with all
of his heart every day, "Deliver me from evil, Lord." God is a God who
delivers. Isn't that good news? He loves to have His children pray for
deliverance. He is a God who sees us in our predicaments and delights
to deliver us. We can confidently call on His name and trust Him to
keep us safe.

---

*Faith, mighty faith, the promise sees and looks to God alone,
laughs at impossibilities and cries, "It shall be done."*

CHARLES WESLEY

March 29

DAY AND NIGHT

Keep this Book of the Law always on your lips; meditate on it day and night, so that you may be careful to do everything in it. Then you will be prosperous and successful.

JOSHUA 1:8, NIV

Imagine a chef who collected cookbooks, took cooking classes, studied recipes, and developed menus—but never cooked. Are you like that when it comes to spiritual food? It's one thing to enjoy Bible study, attend Bible classes, and follow daily reading plans. But are you daily applying the Bible's lessons to your attitudes and behavior?

Joshua 1:8 gives three steps to Bible study. First, keep listening to God's Word. Keep reading it aloud. Don't let it depart from your mouth or your mind.

Second, meditate on it. Mull it over in your imagination. Think about it when you drive to work and when you sit at home. Ponder it when you lie down and when you rise up.

Third, obey it—be careful to do everything in it. Then you will make your way prosperous, and then you will have good success. When we're consistent in our daily devotions, it's easier to be consistent in our daily duties.

I on Thy statutes meditate,
Though evil men deride;
Thy faithful Word is my delight,
My counselor and guide.

THE 1912 PSALTER

> Jesus said to him, "Thomas, because you have
> seen Me, you have believed. Blessed are those
> who have not seen and yet have believed."

JOHN 20:29

Until that moment, Thomas had evidently always struggled with nagging doubts. He was full of questions, and his mind was, by nature, skeptical. Yet Jesus loved him, believed in him, and gave him irrefutable, visible, empirical proof of the Resurrection: "Reach your finger here, and look at My hands; and reach your hand here, and put it into My side. Do not be unbelieving, but believing" (v. 27). Imagine the relief and joy that swelled into Thomas's heart as he replied, "My Lord and my God!" (v. 28). Could there be any greater happiness?

Yes—ours! Jesus used this conversation with Thomas to issue His last beatitude before the Ascension: blessed—happy, joyful, and to be envied—are those who have not seen and yet have believed.

One day we'll behold Him face-to-face, and our eyes will gaze upon the nail prints in His hands. But until then, we're blessed for walking with Him by faith and not by sight. Of all people on earth, we are the most joyful. So shouldn't we be smiling today?

Why should I charge my soul with care? The
wealth of ev'ry mine belongs to Christ, God's
Son and Heir, and He's a friend of mine!

JOHN H. SAMMIS

REGAIN YOUR LOST COMPOSURE

They departed from the presence of the council, rejoicing that
they were counted worthy to suffer shame for His name.

ACTS 5:41

Perhaps the greatest secret of the saints of old was their ability to praise God amid the afflictions of life.

Saint Francis de Sales once wrote to a friend who was undergoing stresses at home, saying, "The many troubles in your household will tend to your edification, if you strive to bear them all in gentleness, patience, and kindness. Keep this ever before you, and remember constantly that God's loving eyes are upon you amid all these little worries and vexations, watching whether you take them as He would desire. Offer up all such occasions to Him, and if sometimes you are put out, and give way to impatience, do not be discouraged, but make haste to regain your lost composure."

Do you have an area of frustration, fear, fretting, pain, or stress? Don't be ashamed about it, but glorify God in the midst of it, and let Him use it for the edification of your soul.

---

*You had better make up your mind to accept what
you cannot alter. You can live a beautiful life in
the midst of your present circumstances.*

J. R. MILLER

APRIL

April 1

THE CUSHION OF THE SEA

Be still, and know that I am God.

PSALM 46:10

A number of years ago, a submarine being tested had to be submerged for several hours. Upon returning to harbor, the captain was asked, "How did that terrible storm last night affect you?" Surprised, the captain exclaimed, "Storm? We didn't even know there was one!" Their submarine was so far beneath the surface that it had reached what sailors refer to as "the cushion of the sea"—a depth at which the waters are never stirred, despite any commotion on the surface.

In our fast-paced world, it is a challenge to slow down and remember that God is in control. We are a society of do-everything, go-everywhere, get-it-done people who mistakenly believe we can handle everything if we just keep going. In reality, we need to become so submerged in God's peace that no matter what's happening in our lives, we are able to remain as calm as "the cushion of the sea."

If you feel overwhelmed, bogged down, or burned out, add one more activity to your daily schedule: spend time with almighty God. That is the only way to reach the depth needed to find true calm in the midst of any storm.

In the name of Jesus Christ, who was never in a hurry, we pray, O God, that You will slow us down, for we know that we live too fast.

PETER MARSHALL

GARMENTS OF GRACE

> Be kind to one another, tenderhearted, forgiving one
> another, even as God in Christ forgave you.
>
> EPHESIANS 4:32

In *Running on Empty*, Jill Briscoe writes about a friend who had been molested by her father as a child. She grew up, met the Lord, and recovered from her childhood wounds. When her father eventually found the Lord and asked his daughter for forgiveness, she was angry that he had been welcomed into God's grace—until she had a dream in which she saw both herself and her father clothed in the same white robes of righteousness.

There is only one garment of grace, and it covers every sinner the same way: completely. When Christ died, it was for all to the same degree. There is not one garment of grace that is richer and finer for the most deserving, and one that is skimpy and thin for the least deserving. The garment of God's grace, provided by the death of Christ on the cross, covers every sinner the same way: from top to bottom, from eternity past to eternity future. When we stand clothed in grace and find it difficult to forgive another who is also clothed in grace, we have misunderstood the nature of Christ's sacrifice and God's gift.

Grace not only forgives; it also provides the power to forgive in the way we have been forgiven.

God appoints our graces to be nurses
to other men's weaknesses.
HENRY WARD BEECHER

SEEDS OF DISCOURAGEMENT

Be strong and do not let your hands be weak,
for your work shall be rewarded!

2 CHRONICLES 15:7

If Satan had a barn for storing his weed seeds, the biggest bins would be filled with discouragement seeds, for he's constantly sowing them in the hearts of faithful Christians. Many pastors are utterly worn out. Missionaries, seeing little tangible progress, are disheartened and ready to give up their work. Lay workers sometimes ask themselves, *Am I doing any good, or is this a waste of time?*

We don't always see immediate and impressive results from our labor, but God promises that our work shall be rewarded. Paul told us to be "always abounding in the work of the Lord," knowing our labor in Him is not in vain (1 Corinthians 15:58).

We have barns, too, filled with gospel seed. The Bible promises, "He who continually goes forth weeping, bearing seed for sowing, shall doubtless come again with rejoicing, bringing his sheaves with him" (Psalm 126:6).

So don't give up or grow weary in doing good, for in due season, we'll reap a harvest if we do not lose heart (Galatians 6:9).

Lord, take my lips, and speak through them; take my mind,
and think through it; take my heart, and set it on fire!
WILLIAM H. H. AITKEN

The fear of the LORD is the beginning of knowledge.

PROVERBS 1:7

You settle into your seat on the airplane and notice the person next to you is reading a novel by an author you like. Casual conversation ensues, and you are amazed at your seatmate's knowledge of the author and his books. Is he a professor of literature? No. A book critic? No. Where does a "layman" get that kind of knowledge?

The same question might have been asked of Stephen, one of the early church's first deacons. This man rose to his feet before the Jewish Sanhedrin and delivered one of the most powerful historical-theological sermons in the entire Bible. Where did Stephen get such knowledge? Remember—this wasn't just knowledge of the facts of the Old Testament. It was the ability to show how Jesus of Nazareth was the fulfillment of those facts—the Jewish Messiah—only weeks after His resurrection. The answer is in Acts 6:5: Stephen was full of the Holy Spirit. Stephen had knowledge, but the Spirit transformed that knowledge into the power to convict and change lives.

Ask the Lord to anoint your knowledge of Scripture so it is always available to minister to those in need of truth.

[The] words "unction" and "anointing" are just a very graphic way of describing the influence and the effect of the Holy Spirit upon the believer.

DAVID MARTYN LLOYD-JONES

April 5
SAMUEL'S EAR

The Lord opened [Lydia's] heart to heed the things spoken by Paul.

ACTS 16:14

More than forty men wrote the Bible, all of them using human letters, syllables, and words. In one sense, then, we should read the Bible as we read other books, applying the same reasonable laws of interpretation. The sentences in the Bible are informational and logical, and even children can understand them.

But the Bible was also breathed out by God as its writers were carried along by the Holy Spirit (2 Timothy 3:16; 2 Peter 1:21). Behind the human authors was a divine, master Author, inspiring the words of Scripture and recording them infallibly as inerrant truth. That makes the Bible a one-of-a-kind volume, unequaled by any other book ever written.

Only with the Holy Spirit's illumination can we really appreciate the Bible's message for our own lives. We must pray as Samuel did, "Speak, LORD, for your servant is listening" (1 Samuel 3:9, NIV). And we must always cultivate tender, willing, open, receptive hearts toward Jesus, loving His Word, our hearts burning within us as we daily study our Bibles.

---

*O give me Samuel's ear, the open ear, O Lord, alive
and quick to hear each whisper of Thy Word.*

JAMES D. BURNS

Take heed, and be quiet; do not fear or be fainthearted.

ISAIAH 7:4

In Isaiah 7, the prophet and his son were sent with a message to King Ahaz, who was facing the combined armies of two neighboring enemies. God's counsel was to "take heed, and be quiet," to be unafraid despite the crisis, for the battle was the Lord's. God intended to give Ahaz the resources necessary to overcome his challenges.

That's a message for us, too. We don't have to be fearful, for God gives us the grace and ability for whatever He calls us to do. We need to be strong and courageous, not fearful and doubtful. We need to have quiet minds and confident souls.

John Ruskin wrote, "God is a kind Father. He sets us all in the places where He wishes us to be employed; and that employment is truly 'Our Father's business.' He chooses work for every creature.... He gives us always strength enough and sense enough for what He wants us to do."

We can do whatever He calls us to do through Christ who strengthens us (Philippians 4:13).

———— ◦☙◦ ————

The same God who guides the stars in their courses, who
directs the earth in its orbit, who feeds the burning furnace
of the sun, and keeps the stars perpetually burning with their
fires—the same God has promised to supply thy strength.
CHARLES HADDON SPURGEON

FEELING THE HEAT

The LORD disciplines those he loves, and he
punishes each one he accepts as his child.

HEBREWS 12:6, NLT

Hot sauce adds a kick to salsa, barbecue, and hundreds of other foods. But some parents use it in a different recipe—one they think will yield better-behaved children. They put a drop of it on their son's or daughter's tongue as punishment for lying, biting, hitting, or other offenses. I do not recommend putting hot sauce on your child's tongue, but those who use this form of punishment say it is effective in teaching their children valuable and long-lasting lessons.

Earthly parents use a wide variety of methods to correct children in order to encourage them to be better people. Our heavenly Father loves His children so much that He sometimes has to discipline us to help us to obey. Our response to God's discipline is incredibly important. We must endure, and we must willingly change our wayward behavior. After all, God's purpose in bringing discipline to our lives is to make us righteous. As it is with parental authority, "feeling the heat," so to speak, proves God's love for you. His discipline proceeds entirely from His love.

*God whispers to us in our pleasures, speaks in
our conscience, but shouts in our pains: it is
His megaphone to rouse a deaf world.*

C. S. LEWIS

A COMMON STORY

Blessed are you when they revile and persecute you, and say
all kinds of evil against you falsely for My sake. Rejoice and
be exceedingly glad, for great is your reward in heaven.

MATTHEW 5:11-12

Boston Common is the oldest public park in the United States, a fifty-acre refuge famous for its swan boats, its suspension bridge (the shortest in the world), and for being the setting of the children's story *Make Way for Ducklings*. So it's surprising to learn that in 1651, the Reverend Obadiah Holmes was tied to a post in this park and whipped for preaching Baptist doctrine in Puritan New England. The blood overflowed his shoes.

In our age of religious freedom and pluralistic beliefs, we're apt to forget about the long line of martyrs whose blood has been spilled for the sake of the Cross, even in America.

When we're faithful to Christ, we, too, will suffer some level of rejection, ridicule, or disdain. All who are godly will be persecuted. But the sufferings of this life cannot be compared with the glory to be revealed. So when you encounter someone who disdains your faith, "rejoice and be exceedingly glad, for great is your reward in heaven."

In truth, as the strokes fell upon me, I had such a spiritual manifestation of God's presence as the like thereof I never had nor felt, nor can with fleshly tongue express.

OBADIAH HOLMES

THE ROAD TO CALVARY: FALSE ACCUSATIONS

Pilate said to [Jesus], "Do You not hear how many things they
testify against You?" But He answered him not one word.

MATTHEW 27:13-14

Before being exonerated by DNA tests, Brandon Moon, of Kansas City, Missouri, served nearly seventeen years for a crime he did not commit. The American Bar Association found that more than 150 people in 31 states and the District of Columbia served a total of 1,800 years in prison before being exonerated by DNA evidence.

Being falsely accused can make you feel helpless, especially when the results can devastate your life. What should you do if this happens to you? When Jesus was falsely accused of blasphemy and other crimes, "He . . . did not revile in return; when He suffered, He did not threaten, but committed Himself to Him who judges righteously" (1 Peter 2:23). Jesus chose to entrust Himself to the Judge of all the earth, who will ultimately do right (Genesis 18:25). It may be that we have to endure the temporal pain of false accusation in order to gain the eternal benefit of integrity and trust.

When you think you have exhausted your defense, realize that you haven't. The same One who was falsely accused on the road to Calvary is your advocate with the Father (1 John 2:1).

---

*There is no other method of living piously and
justly than that of depending upon God.*

JOHN CALVIN

April 10

SCALDED!

> A great persecution arose against the church which
> was at Jerusalem; and they were all scattered
> throughout ... Judea and Samaria.
>
> ACTS 8:1

In Acts 1, Jesus commanded the apostles to preach the gospel throughout Judea and Samaria, but after the Day of Pentecost, the work was largely confined to Jerusalem. God used persecution to move His people to obey. When they didn't go out in obedience, the Lord sent them out by persecution. God will accomplish His will and proclaim His Word to the ends of the earth either with our consent or without it, so it's best to cooperate from the beginning.

John Fletcher, a backslidden young man, was waiting to board a ship when a maid spilled boiling water on his leg, badly scalding him and forcing him to literally "miss the boat." But that ship was lost at sea. Fletcher, meanwhile, was convicted of sin through the preaching of a Methodist evangelist and later became one of John Wesley's closest associates.

God used scalding water to get Fletcher's attention and redirect his life. He might do that with you or me! The Lord, in His goodness, sometimes finds ways to motivate us to obey His will, but how much better to be obedient to begin with!

God is love! Shout! Shout aloud! Oh, it so fills me that I
want a gust of praise to go to the ends of the earth!
JOHN FLETCHER

BIG ENOUGH TO BE
SMALL ENOUGH

A man's pride will bring him low, but the
humble in spirit will retain honor.

PROVERBS 29:23

When Dr. J. Edwin Orr wanted to write a biography of Toronto's famous pastor Oswald J. Smith, he was concerned about how Smith would respond to the complimentary nature of the work. He soon realized, however, that Dr. Smith was gracious and humble enough to take both criticism and compliments in stride. "He is big enough to be small enough to give the glory to the Lord," wrote Orr.

What a quality for us to emulate!

The apostle Paul was like that too. His credentials were outstanding, but he realized that without Christ in his life, he was nothing. His life was honorable because he was consistently saying, "Not I, but Christ" (Galatians 2:20, KJV).

Are you big enough to be small enough to give God the glory for whatever He may do with or through you? God resists the proud but gives grace to the humble.

Not I, but Christ Himself in me....
I take, He gives—the victory.

PAUL RADER

WALKING TORCHES

These who have turned the world upside
down have come here too.

ACTS 17:6

The first Christians were walking torches who weren't afraid to
share their faith, spread their news, praise their Lord, and set the
world on fire. They'd discovered a secret that had turned them inside
out. Gone were their inhibitions, failures, sins, and temporal concerns. The risen Christ was living within them, walking among them,
and working through them. They were filled with the Spirit, and they
shared the Word with boldness, though it sometimes brought the
lash down on their backs and the government down on their heads.
They didn't expect to be here long, so they made the most of every
opportunity.

There are still Christians like that, but the majority of us are content with being middle-of-the-roaders, whose lukewarm Laodicean
faith won't even cause the world to tilt a little.

The gospel isn't going to turn the world upside down until it turns
us inside out and right side up, and we'll not set others on fire until
we become walking torches. But when the zeal of Christ sets a church
afire, people will say of us as was said of old: "These who have turned
the world upside down have come here too" (Acts 17:6).

---

*The Christians who have turned the world upside
down have been men and women with vision in
their hearts and the Bible in their hands.*

T. B. MASTON

THE ROAD TO CALVARY: MOCKING

> Those who passed by blasphemed Him, wagging their heads and
> saying, "You who destroy the temple and build it in three days, save
> Yourself! If You are the Son of God, come down from the cross."
>
> MATTHEW 27:39-40

Everyone in John's office knew he was a Christian. In his own quiet way he lived out his faith by means that were evident to all. But when he went through a number of difficulties in life—things his coworkers learned about—he felt as if everyone must be thinking, *Where is God now? I thought God promised to take care of you Christians. If your faith is so strong, why isn't God helping you with these problems?*

Sometimes being a Christian can be "embarrassing"—embarrassing to our fleshly nature, that is. When Jesus was hanging on the cross, He was mocked by the crowds. But as He had done with all the rest of the injustices of His arrest, trial, and crucifixion, Jesus embraced what He knew instead of reacting to what His mockers didn't know. When you feel a need to apologize for what God *hasn't* done, remember all the things He *has* done.

God's timing and His decisions don't always meet our expectations. But that didn't keep Jesus from trusting Him on the road to Calvary.

Confront your fears by drawing near to God.

AND, IN OTHER NEWS . . .

Let everyone who names the name of Christ depart from iniquity.

2 TIMOTHY 2:19

Watching the evening news can be an emotional roller-coaster ride. The top news story could be that flood victims are still without homes, followed by a report of the number of soldiers who have died fighting for our freedom, rounded out with a court's decision to sentence a man accused of murdering a child to only five years in prison. Viewers hardly have a moment to ponder the evil and injustice that just hit them in the face before they are quickly ushered out with the words, "And, in other news . . ." As a result, we have in part become a desensitized society of tolerance and indifference.

As Christians, we cannot let this same attitude invade our thoughts toward sin. When we encounter sin, we should not tolerate it; it ought to provoke our spirits and call us to action in an effort to eradicate it. Let us never become so desensitized to "everyday sins" that we allow them to slowly creep back into our lives without our even realizing it. Like the soldier who never sleeps, we must be vigilant in our Christian walk, always aware of our adversary—the devil—who "walks about like a roaring lion, seeking whom he may devour" (1 Peter 5:8).

The devil's snare does not catch you, unless you are first caught by the devil's bait.

ST. AMBROSE

April 15

GRACE FOR A SEASON

It is appointed for men to die once, but after this the judgment.

HEBREWS 9:27

Warren Wiersbe tells of a frontier town in which a horse-drawn wagon with a little boy aboard was racing through the streets. A young man risked his life to stop the horse and save the child. The rescued child grew up to become a lawless man and one day stood in a court in front of a judge—the now-grown young man who had saved his life. On the basis of their prior relationship, the convicted man pled for mercy. The judge responded, "Once I was your savior, but now I am your judge. I sentence you to your just punishment."

When the young man risked his life years before to save the child, it was an act of grace. He knew nothing of the young child: Was he worthy of being saved? Was he a respectful child? A rebellious one? It didn't matter, for grace asks no questions concerning worthiness. It acts only out of self-sacrifice and love. But the Bible says that grace is only for a season. The day will come when God extends judgment to all who have rejected His grace and mercy. Those who reject God's grace will be worthy of God's punishment. Have you received His grace?

Don't consider your worthiness to be saved. Only reach out and take the hand that is extended to you by grace.

Grace is love that cares and stoops and rescues.

JOHN R. W. STOTT

100 PERCENT

> My eyes are ever toward the LORD.
>
> PSALM 25:15

Nineteenth-century humorist Josh Billings said cleverly, "Consider the postage stamp: its usefulness consists in the ability to stick to one thing till it gets there." As Christians, we can apply these witty words to our goal of living for Christ until the day He returns.

We are surrounded by distractions every day, and we can easily let them cloud our vision and take our focus off of Christ. But we must learn to recognize when that is happening so that we can put aside those distractions and fix our eyes on Him. As with any area of life that needs to be mastered, focusing on Christ takes discipline and preparation. If we start out by turning our day over to the Lord, it will be easier for us to be aware of His presence throughout the day, and that awareness will help us avoid becoming distracted.

Glorifying God should be our focus in everything we do. The only way to accomplish that is by giving Him 100 percent of ourselves 100 percent of the time, and like the postage stamp, sticking to that goal until we reach heaven.

Let your eyes look straight ahead; fix your gaze
directly before you. . . . Do not turn to the right
or the left; keep your foot from evil.
SOLOMON (PROVERBS 4:25, 27, NIV)

April 17

THE SALESMAN

> My speech and my preaching were not with persuasive words of
> human wisdom, but in demonstration of the Spirit and of power.
>
> 1 CORINTHIANS 2:4

A young salesman was disappointed about losing a big sale. As he talked with his sales manager, he lamented, "I guess it just proves you can lead a horse to water but you can't make him drink." The manager replied, "Son, take my advice: your job is not to make him drink. Your job is to make him thirsty." So it is with evangelism. Our lives should be so filled with Christ that they create a thirst within others for the gospel. Witnessing is really interaction. It's not about just dropping a whole presentation on somebody. The more we practice sensitivity and sincerity in telling others about Jesus, the more responsive people tend to be.

Sometimes we ought to think of ourselves as sales representatives, ambassadors of Jesus. Spend time in prayer today, asking God to give you the courage to witness. Trust that He will give you the right words. And never forget that you can lead people to Christ, but it's through Christ alone that they will come to know Him.

---

*The kingdom of God is not going to advance by
our churches becoming filled with men, but by men
in our churches becoming filled with God.*

HOWARD SPRING

SYMPATHY OF JESUS

I will never leave you nor forsake you.

HEBREWS 13:5

One night at the Salvation Army Citadel after Frederick Booth-Tucker had given a sermon on the sympathy of Jesus, a man from the audience approached him and said, "If your wife had just died, like mine has, and your babies were crying for their mother who would never be coming back, you wouldn't be saying what you're saying." Tragically, Tucker's wife was killed in a train wreck a few days later. The funeral was held at the Citadel, and after the eulogy, Tucker addressed the audience, saying, "The other day a man told me I wouldn't speak of the sympathy of Jesus if my wife had just died. If that man is here, I want to tell him that Christ is sufficient. My heart is broken, but it has a song put there by Jesus. I want that man to know that Jesus Christ speaks comfort to me today."[3]

Because of Jesus' promise to never leave us or forsake us, we can be assured that when we face discouragement or heartbreak, He'll be right there, holding our hand through every moment of sorrow. Lean on that truth, and allow it to give you strength for another day.

God walks with us. . . . He scoops us up in His arms or simply sits with us in silent strength until we cannot avoid the awesome recognition that yes, even now, He is there.

GLORIA GAITHER

---

[3] www.sermonillustrations.com/a-z/e/empathy.htm.

BE AN OPTIMIST

> Why are you cast down, O my soul? And why are you
> disquieted within me? Hope in God, for I shall yet
> praise Him for the help of His countenance.
>
> PSALM 42:5

By nature, Christians are optimists. They realistically assess the headlines and soberly acknowledge problems. They know that a certain amount of rain falls into every life and that some days are cloudier than others. No one knows when the next bomb will explode or war will erupt. Yet Peter said, "Nevertheless we, according to His promise, look for new heavens and a new earth in which righteousness dwells" (2 Peter 3:13).

History is moving irreversibly toward God's preappointed ends, and Jesus is readying Himself to return as promised. We are heirs of life abundant and life eternal. Goodness and mercy follow us every day on this planet, and we will dwell in the house of the Lord forever.

Every stunning sunrise or orange-streaked sunset should remind us of our Lord's return. Every shaft of light through a granite sky should preach us a sermon about it.

As you watch the news today, don't shake your head in denial or hang your head in despair. Lift up your head, for your redemption draws near. Be an optimist. Christ is coming!

Christians are always just a few heartbeats from heaven. It ought to make a difference.

VANCE HAVNER

FIT FOR THE MASTER'S USE

Go, for he is a chosen vessel of Mine to bear My name
before Gentiles, kings, and the children of Israel.

ACTS 9:15

It's remarkable how yesterday's household goods are today's collector's items. Glassware and dish sets that once sold for pennies at a Woolworth store now sell for hundreds or thousands of dollars in antique galleries. Glass made cheaply during the depression era now commands a prized place in museums and private collections.

The Lord isn't interested in beautiful vessels that sit in display cases to be admired. He chooses us to be vessels to bear His name.

Think of yourself as a cup, a glass, or a bowl. You're a vessel in the Master's hand, bearing the water of life to a needy world.

That's a biblical picture. The apostle Paul was described as a "chosen vessel," and Paul himself later said of us: "In a great house there are not only vessels of gold and silver, but also of wood and clay, some for honor and some for dishonor. Therefore if anyone cleanses himself from the latter, he will be a vessel for honor, sanctified and useful for the Master, prepared for every good work" (2 Timothy 2:20-21).

Don't worry if you are not beautiful enough to sit in a museum or old enough to be a fine antique. Just live faithfully and bear the water of life to a needy world.

The pierced hand, which gave thee healing, has appointed thee to thy Lord's service, and made thee a chosen vessel to bear His Name.
CHARLES HADDON SPURGEON

WALDEN'S CABIN

[Jesus] said to them, "Come aside by yourselves
to a deserted place and rest a while."

MARK 6:31

America's great philosopher Henry David Thoreau extolled the
virtue of solitude. Living in his isolated cabin at Walden Pond,
Thoreau wrote, "I find it wholesome to be alone the greater part of
the time. . . . I love to be alone. I never found the companion that was
so companionable as solitude."

Few of us want to live by ourselves for extended periods in an
isolated cabin far from human voices, but our society has gone too far
in the other direction. We can't stand stillness, we disdain meditation,
and we dislike our own company. When we're alone, we feel compelled
to turn on some source of noise. We're alarmed at the thought of being
out of cell-phone range.

Remember, however, that Jesus would rise early in the morning
to hike into the mountains for solitude. Think of Elijah and John the
Baptist, who found strength in being alone. It's impossible to grow
spiritually without learning the secret of withdrawal to be alone with
God. It's not loneliness we need but rather more time alone.

---

*I know of no way to recover that which we have
lost other than to cultivate the practice of being
more frequently alone with [God].*

J. WILBER CHAPMAN

April 22
CLASSIC DUO

Two are better than one, because they have
a good reward for their labor.

ECCLESIASTES 4:9

In Hollywood history there have been but a handful of couples who were so perfectly paired that they created their own brand of magic for the silver screen. For some of us, this movie magic is indelibly etched on our memories. Couples such as Fred and Ginger, Bogey and Bacall, and Lucy and Desi will live on in the classic films and TV shows that made them famous.

Fortunately for us, there was another couple who left a lasting legacy. Aquila and Priscilla were two people who were continually present throughout several chapters of the New Testament and became a wonderful example of a husband-wife mentoring team. They worked together to contribute to the body of Christ, leaving us an example of how married couples can greatly impact just about anyone God leads them to (Acts 18).

If you are married, the Lord may use you and your spouse in mighty ways to minister to people, whether they're newlyweds, young parents, or struggling singles. Make it your aim to leave a lasting legacy as a classic duo for the Lord. If you don't have a spouse to minister with, the Lord has still designed you to serve in the context of community. Perhaps there is a friend or family member you can team up with as you labor for the Lord.

*Lord, please help my teammates and me to work
together to bless and encourage those around us.*

April 23

LIVING IN HARMONY

Live in harmony with one another. Do not be proud, but be willing
to associate with people of low position. Do not be conceited.

ROMANS 12:16, NIV

Want to know where 1,080 people live in Harmony every day?
Just travel to Fillmore County, Minnesota, and visit the town
of Harmony. It bills itself as the "Biggest Little Town in Southern
Minnesota" and features the largest Amish population in the state.
The town may occasionally face misunderstandings and disagree-
ments, but it's fair to say that everyone there lives in Harmony.

The truth is, of course, that we should all live in harmony. Peter
said, "All of you, live in harmony with one another; be sympathetic,
love as brothers, be compassionate and humble" (1 Peter 3:8, NIV).

Harmony is a musical term. In a musical score, the harmony
doesn't always agree with the melody, but it always goes with it. The
harmony adds to the melody so that the overall experience is interesting and enjoyable.

If two people always agree on everything, they double their
chances of being wrong! We don't have to always agree in our opinions, but we should strive to be agreeable in our dispositions.

Are you living in harmony?

---

*How can we live in harmony? First we need to know
we are all madly in love with the same God.*

ST. THOMAS AQUINAS

April 24
NOT SELF-IMAGE BUT
CHRIST-IMAGE

When pride comes, then comes shame;
but with the humble is wisdom.

PROVERBS 11:2

In *Why Leaders Can't Lead*, popular management consultant Warren Bennis wrote, "Magnanimous and/or humble people are notable for their self-possession. They know who they are, have healthy egos, and take more pride in what they do than in who they are. They take compliments with a grain of salt and take intelligent criticism without rancor. Such people learn from their mistakes and don't harp on the mistakes of others. . . . True leaders are, by definition, both magnanimous and humble."[4]

Solomon agreed, saying that God resists the proud but gives grace to the humble (Proverbs 3:34). Humility precedes honor (Proverbs 15:33) and, when coupled with the fear of the Lord, brings "riches and honor and life" (Proverbs 22:4).

By humility, however, the Bible doesn't mean a low self-image. We aren't to put ourselves down or nurture an inferiority complex. We're just to think of Jesus more often than we think of ourselves, and we're to put the needs of others before our own. Today, try keeping a window before your face instead of a mirror.

---

*Humility does not consist simply in thinking cheaply
of oneself, so much as in not thinking of oneself
at all—and of Christ more and more.*

KEITH BROOKS

---

4 Warren Bennis, *Why Leaders Can't Lead* (San Francisco: Jossey-Bass Publishers, 1989), 118.

OBEY AND PRAY

> There is no authority except from God, and the
> authorities that exist are appointed by God.
>
> ROMANS 13:1

When the Founding Fathers of the United States established our system of government, they did something unique in history: they built in checks and balances between the executive, legislative, and judicial branches. No one person or branch of government can rule the country. Everyone is subject to someone else.

The Bible says that all authorities are "appointed by God" (Romans 13:1). That includes authorities at the national and local levels of government, authorities in the church, and authorities in the family. *All* authority is based in God's ultimate authority, and He assigns it to others according to His plan. Since authority comes from Him, authorities are deserving of our prayers—that they might govern in ways that honor the Source of the authority they exercise. It is easy to complain about the authorities in our lives, but God has a solution: pray "for kings and all who are in authority, that we may lead a quiet and peaceable life in all godliness and reverence" (1 Timothy 2:2).

Are the authorities in your life—national, local, spiritual, familial—on your prayer list? You are the beneficiary of your prayers for them.

The real business of your life as a saved
soul is intercessory prayer.
OSWALD CHAMBERS

Not that I speak in regard to need, for I have
learned in whatever state I am, to be content.

PHILIPPIANS 4:11

A popular book on business management has the unique title *Contented Cows Give Better Milk: The Plain Truth about Employee Relations and Your Bottom Line.* Besides having some basis in fact agriculturally speaking, the book's title is an obvious play on the century-old slogan of the Carnation Milk Company: "Carnation Condensed Milk, the Milk from Contented Cows."

The apostle Paul would probably agree with the thrust of that slogan—that there is a connection between contentment and quality. Spiritually and emotionally speaking, the quality of our lives has a lot to do with how content we are. Granted, there can be positive kinds of discontent, such as dissatisfaction with our faith, determination, or service. But if we are discontented with our standing in this world— not enough prestige, power, possessions, or high positions—we are lacking the kind of joy Paul revealed when he wrote about contentment while incarcerated in Rome. How would you assess the connection between quality and contentment in your life?

Consider this as a slogan for your life: "Joy in the Lord—the evidence of a contented Christian."

A little is as much as a lot if it is enough.
STEVE BROWN

Whatever things are true, whatever things are noble, whatever
things are just, whatever things are pure, whatever things are
lovely, whatever things are of good report, if there is any virtue
and if there is anything praiseworthy—meditate on these things.

PHILIPPIANS 4:8

A sleeping dog makes noises, and his legs twitch—he's dreaming, just like we do. In that sense, animals share a cognitive similarity with humans. But try handing your dog a list of house rules and asking him to think about them, and you'll get the proverbial cocked head and blank stare.

Human beings are the only part of God's creation that can be told to think about good things. Not that we always do—we often allow our minds to drift and wander and dwell on random thoughts that come to us without our bidding. But we do have the ability to discipline our minds to think about the kinds of things Paul suggests: truth, matters noble and just, things pure and lovely, things that come highly recommended, and virtuous and praiseworthy things. When we consider how few of those kinds of things would come to us "accidentally," it means we must be proactive in choosing what we think about.

Your mind is a gift from God. Using it wisely is a means of expressing love for Him (Mark 12:30).

———— ❦ ————

[Bring] every thought into captivity to the obedience of Christ.

APOSTLE PAUL (2 CORINTHIANS 10:5)

PREPARE TO BE OPPOSED

Consider Him who endured such hostility from sinners against
Himself, lest you become weary and discouraged in your souls.

HEBREWS 12:3

In 1786, a young Englishman named William Carey raised the subject of world evangelization with a group of ministers. He was reportedly told, "Young man, sit down; when God pleases to convert the heathen, He will do it without your aid and mine." But Carey would not be dissuaded. By 1792, he had published a revolutionary book on the church's responsibility in world missions and founded a missionary society with several other ministerial supporters. When he prepared to sail to India to preach the gospel, his wife refused to accompany him, although she eventually agreed.

The resistance William Carey encountered is not unusual. Young David's family resisted his determination to slay Goliath. Jesus' family and friends thought He was crazy (Mark 3:21). And Paul's friends tried to talk him out of his obedience to God. There will always be opposition against those who desire to carry out God's will for their lives.

If you have something you want to do for God, prepare to be opposed. If you are being opposed now, commit your way to the Lord (Proverbs 3:5-6).

---

*The Word of God never yet prospered in
the world without opposition.*

IAIN H. MURRAY

April 29

A CLOSE SHAVE

> Go rather to the lost sheep of the house of Israel. And as you
> go, preach, saying, "The kingdom of heaven is at hand."
>
> MATTHEW 10:6-7

One of the members of W. E. Sangster's church in Scarborough, England, was a barber who felt it was his duty to witness to his customers, but he wasn't always prudent in how he went about it. One day, after he lathered a man for a shave, he picked up the razor and asked, "Sir, are you prepared to meet your God?" The poor fellow fled with the lather still on his face.[5]

You know, our culture today has convinced us that it is inappropriate and unacceptable to talk about religion. But that shouldn't discourage us, because evangelism is really as simple as testifying about what God has done in your life. It's humorous to think about a barber witnessing at such an odd time. But consider your own life. When was the last time you told someone about how God's grace has turned your world upside down and inside out? Go out and meet people where they are—at the dentist, a neighborhood party, or around the water cooler—and tell them how they, too, can experience God's grace.

---

*Evangelization is a process of bringing the gospel to people
where they are, not where you would like them to be.*

VINCENT DONOVAN

---

5 Warren Wiersbe, *Walking with the Giants: A Minister's Guide to Good Reading and Great Preaching* (Dartmouth: Baker Books, 1976), 173.

In Christ Jesus you who once were far off have
been brought near by the blood of Christ.

EPHESIANS 2:13

The parable of the Good Samaritan helping the injured Jew is widely accepted as an illustration of how we are to treat others who are in need (Luke 10:25-37). There is another side to it, however, a side that becomes clear when you learn that Jews and Samaritans were taught to despise each other and that Jesus was telling this parable to a Jewish audience. Hearing their teacher tell them to "go and do likewise," regardless of cultural differences, was overwhelming for them. In effect, Jesus was trying to open the eyes of their hearts so they could see all human beings as He saw them: in need of a Savior.

Throughout history, the good news of the gospel has broken down the walls of separation between races and religions because of the one thing we all have in common: the need for salvation. The Bible tells us that "there is no difference; for all have sinned and fall short of the glory of God" (Romans 3:22-23).

Everyone, regardless of race, religion, or creed, shares the same title of "Sinner." Because of Christ's sacrifice on the cross, everyone who believes in Him can share the same glorious title of "Forgiven."

We hold these truths to be self-evident,
that all men are created equal.
DECLARATION OF INDEPENDENCE

MAY

You are the light of the world.

MATTHEW 5:14

Two college students responded to God's call in very different ways while being taught by professors who did not believe in God. One of the students diligently studied what the professor taught, always hesitant to mention her belief in God for fear of sacrificing her grade, while the other student knew God was calling him to write his final paper on how to become a Christian, despite putting his grade in jeopardy. At the end of the semester, the first student walked away with an A, while the young man received an F on his paper and barely passed the class. Some time later, the young man ran into his old professor, and during their conversation she confessed to giving him an F because she was angry that he had tried to share the gospel with her. She also thanked him for taking that chance, because his F paper led her to accept Christ as her Savior.

The A student still wonders with sadness about her professor.

It's not always easy to accept the task of shining God's light in this dark world, but we may be the light that God has sent for a soul in need of a Savior. We must not only be ready; we must also be willing.

This little light of mine, I'm gonna let it shine,
let it shine, let it shine, let it shine.
UNKNOWN

I also suffer these things; nevertheless I am not ashamed, for
I know whom I have believed and am persuaded that He is
able to keep what I have committed to Him until that Day.

2 TIMOTHY 1:12

A group of nine-year-olds was asked their opinions on the subject of death. Jim said, "When you die, they bury you in the ground and your soul goes to heaven but your body can't go to heaven because it's too crowded up there already." Judy answered, "Only the good people go to heaven. The other people go where it's hot all the time like in Florida." John thoughtfully replied, "Maybe I'll die someday, but I hope I don't die on my birthday because it's no fun to celebrate your birthday if you're dead." Marsha added, "When you die, you don't have to do homework in heaven, unless your teacher is there too."[6]

It's always amusing to find out what children think of serious issues like death. And what does God's Word have to say about death? For the believer, to be absent from the body is to be present with the Lord. We can have confidence that our loved ones who are believers are immediately taken into the presence of God when their spirit leaves this earth. And that simple truth, that hope that comes from our Maker, can bring a childlike smile to the face of even the most mature.

Death is not extinguishing the light from the Christian;
it is putting out the lamp because the dawn has come.

UNKNOWN

---

[6] Michael Hodgin, *1001 Humorous Illustrations for Public Speaking* (Grand Rapids: Zondervan, 1994), 100–101.

May 3

BIG AND SMALL SACRIFICES

> If I give everything I own to the poor and even go to the stake
> to be burned as a martyr, but I don't love, I've gotten nowhere.
>
> 1 CORINTHIANS 13:3, *THE MESSAGE*

For more than a decade, North Korea has been the most restrictive nation for Christians to live in. The accounts of persecution from those who have fled the nation are sobering. For instance, when authorities destroyed a home near Pyongyang, they discovered a Bible hidden among the rubble. Inside it was a list of Christians, including a pastor, two assistant pastors, two elders, and twenty other members of the church. All of them were called in for questioning, and the five leaders were told they must deny Christ and pledge their loyalty to Kim Jong Il and his father, Kim Il Sung, or die. Refusing to renounce their faith, they became martyrs. They were forced onto the ground, and a steamroller was driven over them. The report continues, "Fellow parishioners who had been assembled to watch the execution cried, screamed out, or fainted when the men were crushed beneath the steamroller."[7]

This account is a good reminder to us that martyrdom still happens today. While you may never be asked to deny God or be killed, each day you have opportunities to show you are dedicated to Him.

*Lord, help me to be sensitive to the ways
I can make small sacrifices today.*

---

[7] www.firstthings.com/onthesquare/?p=79, accessed January 19, 2006.

130 | TURNING POINTS WITH GOD

As for these four young men, God gave them
knowledge and skill in all literature; and Daniel
had understanding in all visions and dreams.

DANIEL 1:17

God is preparing you for the ministry that He is preparing *for* you.
He's working at both ends of the process—preparing you for a
unique role of service, and preparing the work He'll give you in His
timing. So wherever you are right now is God's classroom for future
service.

Joseph's prison term prepared him to be God's man on Egypt's
throne. Moses' years in Pharaoh's court equipped him for his tasks
as leader of Israel. For years Joshua served as Moses' aide, and Elisha
did the same for Elijah; God was preparing them both as successors.
Paul's years in Arabia were readying him for years of missionary service. Even Jesus experienced an extended period of preparation in the
carpenter's shop of Nazareth.

Wherever you are right now, God is giving you experiences that
are training you for future service. The training may extend over a
long period of time or for only a few minutes, but He equips us with
what we need to serve Him.

Think of your circumstances today as God's seminary.

All there is of God is available to the man
who is available to all there is of God.
MAJOR IAN THOMAS

A word fitly spoken is like apples of gold in settings of silver.

PROVERBS 25:11

Newlyweds Sean and Beca Thompson were having trouble adjusting to the pressures of marriage. Whenever they disagreed, they raised their voices, which led to yelling and name-calling. Their words hurt one another and badly damaged their marriage.

We need to realize the destructive power of the tongue, but we also need to grasp its power for good. Do you speak tenderly with your loved one? Do you express affection? Do you compliment and edify? Are your words fitly spoken?

The word *fitly* is an interesting term in Hebrew, the original language of the book of Proverbs. It's the only time this word occurs in the entire Old Testament, and experts suggest two different meanings. The first involves the idea of timing—a word spoken at the right time, or a *well-timed* word. Other experts think this Hebrew term is related to the idea of a wheel, such as a potter's wheel. The idea would be a *well-turned* word.

Both ideas are important. We need to say the right words, and we need to say them at the right time. Ask God for wisdom, and may your words be "fitly spoken" today.

---

*One reason a dog is such a good friend is that
his tail wags instead of his tongue.*

ANONYMOUS

May 6

HIGH CALLING

Train up a child in the way he should go, and
when he is old he will not depart from it.

PROVERBS 22:6

In the film *Cheaper by the Dozen*, Steve Martin's character, Tom Baker, decides to walk away from his dream of coaching college football because of the strain it has been on his family. When his boss asks if he'll have any regrets for such a decision, Baker says, "If I screw up raising my kids, nothing I achieve will matter much."

Jesus says it a different way: "Whoever causes one of these little ones ... to stumble, it would be better for him if a millstone were hung around his neck, and he were thrown into the sea" (Mark 9:42). In other words, raising children is a serious responsibility and privilege; we should treat it that way and give our best to this high calling.

The world says we ought to pursue degrees, titles, salaries, and accomplishments. But if you look intently into the eyes of your child, the things that are truly important will become clear. The title you hold will fade, and your accomplishments will someday be forgotten; it is the investment you make in the spiritual lives of your children that will outlive you and carry on into eternity.

---

*The first and most natural condition of things is
for Christian parents to train up their own children
in the nurture and admonition of the Lord.*
CHARLES HADDON SPURGEON

So shall My word be that goes forth from My
mouth; it shall not return to Me void.... It shall
prosper in the thing for which I sent it.

ISAIAH 55:11

Noted Quaker missionary Stephen Grellet once felt burdened to preach the gospel to the men in an American lumber camp. When he arrived, however, the camp was empty; the men had gone farther into the forest. Still believing he had been sent there to preach the gospel, he stood up and delivered his sermon to a deserted mess hall.

Years later a man stopped him and proclaimed, "I have found you at last!" Thinking there was some mistake, Grellet inquired as to how the man knew him. He explained that he had been working at the lumber camp and had returned from where the other men were to get a saw. Startled at hearing a man's voice, he peeked through a chink of the logs and saw Grellet preaching to an empty room. He listened to the sermon, felt conviction of his sins, got hold of a Bible, was saved, and led others to a saving knowledge of Christ Jesus. Is God calling you to speak His Word into someone's life?

God's Word is powerful; whenever it is spoken, the Spirit of God will work in the hearts of seen and unseen listeners.

---

*After awhile, the power of truth came so forcibly over them
that they trembled under it, and many tears were shed.*
STEPHEN GRELLET

THE GREAT COMFORTER

As a mother comforts her child, so will I comfort you.

ISAIAH 66:13, NIV

This time of year can be especially difficult for those whose mothers are no longer living. For them, Mother's Day is a painful reminder of the void left by the dear person who gave them life. For some, it may be the loss of a grandmother or aunt who raised them. For others who never knew their mothers, this time of year reminds them of that cruel reality. In each case, it is not easy to feel celebratory on the day we honor and commemorate our mothers. However, God understands the comfort only a mother can give, and He promises to comfort us "as a mother comforts her child" through heartache.

Sadly, an author once said that "time is the only comforter for the loss of a mother." But if we know the love of Christ Jesus, then we know a greater Comforter than time. We know a Savior who experienced loss and a Creator who gently brushes the tears from our cheeks, just as our mothers did.

During any loss or sadness, depend on the God of all comfort to take you in His arms and soothe you with His Word. Though our earthly mothers can never be replaced, Christ Jesus can comfort us with the tenderness and strength of a mother's love.

The LORD is near to those who have a broken heart.

KING DAVID (PSALM 34:18)

May 9
GREAT MOMS WHO MADE A DIFFERENCE: RUFUS'S MOTHER

> Greet Rufus, chosen in the Lord, and his mother and mine.
>
> ROMANS 16:13

You may be surprised to learn that some pastors have mixed feelings about celebrating Mother's Day. The reason: many women sitting in the pews long to be mothers but aren't—those who are single and celibate, those who struggle with infertility, or those who have suffered a miscarriage or lost a child—and for them the day is painful.

But every woman can be a mother to someone. The apostle Paul had an "adopted mother" whom he greeted in Romans 16:13. "Greet Rufus for me," he wrote, "and also his dear mother who has been such a mother to me" (TLB).

American Greetings, the card company, has a Mother's Day card that says, "Because you're like a mother to me, I'm thinking of you on Mother's Day. Whenever I need advice, you're always there with an open mind and an understanding heart. I can't tell you how much that means to me."

According to Isaiah 66:13, even the Lord longs to be like a mother to us.

Perhaps you're more of a mother than you realize. Or perhaps there's more than one "mother" whom you need to appreciate this year on Mother's Day.

"Like as a mother comforteth"
O words of gentle worth!
"So I will comfort you," declares
The Lord of all the earth.

WILLIAM RUNYAN

HE GIVES ME RULES

Keep the commandments of the LORD and His statutes
which I command you today for your good.

DEUTERONOMY 10:13

James Hatch, beloved professor at Columbia International University, once opened class by leading students in the chorus "God Is So Good." After several stanzas like "He cares for me" and "I love Him so," Hatch added one of his own: "He gives me rules, He gives me rules, He gives me rules. He's so good to me." The students were surprised, but Hatch was right. God has given us His rules for our good, and when we obey them, we're healthier, happier, and holier.

Consider the command in Ephesians 4:32 to be kind to one another, tenderhearted, and forgiving. When we carry resentment in our hearts, it's like a little pocket of poison that pollutes our personalities and sours our spirits. But being kind and pleasant lightens our burdens and brightens our days—not to mention what it does for others.

The Creator knows how we best function, and He's an expert on the care of the soul. Obedience not only glorifies Him; it also blesses our lives.

He gives us rules; He's so good to us.

God knows we need help, and thankfully in His love He blessed us with a few really important rules. As the psalmist says, Blessed is the person who doesn't scoff at God's law!

JOE STOWELL

A CITY BIG ENOUGH

> The city is laid out as a square; its length is as great as its
> breadth. And he measured the city with the reed: twelve
> thousand furlongs. Its length, breadth, and height are equal.
>
> REVELATION 21:16

Picture this: a city shaped like a cube that covers the United States from the Atlantic Coast to the middle of Kansas, and from Texas to the Canadian border—1,400 miles long, wide, and high. It covers about two million square miles of land; but because it's a cube with room for about 600 "floors," in total it has 1.2 billion square miles of living space. That's the city the Bible calls the New Jerusalem (Revelation 21:2).

Sometimes people wonder whether there will be room in heaven for all the millions of believers destined to go there. Based on the above dimensions, it would appear so! The New Jerusalem is not heaven—it's a city in heaven that will serve as the "capital" of heaven. In it are the thrones of God and the Lamb, a river of the water of life, and the tree of life: food, water, and Jesus Christ—everything needed to live forever. The question is not whether there will be room in the New Jerusalem for everyone—there will be—but whether you will be one of the "everyone."

Jesus has invited you to spend eternity in the New Jerusalem. Have you made your reservation?

The best is yet to be.
JOHN WESLEY

Let your speech always be with grace, seasoned with salt,
that you may know how you ought to answer each one.

COLOSSIANS 4:6

Evangelist Michael Guido once learned an interesting lesson from snails: they are created with teeth on their tongues. A well-known scientist examined a snail's tongue under a microscope and counted thirty thousand teeth. Usually the snail keeps its tongue rolled up like a ribbon; but when necessary, it sticks it out and the teeth do their damage.

Sometimes people have teeth on their tongues too, teeth that can snap, bite, and inflict damage. The Bible tells us to let our speech always be with grace. Not sometimes, but always, according to this verse. And we shouldn't be boring. The phrase "seasoned with salt" specifically refers to salt's power not as a preservative but as a seasoning. Salt keeps food from tasting bland or insipid. It makes a dish flavorful and enjoyable. That's the way our talk should be.

Don't be biting or boring in your conversations today; be edifying and interesting, knowing how to answer each one.

Father, take control of our tongues. Guard our lips from telling lies. Help us to speak the truth in love. In Jesus' name, amen.
MICHAEL GUIDO

SEARCH ME

Grow in the grace and knowledge of our
Lord and Savior Jesus Christ.

2 PETER 3:18

There are two words we should say less and less as we grow in the Lord: "I'm sorry." Or, if you prefer, "Forgive me." Those are vital words when we need them—and we need them frequently, for James 3:2 tells us, "We all stumble in many things." But how much better to avoid the offense before it's committed. How much better to grow in grace.

Psalm 139 offers a prayer for God to search us and know our hearts, to try us and know our ways. "See if there is any wicked way in me," pleads the psalmist, "and lead me in the way everlasting" (v. 24).

When we get a good night's sleep ("He gives His beloved sleep"—Psalm 127:2) and we begin the day with the Lord ("In the morning, having risen a long while before daylight, He went out . . . and . . . prayed"—Mark 1:35), we're less likely to stumble during the day. And as we progress in Christ, we're more likely to grow in wisdom, love, graciousness, and maturity.

May the Lord help us to say "Praise the Lord!" more often and "I'm sorry" much less.

He who loves the Savior desires to grow in the knowledge of him; he cannot read or hear too much or too often concerning his great Redeemer.

CHARLES HADDON SPURGEON

FERVENT AND PREVAILING

> Peter was kept in the prison, but prayer for him was
> being made fervently by the church to God.
>
> ACTS 12:5, NASB

*F*ervent is one of those great old-fashioned Bible words that has fallen into disuse. James 5:16 says: "The effective, fervent prayer of a righteous man avails much." Paul wrote to the Colossians that Epaphras was "always laboring fervently for you in prayers" (4:12). The English word *fervent* comes from a term meaning "to boil," and it implies intensity of feeling.

Is that the way we pray?

Another nearly forgotten prayer adjective is *prevailing*, which was a favorite term of an earlier generation. Charles Finney wrote, "In prevailing prayer, a child of God comes before Him with real faith in His promises and asks for things agreeable to His will, assured of being heard according to the true intent of the promises; and thus coming to God he prevails with Him."

Matthew Henry, the old Bible commentator, wrote, "It is the prayer of faith that is prevailing prayer. . . . It is the believing prayer that will be the prevailing prayer."

In order to grow strong, we have to exercise our prayer muscles. Learn to pray fervently. Learn the secrets of prevailing prayer.

Prevailing prayer is the pathway to the
outpouring of the Holy Spirit.
JOHN PIPER

CHIEF CORNERSTONE

> The stone which the builders rejected has
> become the chief cornerstone.
>
> PSALM 118:22

The idea of setting a large stone with perfectly squared corners at the corner of a new building is an ancient one. The tradition is carried on today but for different reasons. Today the cornerstone of a building is laid for commemorative or memorial reasons. But in ancient times, the squared corners of the cornerstone served an engineering purpose: to set the direction of the two walls connected at the corner.

Interestingly, in modern Greece the blood of a sacrificial animal is sometimes sprinkled on a new cornerstone to give it strength and endurance. What an amazing picture of the cornerstone the Bible describes: Jesus Christ. Indeed, the Bible calls Christ the "chief" cornerstone. Christ sets the standard and measurements for the building for which He shed His blood—the temple made of living stones, the church (1 Peter 2:5). Whenever anything is built in the Kingdom of God, it must draw its direction and standards from the Chief Cornerstone, Jesus Christ.

The same is true for each Christian. The only way to adjust one's life is to measure it by the standard of the Chief Cornerstone.

Jesus is the Cornerstone, came for sinners to atone.
Though rejected by His own, He became the Cornerstone.

LARI GOSS

WORSHIP AS CONFESSION

> Please pardon my sin, and return with me,
> that I may worship the LORD.
>
> 1 SAMUEL 15:25

It is said that when former President John Kennedy and then Soviet Premier Nikita Khrushchev were meeting together, their opinions were strong and the exchange heated. In exasperation, Kennedy asked the Soviet leader, "Do you ever admit a mistake?" The premier responded, "Certainly I do. In a speech before the Twentieth Party Congress, I admitted all of Stalin's mistakes."

That could be categorized as confession of the Soviet sort, but not biblical confession. The Greek word translated "confession" (*homologeo*: *homo* = same, *logeo* = say) means "to say the same thing as." Therefore, when we confess to God, we agree with what He says about sin. And in personal confession, we say what He says about *our* sins. Jesus was clear to the Pharisees of His day that coming to worship God without confessing our sins (that is, having a heart far from God) is a futile exercise. Our worship of God must start where David's did: "Against You, You only, have I sinned, and done this evil in Your sight" (Psalm 51:4). The next time you purpose to worship God, begin with confession of your sin.

Not to agree with God is an exercise in deception—of ourselves, not God.

---

*The confession of evil works is the first
beginning of good works.*

ST. AUGUSTINE

May 17

FIDELIS IN PARVO

He who is faithful in what is least is faithful also in much.

LUKE 16:10

The Mount School in York, England, started by Quakers in 1831, is a boarding school for teenage girls. The school motto is *Fidelis in Parvo*, a Latin phrase meaning "Faithfulness in Little Things."

That's a great motto for all of us. Jesus stressed this principle in His parable of the talents. Some servants were given more coins than others, but all were expected to invest them faithfully. Those who did so proved they could be trusted with more.

It reminds us of the old adage "If you need help getting something done, find the busiest people you know and get 'em involved." The point is that busy people tend to be productive, efficient, organized, and motivated.

Well, it's possible to be too busy, of course. But when God is looking for workers, He doesn't select those sitting around doing nothing. He wants people who are working where they are, blooming where they're planted, faithful in whatever He has already given them, and dependable in little things. If we'll be faithful where we are, the Lord will entrust us with more.

---

*Little things are little things; but faithfulness
in little things is a great thing.*

UNKNOWN

PROFITING FROM PERSEVERANCE

> We also glory in tribulations, knowing that tribulation produces
> perseverance; and perseverance, character; and character, hope.
>
> ROMANS 5:3-4

Most people are familiar with this famous quote from a speech by Winston Churchill: "Never give in. Never give in. Never, never, never, never—in nothing, great or small, large or petty—never give in, except to convictions of honor and good sense. Never yield to the apparently overwhelming might of the enemy." Not everyone knows to whom he gave this speech: it was to a group of young schoolboys at the Harrow School in England, Churchill's own alma mater, at a time when England was under attack by Germany in World War II.

Young people can be easily discouraged in the face of adversity—like John Mark, the cousin of Barnabas, who accompanied Paul and Barnabas on the opening leg of their first missionary journey. As they prepared to enter the difficult region of Asia Minor, John Mark left and returned to Jerusalem (Acts 13:13; 15:36-41). John Mark had not yet learned that "tribulation produces perseverance; and perseverance, character; and character, hope."

If you are thinking of quitting something that is difficult, think of the character and hope you will forfeit if you do.

Genius, that power which dazzles mortal eyes,
Is oft but perseverance in disguise.
HENRY AUSTIN

PREDICTING THE FUTURE

The LORD ... by no means clears the guilty, visiting the iniquity
of the fathers on the children to the third and fourth generation.

NUMBERS 14:18

Repentance and forgiveness accomplish much, but there is one thing they can't do: change the past. What's done is done. Like the ripples that cross a pond where a pebble has been thrown, the effects of even small choices reverberate far and wide. Take Abraham's acquiescence to fathering a son with Hagar (Genesis 16). The descendants of that son, Ishmael, became a thorn to the descendants of Isaac, Abraham's son of promise. That antagonism rages on in the lands of the Middle East today.

God warned that the effects of iniquity would be visited on the third and fourth generations. But He also promised that He would maintain His covenant and mercy for a "thousand generations with those who love Him and keep His commandments" (Deuteronomy 7:9). If the effects of good and bad choices have an impact on future generations, would a thousand generations of mercy be better than four generations of judgment?

Parents who teach their children how to make wise choices today are blessing future generations. It's a biblical way to predict the future.

Men are free to decide their own moral choices, but they are
also under the necessity to account to God for those choices.

A. W. TOZER

A soft answer turns away wrath, but a harsh word stirs up anger.

PROVERBS 15:1

Leslie Flynn tells a story from the days when many people traveled by rail. A baby cried throughout the night, keeping the passengers awake. One exasperated traveler finally shouted to the man who was caring for the baby, "Why don't you take that baby to its mother?" The answer was a soft reply, "I'd like to, sir, but its mother is in the baggage car in a coffin. We're taking her home for burial."

When we're angry, we seldom speak our words wisely. It is possible, of course, to speak as Jesus did, with righteous indignation, when warranted. But most of the time we just blow our tops, and our rash words come back to haunt us. Someone quipped, "Happiness is often punctured by a sharp tongue."

It's not easy to learn to hold our tongues, but memorizing Proverbs 15:1 has helped multitudes of believers through the ages. It's one of Scripture's most powerful verses for learning to underreact to provocation. If you've never memorized it, commit it to memory today. If you have learned it, remind yourself of it.

You might have an occasion today to use it.

He who has a sharp tongue soon cuts his own throat.

ANONYMOUS

> The things which are seen are temporary, but
> the things which are not seen are eternal.
>
> 2 CORINTHIANS 4:18

Ever been to a "howl-in"? For several years, animal-rights activists have staged howl-ins across Alaska to protest the state's predator-control program, which allows the killing of wolves that threaten moose and caribou numbers. Protestors dress up in wolf costumes and howl at the top of their lungs.

Well, all things in balance. The earth is the Lord's, and we are stewards of it. We should be concerned for our environment; we should recycle and not litter; and we should certainly appreciate the plants, animals, and other natural blessings God has given us.

But in Genesis 1:28, Adam and Eve were instructed to subdue the earth, which indicates that people are more important than animals in God's sight. Sometimes animal-rights protesters and plant-life advocates give the impression that plants and animals are more important than human souls.

Be a responsible Christian who maintains a healthy concern for the environment, but never forget the worth of an eternal soul. Winning others to Christ—that's something to howl about!

If I had my life to live over again, I would live it to change the lives of people, because you have not changed anything until you've changed the lives of people.

WARREN WEBSTER

> This is eternal life, that they may know You, the only
> true God, and Jesus Christ whom You have sent.
>
> JOHN 17:3

At the world's trendiest nightspots and restaurants, long lines are formed by those who want to be admitted. They stand behind velvet ropes under the watchful eye of those who keep the door. Suddenly, an individual walks past the long line of hopefuls, catches the eye of the doorkeeper, and is motioned forward. The clasp on the velvet rope is released, the door is opened, and the favored guest is granted entrance, leaving all the rest to wonder, *Who does he know that we don't know?*

It's from those kinds of situations in life that the familiar expression arose: "It's not what you know but who you know that matters." And that is definitely true when it comes to eternal life. Jesus said that not everyone who called Him "Lord" would enter the Kingdom of Heaven. To those who practice lawlessness, His reply to their "Lord, Lord," will be, "I never knew you" (Matthew 7:21-23). There is a difference in knowing *about* God and actually knowing *Him*. And only by knowing Him do the doors to the Kingdom of Heaven and eternal life open.

Do you *know* God or only know *about* Him? Gaining access to a restaurant brings enjoyment for an evening. Gaining access to heaven brings joy forever.

Oh, the fullness ... of knowing God on earth!

JIM ELLIOT

I DON'T LIKE THE DIRT!

> I know what I'm doing. I have it all planned
> out—plans to take care of you.
>
> JEREMIAH 29:11, *THE MESSAGE*

A little girl walking in a garden saw a particularly beautiful flower and promptly picked it because she felt it was too pretty to be in the dirt. She then took the flower home and rinsed the dirt off with water. Shortly thereafter, the flower wilted and died. When the owner of that garden saw what the little girl had done, he exclaimed, "You have destroyed my finest bloom!"

"I'm sorry, but I didn't like it in all that dirt," said the girl.

The gardener responded by saying, "I chose that spot and mixed the soil because I knew that only there could it grow to be a beautiful flower."

Sometimes we become like that little girl, fixated on the dirt of our lives instead of seeing the beauty and growth that will emerge in time. But once we have seen the hand of God in our lives, we have assurance that we can trust His sovereignty. So if it feels as if nothing good will ever come from what you are going through, be patient and steadfast, knowing that God "plans to give you hope and a future" (Jeremiah 29:11, NIV).

> *I have lived a long time; and the longer I live,*
> *the more convincing proofs I see of this truth,*
> *that God governs in the affairs of men!*
>
> BENJAMIN FRANKLIN

Remember the word that I said to you, "A servant is not
greater than his master." If they persecuted Me, they will also
persecute you. If they kept My word, they will keep yours also.

JOHN 15:20

Sir Isaac Newton published his Three Laws of Motion in 1687. The
third law said, "All forces occur in pairs, and these two forces are
equal in magnitude and opposite in direction." That law has been
paraphrased into the modern form we know today: "For every action
there is an equal and opposite reaction."

What the great scientist didn't include in his 1687 treatise is that
his third law of motion applies to the spiritual world as well. If you
push in the spiritual realm, you are going to get pushed back. This
world system is under the control of Satan (1 John 5:19); when we
spread the gospel into his domain, there is going to be strong resistance. Jesus told His original disciples that they would be resisted just
as He was—and that applies to you as well. Unless God has prepared
the heart of your listener to receive the Word, don't be discouraged if
there is "push back." It's a law in both the physical and the spiritual
world.

Here's another spiritual law for those situations: "My word . . .
shall not return to Me void" (Isaiah 55:11).

---

*Jesus promised His disciples three things: They would be
completely fearless, absurdly happy, and in constant trouble.*

G. K. CHESTERTON

May 25

WHO MADE THIS MESS?

From childhood you have known the Holy Scriptures,
which are able to make you wise for salvation
through faith which is in Christ Jesus.

2 TIMOTHY 3:15

Every inch of the kitchen floor was covered with flour. And in the center of it was the bright-eyed three-year-old Savannah, clapping her hands. She was having a great time making handprints on the cupboards, until her mother came in. "Savannah! Who made this mess?"

"God did!" Savannah replied confidently.

"No, Savannah, God didn't make this mess, *you* did!"

"But in Sunday school this morning we learned that God created everything, Mommy. So He must have made this mess too."

From the mouths of babes! Although Savannah's interpretation was a little off, her observation is a reflection of her parents' investment in her spiritual growth. Only when Christian parents raise their children in the context of the gospel will those children be sensitive to the Lord. If we teach our children to pray, they must see us praying. If we teach them that the Bible is God's Word, they must see us reading it and loving it. If we insist that they go to church, we must go with them. You know, one of the greatest needs in the church today is for a revival of solid Bible teaching in the Christian home. After all, the home is where the next generation of Christians is being molded.

Let the little children come to Me.

JESUS CHRIST (MARK 10:14)

May 26
THE WELLSPRING OF LIFE

Keep your heart with all diligence, for out
of it spring the issues of life.

PROVERBS 4:23

Underground water reservoirs are being contaminated with all manner of chemicals, some of them carcinogenic. The gasoline additive MBTE has been leaking from storage tanks nationwide; arsenic has been found in New England well water; and chemicals from fertilizers are polluting wells in agricultural areas.

The water that comes out of a rural kitchen faucet is only as pure as the well water that supplies it. A tiny bit of a deadly chemical is enough to cause authorities to seal the well out of concern for its users' health. The human heart is like an underground reservoir: what comes out of the mouth of man will be only as pure as the heart-reservoir that supplies it (Mark 7:17-23). Just as governments are getting tough on polluters, we need to get tough with ourselves about what goes into the spiritual reservoir of the heart. We cannot willingly be contaminated by the world and then expect our hearts to flow with purity and life. It is up to us to safeguard our hearts. How tough are you being on yourself when it comes to keeping your heart pure with all diligence?

A pure external life—speech, thoughts, actions, desires—begins at a deeper level. The heart is the wellspring of life. Purity begets purity.

Make and keep me pure within.
CHARLES WESLEY

WHAT PRICE UNITY?

Let each of you look out not only for his own
interests, but also for the interests of others.

PHILIPPIANS 2:4

The greater good is a phrase we hear often today. It has good implications (when a family member gives up a personal preference for the sake of family harmony) and bad (when society decides the unborn and infirm are too big a burden). In other words, the needs of the majority do not always take precedence. But sometimes they do.

In the early church, a situation arose that had the potential to keep the church from becoming the unified body God intended. Initially, the church had a distinctly Jewish flavor—faithful Jews found it hard to immediately give up centuries of laws and traditions that were meaningless to Gentiles. Then Gentiles came into the church, and they found it hard to give up centuries of pagan practices that were offensive to Jews. In Acts 15, we find the church leaders working out a compromise: Jews were to stop insisting the Gentiles keep Jewish laws, and Gentiles were to avoid practices that offended the Jews. The result: peace and unity in the church.

Don't be afraid to put the interests of others ahead of your own when necessary. The church's greater good, and God's glory, will be the result.

In essentials, unity; in non-essentials,
liberty; in all things, charity.
ST. AUGUSTINE

> The righteous shall flourish like a palm tree,
> he shall grow like a cedar in Lebanon.

PSALM 92:12

Most plants grown by gardeners change imperceptibly day by day. Check a plant one day, and you'll see little difference from the day before. But such is not the case with various species of bamboo. Bamboo is actually a type of grass and is said to be the fastest-growing plant in the world. Some bamboo shoots have been known to grow two feet or more in a twenty-four-hour period.

Some new Christians think they should grow as quickly as bamboo. In other words, they wonder why change is taking so long. Those believers are hungry to put off the old self and put on the new (Ephesians 4:22-24, NIV). Sadly, other Christians don't seem to worry about growth at all. For them, Christianity is more about a ticket to heaven than about life change on earth. But the Bible is clear that growth is not an option. Just as we grow physically when we are born physically, we should grow spiritually when we are born again. Every living organism that is healthy will grow. If over time there is no noticeable evidence of spiritual growth—recognizable changes in your life—you should be concerned.

Better to be concerned that you're not growing fast enough than to have others be concerned that you're not growing at all.

---

*Some people's religion reminds me of a rocking
horse, which has motion without progress.*
ROWLAND HILL

NEW-FASHIONED SALVATION

By grace you have been saved through faith, and
that not of yourselves; it is the gift of God.

EPHESIANS 2:8

In the 1980s, the Smith-Barney company made a series of commercials in which distinguished actor John Houseman spoke the famous line "We make money the old-fashioned way. We *earn* it!" Sometime later, based on that commercial, a Christian cartoonist showed some Pharisees arguing with Jesus about salvation. Their punch line? "We get our salvation the old-fashioned way. We *earn* it!"

Those Smith-Barney commercials were a success partly because they appealed to something in fallen human nature: the desire to work and pay our own way. The Bible commends that attitude in many respects (2 Thessalonians 3:10), but not when it comes to salvation. The problem with earning our salvation is that we can never do enough. Committing one sin is the same as committing them all. And once a sin is committed, it's like a spoken word—there's no getting it back. The biggest challenge facing the early church was helping Jewish believers set aside law and tradition as ways of trying to earn God's approval.

Don't try to be saved the old-fashioned way. Receive salvation the way God offers it—through Christ—as a gift of grace through faith.

---

*The sinner, apart from grace, is unable to
be willing and unwilling to be able.*

W. E. BEST

> Godliness with contentment is great gain.
>
> 1 TIMOTHY 6:6

Internet matchmaking sites differ in purpose. Some are dating sites that allow singles to meet and get together. Other sites are marriage oriented, requiring interested parties to fill out extensive questionnaires about themselves and the kind of person they're looking for. All these sites are based on a single premise: few people are happy being single.

God Himself said to Adam, "It is not good that man should be alone; I will make him a helper comparable to him" (Genesis 2:18). God said that, ideally, men and women should meet, marry, and populate the earth. What He didn't say was that it's okay to be unhappy until that meeting and marrying take place. The apostle Paul pointed out that singleness can be a rare blessing—the chance to be wholly committed to serving Christ. His point is this: whether you are single or married, use that condition as an opportunity to serve the Lord with all your heart. Are you happy where you are, taking advantage of the opportunity you have today?

Happiness is not a state of companionship. Rather, true joy is a by-product of being in the center of the will of God.

There is never a place in the Bible where it says that marriage makes you happy. It says over and over again that God makes you happy.

DICK PURNELL

Let him who thinks he stands take heed lest he fall.

1 CORINTHIANS 10:12

On September 26, 1960, Vice President Richard Nixon debated John Kennedy, the Democratic presidential candidate, in the first-ever televised presidential debates. Nixon was warned not to accept Kennedy's challenge to debate, but he didn't listen. Instead, he arrived at the debate tired, needing a shave, and baggy-eyed, while Kennedy was tanned, youthful, and rested. Nixon lost both the debate and the election.

Pride makes us believe things that are not true. Vice President Nixon was an experienced debater and felt he didn't need to prepare in order to beat his youthful challenger. Nor did he take into account the power of television to project an image, good or bad. That's what pride does—it makes us think reasonable things are unreasonable, and vice versa. The Bible warns us often about the deceitfulness of pride—about thinking we are invincible and not able to fall. It is at that moment that we are most vulnerable, most likely to be proven wrong. If you are feeling prideful right now, be forewarned.

God loves to lift the humble up and will not hesitate to allow the prideful to fall. Choose the upward direction. It's a much softer landing than the alternative.

He that is down need fear no fall,
He that is low, no pride.

JOHN BUNYAN

JUNE

GOD THE ARCHITECT

Unless the LORD builds the house, they labor in vain who build it.

PSALM 127:1

Frank Lloyd Wright, one of the twentieth century's most well-known architects, practiced "organic architecture"—designs that flow out of and reflect the context of their environment. His designs are easily recognizable, perhaps the most famous being "Falling-water," a private Pennsylvania residence with a waterfall and stream running beneath it.

We ought to be able to recognize what God builds as well, since He also is an "architect and builder" (Hebrews 11:10, NIV). If you looked at the homes on your street, which ones would you identify as having been built by God? Would you pick your own home? Solomon wrote that unless God is building our homes, we are laboring in vain. The family we build in our own strength will not be recognized as one of God's homes. The Bible calls God's works the fruit of the Spirit and humans' works the deeds of the flesh (Galatians 5:16-23). God's buildings are characterized by love and encouragement, humanity's by enmity and strife.

The only way to end up with a home that reflects God as the Architect is to build according to His plan—the Word of God.

---

*The Christian home is the Master's workshop where
the processes of character molding are silently,
lovingly, faithfully, and successfully carried on.*

RICHARD MONCKTON MILNES, LORD HOUGHTON

ENDURING MERCY

Praise the LORD! Oh, give thanks to the LORD, for
He is good! For His mercy endures forever.

PSALM 106:1

Many people, Christians and non-Christians alike, who read the story of King David in the Old Testament are shocked at his double sins of adultery and ordering the death of Uriah the Hittite. They are even more surprised to learn that David was not punished for his sins in accordance with the statutes of Israel.

According to Leviticus 20:10 and 24:17, the punishment for adultery and murder in Israel was death. (While it was not David's hand that took the life of Uriah, it was by David's order that he was killed, so he was certainly responsible.) God forgave David's sin (2 Samuel 12:13; Psalm 32), and in doing so, extended mercy to him. We receive mercy when God withholds from us a judgment we deserve (as opposed to grace, which we receive when God gives us favor that we don't deserve). No wonder David said, "His mercy endures forever," thirty-three times in Psalms! The basis of God's mercy toward David was the same as the basis of His mercy toward us: the death of Christ for the sins of the whole world (1 John 2:2). Christ took the punishment David deserved.

The next time you sin and are not immediately punished, thank God for His mercy, extended through Jesus Christ.

---

*Mercy, also, is a good thing, for it makes men
perfect, in that it imitates the perfect Father.*

ST. AMBROSE

TO DO: REMOVE TROUBLES

> Jesus answered and said to her, "Martha, Martha, you
> are worried and troubled about many things."
>
> LUKE 10:41

Achan, an infamous Israelite in the Old Testament, brought great trouble into Israel's camp by violating the ban on taking plunder from the conquered city of Jericho (Joshua 7). By the time of the monarchy, Achan's name (in a play on words) was being spelled "Achar"—the Hebrew word for trouble or disaster (1 Chronicles 2:7). Until Achar—Israel's troubler—was dealt with, there was no peace or victory in the camp.

Trouble doesn't always enter our lives on two legs. It's usually more subtle, coming in the form of schedules, finances, family matters, vocational problems, personal challenges, and the endless to-do lists that rob us of time we could be spending with God. Like Joshua, we must remove trouble from the camp if we are going to have peace. Nowhere were trouble and tranquillity so clearly juxtaposed as in the house of Mary and Martha. Jesus chided Martha for being distracted—"worried and troubled about many things"—but praised Mary for focusing solely on Him (Luke 10:38-42).

What troubles have you allowed to separate you from Jesus? There'll be no peace until they have been removed.

---

*Peace is such a precious jewel that I would
give anything for it but truth.*
MATTHEW HENRY

THE WORD OF THE CONCERTMASTER

Forever, O LORD, Your word is settled in heaven.

PSALM 119:89

Second only to the conductor in importance in an orchestra is the concertmaster or concertmistress, sometimes referred to as the first-chair violinist. He or she sets the standard for the other string players in two regards: bowing and pitch. Before rehearsals of a particular work the concertmaster decides which bow strokes will be used and annotates the violin score, from which copies are made for the other string players. When tuning the orchestra, the concertmaster usually gets an A note from the oboist, tunes his or her violin to that tone, and then plays that note as the standard to which the other strings tune their instruments.

Life is full of standards: weights, measures, time, color, and others. Think of what chaos would ensue if standards didn't exist! There is a standard when it comes to truth as well. Jesus said it best, referring to God's Word: "Your word is truth" (John 17:17). And the psalmist declared God's Word to be "settled in heaven." Because God's Word is eternal and "settled," the standard never changes. It remains the "pitch" to which our lives and hearts must be tuned.

If your life feels a bit off-pitch at present, check to see if you are tuned to the pitch of *the* Concertmaster as revealed in His Word. All truth is God's truth, and the Bible is the standard by which it is measured.

The Word of God is either absolute or obsolete.

VANCE HAVNER

YOUR GRAND CANYON

The LORD will guide you continually, and satisfy
your soul in drought, and strengthen your bones;
you shall be like a watered garden.

ISAIAH 58:11

No one said that marriage was easy. And when people enter into nuptials with preconceived notions about being fulfilled by their spouses, problems begin. That's what one couple experienced. After much dissatisfaction in their marriage, a husband carefully approached his wife and said, "Dear, you have a Grand Canyon of emotional needs. And if every man in the United States lined up to spend time with you, it would not be enough." She realized that what her husband said was true. Until she went to God to have her emotional needs met, there was nothing that her husband or any other man on the planet could do to satisfy her.

Every one of us deals with a lack of fulfillment when we try to find ultimate joy in anything or anyone but Jesus Christ. Do you know that God wants to reveal Himself to you as the Lover of your soul? He will bring you into an incredible, intimate relationship filled with unconditional love—enough love to fill your Grand Canyon of emotional needs. Go to Him now. Share with Him how you feel, and allow Him to fill you up.

*God, show me what is causing me to feel so
empty and so dissatisfied with my marriage.
Let this be a time of healing and growth.*

HIS STRONG HAND

[Jesus said,] "I give them eternal life, and they shall never
perish; neither shall anyone snatch them out of My hand."

JOHN 10:28

The scene is usually a cliff, a waterfall, a window ledge, or some
other precipice, a fall from which would result in certain death.
One person is hanging over the precipice, kept from falling only by
holding on to the outstretched hand of another. Three things can happen to the one hanging over the edge: (1) the grip is unintentionally
broken because of a failure in strength, (2) the grip is released intentionally because of malevolence, or (3) the person is pulled to safety
through the strength of a rescuer.

One of the strongest images of the believer's eternal security in
Christ was painted by the Savior's own words: "Neither shall anyone
snatch them out of My hand." Too often, Christians feel that eternal
security depends on their own strength, their own faithfulness, their
own perseverance—their ability to hold on to the Savior's hand. The
opposite is actually the truth: it is Christ's strength, Christ's faithfulness, Christ's perseverance—Christ's ability to hold on to the believer's hand—that keeps the Christian eternally secure.

When you wonder if you have been faithful enough, hold out your
hand—and picture it enveloped in the strong hand of Christ.

Once a man is united to God, how could he not live forever?

C. S. LEWIS

June 7
UNCERTAIN TIMES: GOD, A ROCK, AND A HARD PLACE

> Miriam answered them: "Sing to the LORD, for He has triumphed
> gloriously! The horse and its rider He has thrown into the sea!"
>
> EXODUS 15:21

By a series of amazing miracles, Moses reintroduced the Hebrew slaves in Egypt to the God of their fathers. By the time Pharaoh let the people go, the slaves had become believers. But like so many baby believers, the first crisis made them rethink their new faith. They were stuck between the rock of the Red Sea and the hard place of the hordes of Egyptian chariots bearing down on them. But God proved Himself faithful to Moses and the Hebrews: He parted the sea, and the rest is biblical history.

When you get between a rock and a hard place, what do you do? Does your faith vanish faster than an Egyptian chariot? We have to admit that what God did once—rescue His people dramatically—He is not obligated to do again in the same way. But the promise Moses made to the Hebrews is repeated throughout Scripture: "The LORD will fight for you; you need only to be still" (Exodus 14:14, NIV). In other words, don't panic and run.

The question is not *if* God will prove Himself faithful to you but *how*. If you panic and run, you might miss the miracle.

You can never understand the faithfulness
of God by taking the short view.

PAUL S. REES

> The Scripture cannot be broken.

JOHN 10:35

A thousand times over," wrote Barnard Ramm, "the death knell of the Bible has been sounded, the funeral procession formed, the inscription cut on the tombstone, and committal read. But somehow the corpse never stays put."

You can't keep the Good Book down. The psalmist said, "The words of the LORD are pure words, like silver tried in a furnace of earth, purified seven times" (Psalm 12:6). The Hebrew term translated "pure" is used elsewhere to describe metals such as gold that were refined and absolutely pure, without the slightest defect or flaw.

This is the consistent teaching of Scripture about itself. On 3,808 occasions in the Old Testament, the biblical writers claimed to be writing the very words of God. In the New Testament, Christ confirmed the integrity of the Scriptures without the slightest doubt. The apostles trusted the Scriptures to the very word, and James called it "the perfect law of liberty" (James 1:25).

It is flawless. Because God inspired the Bible, it is inerrant and infallible. And because it's inerrant and infallible, it is trustworthy and authoritative—to be trusted and obeyed.

Only the Book without error can correct and control our erring lives.

By affirming the inerrancy of the Scriptures, we place ourselves under the authority of all the teachings of the Bible.

ROBERT SAUCY

JOYFUL OBEDIENCE

God gives wisdom and knowledge and joy
to a man who is good in His sight.

ECCLESIASTES 2:26

It has been said that "God prefers reluctant obedience rather than joyful disobedience." But this statement is misleading. When we first learn to obey God, we sometimes do so reluctantly because we leave the familiar territory of doing as we please to embark on the uncharted waters of yielding our will to His. But once we understand that obedience to the Lord produces joy in our lives, we also begin to realize that there is no such thing as "joyful disobedience." For, in fact, ignoring God's directives is a joy stealer.

Alan Redpath states it this way: "When there's disobedience in the Christian life, the fullness ceases. . . . And you soon know when you've lost the fullness, because the joy is gone."

If you find that you are resisting obedience to God in some area of your life, ask yourself, *Is it worth it?* Because no matter how vigorously you try to justify disobedience in your life, you can never replace the joy that is lost when you say no to God.

Dear Christian, run to do His will, and lay hold of the resulting joy that God has provided for those who obey Him. There is nothing to lose and everything to gain, for a joyful heart stems from an obedient heart.

Obedient submission is the only way to joy.
CHARLES STANLEY

BARNABAS

When [Barnabas] arrived and saw what the grace of
God had done, he was glad and encouraged them all
to remain true to the Lord with all their hearts.

ACTS 11:23, NIV

Did you learn about "junctural metanalysis" in grammar class?
Not to worry—it means the process of forming new words when
the boundaries between existing words get confused over time. For
example, Old English "a napron" (little tablecloth) became "an apron."
Likewise, "an eke name" ("eke" meant "little" or "extra") became "a
nickname."

One of the most famous nicknames in church history was
given to a Jewish man named Joseph, from the island of Cyprus in
the Mediterranean Sea. When he became a follower of Christ, the
apostles immediately began calling him Barnabas, which means "son
of encouragement" (Acts 4:36). What kind of person would a "son of
encouragement" be—a self-centered person or an others-centered
person? Obviously, the latter. From what Scripture tells us about
Barnabas—especially his ministry relationship with Mark (Acts
15:37-39)—it is clear that he was focused on others. If you became
part of a new group of friends, what kind of nickname would they
give you?

Those who insist on living self-centered lives will never be known
as others-centered.

Self is the opaque veil that hides the face of God from us.

A. W. TOZER

June 11

TAKE GOD'S HAND

You shall do what is right and good in the sight of the LORD.

DEUTERONOMY 6:18

Standing up for what's right is not an easy thing to do. In fact, some people feel it is easier to go with the flow of whatever is popular at the time or avoid the issue altogether. Sadly, this can lead to an entire culture of weak, misguided, and apathetic people. As one person stated, "When forty million people believe in a dumb idea, it's still a dumb idea. So if you believe in something that's good, honest, and right, stand up for it."

There is one person in the Bible who perhaps understood this better than anyone else. When Joseph was approached by his master's wife, he not only stood up for what was right, he *ran*, leaving his coat behind (Genesis 39:12). Most people would think he was crazy for running away from such a proposition; but he knew what was right, and he stood by it. For that, he was immeasurably blessed by God.

Whether you're dealing with ethical issues at work or moral issues with friends and family, don't be afraid to stand up for what you know is right. It may be difficult, but it will be worth it. Take God's hand, and take a stand!

My basic principle is that you don't make decisions because they are easy; you don't make them because they're popular; you make them because they're right.

THEODORE HESBURGH

NEVER-CHANGING TRUTH

The entirety of Your Word is truth, and every one of
Your righteous judgments endures forever.

PSALM 119:160

People who lie have a problem: trying to remember what they have said to whom, or what version of the truth they last conveyed. It has often been said that the greatest advantage to telling the truth is that you don't have to remember what you have said: the version of the story you told ten years ago is the same one you tell today.

The Bible is the repository of the truth God has delivered to humankind—and it is truth that never changes. The same truth that God delivered in the Old Testament is the truth we find in the New Testament. For instance, nine of the Ten Commandments given to Israel are repeated as commands for the church (meeting on the Sabbath being the exception; however, the writer of Hebrews tells us we're not to forsake the assembling of ourselves together). When it comes to practical and holy living, the same solutions God gave saints of old work in the lives of today's Christian believers. Because God's Word (whether spoken or written) is settled in heaven (Psalm 119:89), we need never wonder what God says about life's most important questions.

When seeking guidance from God in prayer, it does no good to ask if He has changed His mind on a moral question. God's truth is the same yesterday, today, and tomorrow.

---

*The Bible is alive, it speaks to me; it has feet, it runs
after me; it has hands, it lays hold on me.*
MARTIN LUTHER

NO SUBSTITUTE FOR VICTORY!

Thanks be to God, who gives us the victory
through our Lord Jesus Christ.

1 CORINTHIANS 15:57

Don't you get tired of Christians going around with their heads down? The Bible says that God "commands victories" for us (Psalm 44:4). "His holy arm" has "gained Him the victory" (Psalm 98:1). "[Whoever] is born of God overcomes the world. And this is the victory that has overcome the world—our faith" (1 John 5:4). "We are more than conquerors through Him who loved us" (Romans 8:37), and our attitude should be "Thanks be to God who gives us the victory through our Lord Jesus Christ" (1 Corinthians 15:57).

We should be excited about that. We are children of the King. He causes all things to work together for good. We have abundant life promised now, and mansions are being prepared for us in glory. Satan was defeated at Calvary, and he'll be condemned to hell at the end of the age. We have the Holy Spirit within us and all the promises of God inscribed in our favorite Book.

It's time to put our shoulders back and our heads up. You're a victor in Christ today, and the joy of the Lord is your strength!

There is no substitute for victory.
DOUGLAS MacARTHUR

CULTIVATED HEART

He who received seed on the good ground is he who hears
the word and understands it, who indeed bears fruit and
produces: some a hundredfold, some sixty, some thirty.

MATTHEW 13:23

If you had to choose the most important of all the stories Jesus told, which would you choose? You should consider the one He said was most important: "Do you not understand this parable? How then will you understand all the parables?" Jesus seemed to indicate that the parable of the four soils was a key to understanding the rest of His parables.

Why was it so important? Because the parable of the soils (Matthew 13:1-23) has to do with what is required for the Word of God to bear fruit in the life of the one who receives it. When the Word is sown in the heart, the condition of the "soil" (the heart) makes all the difference. If the heart is hard, Satan can snatch the Word away. If the heart is troubled or enamored with the world, the Word can die before it bears fruit. But if the heart is tender and ready to receive the Word, it will spring up and bear fruit, "some a hundredfold, some sixty, some thirty." The key to spiritual fruitfulness is a heart in which the Word of God can be sown and take root.

Spend time daily cultivating your heart so it will be ready to receive the Word.

Plato located the soul of man in the head;
Christ located it in the heart.

ST. JEROME

THE ROAD MAP FOR LIFE

Your word is a lamp to my feet and a light to my path.

PSALM 119:105

In his book *Jesus Loves Me*, Dr. Calvin Miller writes, "The Bible is God's diary, his last will and testament, his autobiography, his tied and bundled sheaf of love letters to the human race. It was written over 1500 years of time while empires were forged. Its authors were alternately poets and convicts, adulterers and mystics. Yet I go again and again to these diverse writers to feast on their words of God."[8]

The Bible *is* a feast, and a lamp, and a light. It's a road map that unerringly guides us in our greatest decisions. The entrance of His Word brings light. The Bible provides moral clarity in our dilemmas, marvelous strength in our difficulties, and precious promises for all our days.

If you have a decision to make, try kneeling by your desk or bedside with an open Bible before you. God may not use a specific verse to give you a specific answer, but His Word and the inner guidance of the Holy Spirit will give you the wisdom and peace to know what you ought to do.

The Scriptures! How deeply they reach into our very interiors.

CALVIN MILLER

---

[8] Calvin Miller, *Jesus Loves Me: Celebrating the Profound Truths of a Simple Hymn* (New York: Hatchette, 2002).

It came to pass, when Pharaoh had let the people go, that
God did not lead them by way of the land of the Philistines,
although that was near; for God said, "Lest perhaps the people
change their minds when they see war, and return to Egypt."

EXODUS 13:17

A quick glance at a map of the Mediterranean world in the time of the Exodus shows the proximity of Egypt to the Promised Land. It should have taken only a matter of weeks for Moses and the Israelites to walk around the southeast corner of the Mediterranean Sea to Canaan. But Moses led the people into the Sinai desert so they would not encounter the warlike Philistines and flee back to slavery in Egypt. The Israelites complained, not understanding that being alive at the hand of Moses was better than being dead at the hands of the Philistines.

How many times do we complain about life's circumstances without knowing what's going on behind the scenes? God's hand of mercy and grace is at work, protecting us and guiding our steps more times than we are aware. Our response ought to be, "Lord, thank You for this delay," instead of, "Lord, why are You allowing me to be inconvenienced?"

Make it a habit to thank God for His providential protection—the shield of His faithfulness that surrounds you moment by moment.

God has His hours and His delays.

J. A. BENGEL

JONATHAN

Jonathan said to David, "Whatever you
yourself desire, I will do it for you."

1 SAMUEL 20:4

In John 15:7, Jesus Christ said something to His disciples that Christians have wrestled with ever since: "Ask what you desire, and it shall be done for you." What? Does that mean *anything*? To be fair, there are two conditions: abide in Christ, and have His Word abide in you. Do those two things and then ask—yes, anything.

The implication is that when we abide in Christ, we will make Kingdom-centered requests that He is only too happy to grant. But if the disciples had done their Old Testament homework, they would have discovered Jesus' words were spoken first by Saul's son Jonathan to his friend David. These two young men had made a covenant with one another, pledging their all. So Jonathan told David, "Ask me anything, and I'll do it for you." That is the epitome of others-centered living. What we fail to remember is that, based on the New Covenant, every Christian is in a covenant relationship with every other believer. When we live for one another, self-centeredness loses its place. Look around you—every follower of Christ is someone for whom you should be living.

Is there someone to whom you could say this week, "Ask me anything, and I'll do it for you"?

Many things are lost for want of asking.

ENGLISH PROVERB

WHEN GOD CHOOSES

One and the same Spirit works all these things,
distributing to each one individually as He wills.

1 CORINTHIANS 12:11

When Jesus said, "My kingdom is not of this world" (John 18:36), there were implications that stretched far beyond His immediate setting. For instance, in this world human beings make choices on the basis of personal preference, as long as those choices break no laws. But in the Kingdom of God, human beings don't make ultimate choices—they submit to the choices of God the King.

Take spiritual gifts, for example. Based on our desires, pre-Christian involvements, or talents and abilities, we might like to choose our own spiritual gifts and, thereby, our roles in the body of Christ. But God does not pass out a "Spiritual Gifts Request Form" when we become followers of Christ. He makes the choice and assignment of spiritual gifts for us, the Holy Spirit "distributing to each one individually as He wills." Acceptance of our gift(s) is another of many opportunities to be submissive and obedient to God, trusting that He knows what is best for us and for His church.

Are you enjoying a ministry in the church that allows you to use your spiritual gift? If not, you may be missing out on a blessing God designed for you.

Nothing is really lost by a life of sacrifice:
everything is lost by failure to obey God's call.
HENRY P. LIDDON

June 19

WONDERMENT AND AWE

> *God is greatly to be feared in the assembly of the saints,*
> *and to be held in reverence by all those around Him.*
>
> PSALM 89:7

Every week, thousands of worshipers flock into the great cathedrals of Europe to experience the majesty of the architecture—the high ceilings, massive pillars, stained-glass windows, and reverberating sounds. The ancient builders wanted to inspire us with a sense of the majesty of God, and they designed their cathedrals with that in mind.

Every week, thousands of visitors flock to America's national parks for the same reason. We're awestruck by the vast desolation of Big Bend, the immensity of the Grand Canyon, and the sheer cliffs and plunging waterfalls of Yosemite. The towering peaks of the Tetons and the Rockies are a wonderment. The human heart is hungry for a sense of God's majesty.

Yes, we are God's friends who, in prayer, can call Him, "Abba, Father" (Romans 8:15); but He is also clothed with majesty and girded with strength (Psalm 93). Our worship should be warm and personal, but we shouldn't forget the awe and reverence due His name.

Let's meditate on the "majesty" passages of Scripture and sing the old hymns that uphold the Lord's greatness. Remember that bowing before Him in fear and reverence is an important part of worship.

It is always true that an encounter with
God brings wonderment and awe.

A. W. TOZER

COFFEE STAINS

You meant evil against me; but God meant it for good.

GENESIS 50:20

J. I. Packer wrote, "Our God is a God who not merely restores but also takes up our mistakes and follies into his plan for us and brings good out of them."

Many people have trouble forgiving themselves because the scars of sin remain in their lives and relationships. But don't underestimate God's grace. Joseph's brothers chastised themselves for their past sin, but Joseph reassured them that the Lord had turned even their vicious betrayal and evil deeds into something good.

Remember the old story of the artist and the coffee? A painter was drinking coffee in a French café. One of his companions became enraged and threw his coffee against the wall, creating an ugly stain. Taking his paints, the artist created a beautiful mural that incorporated the stains into the scene.

It's true that sin leaves stains on the walls of our lives, but when we love God, even these things can be worked together for good in His glorious plan.

Only the Lord can turn our spiritual scars into trophies of His grace. If you've been forgiven by Him, you can learn to forgive yourself and to thank Him for turning your spiritual scars into something good.

He most graciously overrules our folly, and causes the influences of our self-chosen circumstances to work for our spiritual benefit.

C. H. MACKINTOSH

> I heard the voice of the Lord, saying: "Whom shall I send, and
> who will go for Us?" Then I said, "Here am I! Send me."
>
> ISAIAH 6:8

An old Yiddish proverb says, "If you don't want to do something, one excuse is as good as another." One schoolteacher received an apt example of that when a note arrived from the mother of an absent student. "Please excuse Jennifer for missing school," said the note. "We forgot to get the Sunday paper off the porch, and when we found it on Monday, we thought it was Sunday."

Another teacher was handed a note that read: "Please excuse Lisa for being absent. She was sick and I had her shot."

When it comes to working for Christ, no excuse will do. Don't say, "I don't have time," "I don't have what it takes," "I'm not the right person," "That's not my gift," "I'll do it later," "I'm too shy," "I don't know how," "I think someone else would be better," "I'm not good enough," "I'm not old enough."

Jesus once told a parable about those who "with one accord began to make excuses" (Luke 14:18).

Instead, just prayerfully kneel before the Lord and say: "Here am I! Send me."

---

*He that is good for making excuses is
seldom good for anything else.*
BENJAMIN FRANKLIN

> Be kindly affectionate to one another ... distributing
> to the needs of the saints, given to hospitality.
>
> ROMANS 12:10, 13

From 1986 to 1990, Frank Reed was held hostage by Lebanese terrorists. He was beaten and tormented and kept in total darkness, but the worst thing he suffered was the feeling that no one cared. In an article in *Time* magazine he said, "I began to realize how withering it is to exist with not a single expression of caring around [me]....
I learned one overriding fact: caring is a powerful force. If no one cares, you are truly alone."

God instituted two social systems on planet Earth so that no one would ever be without care: the family and the church. In a day when even Christian families are failing to care for their own, the church must step in and be a community's "Care Central"—a place where love, healing, and acceptance can be found. The New Testament is filled with admonitions to care for those in need, both within the church and without. As Jesus Himself said, "The world will know you are Christians by how you love one another" (John 13:35, paraphrase).

If you are in need of care, begin by caring for others. If you are "healthy," look to see whom God has put in your path who needs His love.

God ... doesn't look at just what we give.
He also looks at what we keep.
RANDY ALCORN

ILLUMINATION

> The Helper, the Holy Spirit, whom the Father will send
> in My name ... will teach you all things, and bring to
> your remembrance all things that I said to you.

JOHN 14:26

A braham Lincoln studied his schoolbooks by the flickering glow of the fireplace, but most of us have trouble reading in dim light. We've all had the experience of reading or studying in the late afternoon, only to realize the room is growing darker. A sudden flip of the light switch corrects the problem, bathing the words of our book in light.

The illumination of the Holy Spirit is like that.

People read the Bible every day without the Holy Spirit's aid—even skeptics and atheists can read the words. But when, as God's children, we ask the Holy Spirit to open this Book to our hearts, it's like reading with the light on. Paul wrote, "Now we have received, not the spirit of the world, but the Spirit who is from God, that we might know the things that have been freely given to us by God" (1 Corinthians 2:12).

Let's learn to pray as the psalmist did, "Open my eyes, that I may see wondrous things from Your law" (Psalm 119:18).

---

*We should pray that the Holy Spirit would give us his
illumination and thereby help us to understand rightly when
we study Scripture or when we ponder situations in our lives.*

WAYNE GRUDEM

IT IS FINISHED

When Jesus had received the sour wine, He said, "It is
finished!" And bowing His head, He gave up His spirit.

JOHN 19:30

In Beth Moore's devotional book *Voices of the Faithful*, a South
Asian missionary named Janessa tells of how her Muslim neighbors prepared for the Eid Al-Adha festival, in which cows are sacrificed in commemoration of Abraham's sacrificing his son on Mount
Moriah. On the morning of the slaughter, Janessa sensed a somber
feeling in the air. The Muslim pastor came to kill the cows, holding in
his hands the names of those for whom the sacrifice was made, and
Janessa could hear the moaning of the cows as their throats were cut.
Shortly thereafter, the neighbor, covered with blood, passed by with a
smile and said to her, "It is finished."

Janessa later recalled, "That statement sent chills up my spine as I
remembered the words of Jesus on the cross, the *true* sacrifice for sin."

Because Jesus offered Himself on the cross, we should bow in
humble adoration. He finished the work of redemption that we, His
people, might gaze in wonder at the cross and worship Him.

'Tis finished—let all the joyful sound
Be heard through all the nations round.
SAMUEL STENNETT

THE SELF-CORRECTING SOUL

If we would judge ourselves, we would not be judged.

1 CORINTHIANS 11:31

The unexamined life is not worth living, Socrates famously said. Well, in a sense, the Lord agrees. First Corinthians 11:28 says, "Let a man examine himself"; the reason is in verse 31: "For if we would judge ourselves, we would not be judged."

The context of this passage has to do with treating the Lord's Supper with carelessness. Because of their flippant observance of Communion, some of the Corinthians were experiencing sickness and even death as a form of divine discipline (verse 30). The apostle Paul was telling them to look into their own hearts, to recognize their sin, and to confess it and turn from it.

It's always better for us to correct our own behavior before someone else does it for us, or before the Lord steps in with loving discipline. Honest, prayerful self-evaluation is the habit of maturing people.

Where to begin? Ask yourself, *Is there anything nagging at my conscience?* And if so, sincerely offer the psalmist's prayer: "Search me, O God, and know my heart; try me, and know my anxieties; and see if there is any wicked way in me, and lead me in the way everlasting" (Psalm 139:23-24).

The healthy soul is both self-controlled and self-correcting.

UNKNOWN

THE BLESSING OF BROKENNESS

My heart within me is broken because of
the prophets; all my bones shake.

JEREMIAH 23:9

The word *broken* occurs twenty-eight times in the book of Jeremiah, and three more times in his book of Lamentations. Jeremiah was a man whose heart was broken by the sins of his people and the tragedies of his times. We feel his sadness throughout the book as he says things like, "Why did I come forth from the womb to see labor and sorrow?" (Jeremiah 20:18).

Yet think of how greatly God used Jeremiah despite—or because of—his broken heart! He drew people to God in his own day, he predicted the return of Israel from exile in future days, and his book has been ministering to the world for 2,600 years!

The Bible says that we are able to comfort others with the comfort God gives to us in broken times (2 Corinthians 1:3-7).

We can't always avoid broken hearts, broken relationships, broken promises, and even broken items. But when our brokenness is laid at the feet of Jesus, He can use our shattered circumstances to draw others to Him, and we can rejoice in spite of our pain.

After all, Jesus Himself was broken and spilled out for us.

Come, oh come, with thy broken heart, weary and worn with care;
Come and kneel at the open door, Jesus is waiting there.
FANNY CROSBY

ITS SURVIVAL THROUGH THE AGES

Heaven and earth will pass away, but My
words will by no means pass away.

MATTHEW 24:35

In AD 303, Emperor Diocletian ordered Bibles everywhere rounded up and burned and the Christian Scriptures destroyed. Instead, Diocletian perished, and within twenty-five years the next emperor commissioned Eusebius to prepare fifty copies of the Bible at the expense of the government.

Centuries later, the French infidel Voltaire claimed that within one hundred years the Bible would be forgotten and Christianity would be swept from existence. But Voltaire died in 1778, and according to some accounts, within fifty years a Bible society was using his press and his house to print Bibles.

No other book has been so hated, vilified, attacked, abused, burned, banished, criticized, and despised. Yet it is history's best seller, read today and loved by billions. As H. L. Hastings put it: "Infidels for 1,800 years have been refuting and overthrowing this book, and yet it stands today as solid as a rock. Its circulation increases, and it is more loved and cherished and read today than ever before."

That's our Bible!

---

*If this book had not been the book of God, men would
have destroyed it long ago. Emperors and popes,
kings and priests, princes and rulers have all tried
their hand at it; they die and the book still lives.*

H. L. HASTINGS

FORTUNE-TELLERS

> Blessed is he who reads and those who hear the
> words of this prophecy, and keep those things
> which are written in it; for the time is near.
>
> REVELATION 1:3

Fortune-telling is the practice of seeming to predict the future, usually of an individual, through mystical or supernatural means and often for financial gain. Virtually all scientists regard fortune-telling as pseudoscience. They believe that several factors explain its popularity and anecdotal accuracy: mainly that predictions almost always use vague terms and do not lend themselves to being false. Therefore, the forecast is never wrong, but a person's interpretation of it can be wrong.

What about biblical prophecies? We can believe them to be valid because of the many prophecies that have already been fulfilled. Jesus told many parables to illustrate the importance of being prepared for His coming. One such parable was about a master of the house, who had been robbed. If the master had known the hour the thief would come, he would surely have kept watch to prevent the robbery.

The lesson of the parable is simple: be prepared. Always be ready for the Lord's return, which will be as unpredictable as a thief in the night. Don't trust fortune-tellers; entrust your future to God.

Heavenly Father, I want to be more like You.
I want to know what the Bible has to say about the
future. Thank You for making both possible.

June 29

THE PLEASURE OF GRACE

Most gladly I will rather boast in my infirmities,
that the power of Christ may rest upon me.

2 CORINTHIANS 12:9

God's faithfulness is not proved by the absence of trouble, tension, calamity, disaster, or personal pain. Indeed, His faithfulness is seen most clearly in those times when we question His plan and feel the pain of our circumstances.

Besides Jesus Himself, no one suffered as consistently for God's sake as did the apostle Paul. In 2 Corinthians 6:3-10 and 11:21-30, he catalogs the varieties of pain and hardship he experienced. God's faithfulness to Paul was not seen in the avoidance of pain but in the supply of grace needed to endure it. Paul had such a deep understanding of the role of grace in his life that he said he took "pleasure" in what he suffered for Christ's sake because it resulted in a greater revelation of God's grace (2 Corinthians 12:10). When we arrive at the place where we glory more in the presence of grace than in the absence of pain, we know we are making strides toward maturity.

If you are in the midst of trouble right now, develop the discipline of finding pleasure in the experience of grace—the greatest indicator of God's faithfulness.

Nothing whatever in the way of goodness
pertaining to godliness and real holiness can
be accomplished without [grace].
ST. AUGUSTINE

THANKS BE TO GOD!

Honor the LORD with your possessions, and
with the firstfruits of all your increase.

PROVERBS 3:9

The apostle Paul devoted two full chapters—2 Corinthians 8 and 9—to a special offering he was receiving for the poor saints in Jerusalem, and he told the Corinthians to give as God had prospered them, to give cheerfully, and to give as each had determined in his heart to give. He ended his appeal with a simple yet profound sentence: "Thanks be to God for His indescribable gift!" (2 Corinthians 9:15).

That's the Bible's view of Jesus. He is "God's Indescribable Gift" to the human race, to each of us. But it's awkward if we have nothing to give in return. Have you ever felt uncomfortable when you received a Christmas present because you hadn't anticipated exchanging gifts and you had nothing to give in return?

What, then, can we give God in exchange for His indescribable gift? Nothing, except our hearts, our worship, our thanksgiving, our trust, our obedience—our all. And when we place a gift in Sunday's offering plate, that simple gift is symbolic of all of those things. We are honoring the Lord with our possessions and with the firstfruits of all our increase.

We are saying, "Thanks be to God for His indescribable gift!"

Thank you, Lord, for giving to me
Thy great salvation, so rich and free!
SETH SYKES

JULY

Take ... the sword of the Spirit, which is the word of God.

EPHESIANS 6:17

It seems as if everywhere you look these days, someone is pushing a new philosophy—one that won't offend anyone, exclude anyone, or make any absolute claims about anything. According to some, all paths lead to heaven, and there are no eternal consequences for our actions. Others believe in karma, the idea that what goes around comes around. Unfortunately, these beliefs are not just floating around on the pages of obscure alternative books or in clips of a late-night television show; they are in our faces. There are popular sitcoms based on these beliefs and bestselling books making these false claims. They are inescapable but not unconquerable.

As Christians, we have to be careful what we read, listen to, and watch on TV, for Satan's deception through false teaching is ever so subtle and cunning, even capable of capturing the minds of believers if we are not grounded in Scripture.

The Bible says that in order to stand strong against this deception "you must continue in the things which you have learned ... the Holy Scriptures" (2 Timothy 3:14-15). We must keep ourselves grounded in the Word of God, for it is our weapon against the worldly philosophy of the day.

Truth lives on in the midst of deception.
JOHANN FRIEDRICH VON SCHILLER

IN HIS STRENGTH

Jesus answered and said to them, "Most assuredly, I say to you,
the Son can do nothing of himself, but what He sees the Father
do; for whatever He does, the Son also does in like manner."

JOHN 5:19

In Hannah Whitall Smith's journal in October of 1866, she jotted down some interesting observations about holiness: "The Lord has been teaching me in many ways lately about my utter weakness in the presence of temptation." Hannah was troubled because she felt she had no more power over sin then than when she was first converted. "My own efforts have been worse than useless," she lamented. Then it dawned on her that only Jesus Himself perfectly resisted temptation, and He did it through the power of the Holy Spirit.

Likewise, when we're fully yielded to God and filled with His Spirit, the indwelling Christ is able to keep us from falling and to give us daily victory over sin.

"I realize that Christ dwells in my heart by faith," Hannah wrote, "and that He is able and willing to subdue all things to himself."

He not only *gives* us victory—He *is* the victory.

*If I am to be sanctified, if I am to be preserved
blameless and harmless, it must be by the power
of God for my own efforts have utterly failed.*
HANNAH WHITALL SMITH

July 3

ESCAPING THE FIRE

Because you have kept My command to persevere, I also will keep
you from the hour of trial which shall come upon the whole world.

REVELATION 3:10

An offshore oil platform in the North Sea caught fire, and as flames
swept over the rig, workers thought they were doomed. Just in the
nick of time, however, a fleet of Scottish helicopters appeared, and all
the workers were rescued.

We usually thank God for the blessings He gives, but we should
also praise Him for the escapes He provides.

Take, for example, the period of Great Tribulation. If, as many
believe, the church of the Lord Jesus will be taken out of the world
before the time of God's wrath, why should we study chapters (such
as Revelation 6–18) that describe Tribulation events?

They show us how thankful we should be for what we're missing!

Today thank the Lord for His oversight, His protection, and even
for the blessings of unanswered prayer. As Christians, we should be
thankful for what God has given us by His grace, and also for what He
withholds in His mercy.

---

*You ought to be thankful to God that He has not yet
recompensed you—that He has not dealt with you
after your sins, nor rewarded you according to your
iniquities. . . . "Behold, I make all things new," says
Jesus, and then He makes His people into sons.*

CHARLES HADDON SPURGEON

July 4

RECKON ON HIS FAITHFULNESS

Watch, stand fast in the faith, be brave, be strong.

1 CORINTHIANS 16:13

In his book *People My Teachers*, British preacher John Stott recalls discovering a literary genre called Christian Biography as an undergraduate at Cambridge University. Stott said that in reading about the lives of giants in the faith, he found his own life mentored by a host of heroes. Especially impressive was J. Hudson Taylor, the memorable missionary to China, who, through his biography, taught Stott the power of steadfastness in faith.

Hudson Taylor's primary principle was "dependence on God alone," and it's no accident that one of his biographies was titled *The Man Who Believed God.* Hudson Taylor taught that *faith* rests on God's *faithfulness*, and he liked to render Jesus' command to "have faith in God" (Mark 11:22) as "Reckon on the faithfulness of God."

"This paraphrase, although not exegetically exact, is theologically correct," said Stott. Because God is faithful, we can reckon on His faithfulness, believe His promises, depend on His help, and have faith in His watchful care.

Trust Him today. Reckon on His faithfulness.

I have found that there are three stages in every great work of God: first, it is impossible, then it is difficult, then it is done.

J. HUDSON TAYLOR

PERFECTLY SPOKEN TO THE LEPER

Jesus reached out his hand and touched the
man. "I am willing," he said. "Be clean!"

MATTHEW 8:3, NIV

We often use the word *willing* when talking about our own commitment to Christ: Lord, I am willing to follow You. I am willing to obey and serve You however You lead.

In Matthew 8:2, it was the leper who asked Jesus about *His* willingness. "Lord," said the man humbly, "if You are willing, You can make me clean."

Reaching out His hand, Jesus touched the man's leprous skin and spoke the five greatest words the man had ever heard: "I am willing. Be clean!" Instantly the man was cured.

The Lord may not answer our every prayer in the affirmative, for He alone knows what's best for us. But because of His marvelous grace, He is inclined toward blessing us. He is willing to love us, willing to save us, willing to bless us with goodness and mercy all our days. He is willing to forgive our sins, willing to guide our lives, willing to use our efforts, and willing to enrich our homes.

He is not a stingy God; He is willing.

---

*They who by faith apply themselves to Christ for mercy
and grace, may be sure that he is willing, freely willing,
to give them the mercy and grace they come to him for.*
MATTHEW HENRY

July 6
STANDING IN THE DOCK

How shall we escape if we neglect so great a salvation?

HEBREWS 2:3

Every day in courtrooms around the world, the tension is palpable as impartial juries deliver their verdicts. Lives hang in the balance, and ideally, justice is meted out swiftly and objectively.

Recently in a South Carolina murder trial, the defendant, hearing the guilty verdict, collapsed in the courtroom and had to be carried out by deputies. In a recent Missouri case, the defendant was declared innocent. Family members of the victim, feeling justice was denied them, screamed aloud and fell into each other's arms like toppling dominoes.

Can you imagine the soul-crushing strain of standing before the Judge of the entire universe, awaiting the condemnation that will banish you swiftly and inexorably to hell? That will never be the Christian's experience, for the blood of Christ saves us from having to stand before the Great White Throne of God. Jesus bore our sins, accepted our death, and issued His abundant pardon on Calvary's cross. Today, praise God that His "so great a salvation" is for you and me and that there is no condemnation to those who are in Him!

Hallelujah! Hallelujah! Hallelujah for the cross!

HORATIUS BONAR

> Be ready, for the Son of Man is coming
> at an hour you do not expect.
>
> MATTHEW 24:44

Lawmakers and military experts work day and night to keep America's armed forces at a high state of readiness. How about you? Are you living in a state of readiness? Depending on the version, sixteen times in the Bible we find the little phrase *Be ready*. It first occurs in Exodus 19, when the children of Israel were told to "be ready" for the Lord to descend on Mount Sinai.

In the New Testament, we're told to always be ready to give an answer to those asking us the reason for our hope (1 Peter 3:15). We're also to "be ready for every good work" (Titus 3:1), to be ready to give generously (2 Corinthians 9:3, 5), and to be ready to preach the Word in and out of season (2 Timothy 4:2).

If the Boy Scout motto is "Be Prepared," the Christian's motto is "Be Ready." We can never take a break from our Christianity or relax our spiritual vigilance. Be ready to share, to give, to preach, to work. Most of all, be ready for Christ's return.

It might be today!

Ready to go, ready to stay, ready my place to fill,
Ready for service, lowly or great, ready to do His will.
CHARLES D. TILLMAN

> [Jesus] said to them, "It is not for you to know times or
> seasons which the Father has put in His own authority."
>
> ACTS 1:7

A story is told of a man who rushed into a suburban railroad station one morning and, almost breathlessly, asked the station agent, "When does the 8:01 train leave?"

"At 8:01, sir" was the answer.

"Well," the man replied, "it's 7:59 by my watch, 7:57 by the town clock, and 8:04 by the station clock. Which am I to go by?"

"You can go by any clock you wish," said the agent, "but you can't go by the 8:01 train, for it has already left."

It is easy for us to be tempted into one of two errors concerning time. The first is to believe that things just happen when they happen, totally at random, without rhyme or reason. The other is to suppose that we can schedule and manage—and thus control—every detail of our lives. God, our sovereign Lord, stands outside of time and controls it. This realization can either make us fatalistic or incredibly confident and patiently trusting. Everything in our individual lives occurs when it occurs because our loving Lord commands or allows it. Therefore, we can go into the future knowing that history has a purpose and that God awaits us there.

Work as if you were to live a hundred years.
Pray as if you were to die tomorrow.
BENJAMIN FRANKLIN

> Behold, you will be mute and not able to speak until the
> day these things take place, because you did not believe
> my words which will be fulfilled in their own time.
>
> LUKE 1:20

Throughout the Bible there are special promises regarding the births of certain babies: the promise to Abraham about Isaac, the prediction of Samson's birth, the message to Mary regarding Christ, and the encounter of Zacharias with the angel who foretold the birth of John the Baptist.

Whenever God speaks, He expects us to trust. Mary had confidence in the promise, saying, "Let it be to me according to your word" (Luke 1:38). Zacharias was more incredulous: "How shall I know this? For I am an old man, and my wife is well advanced in years" (1:18). His doubt silenced his tongue, and for nine months Zacharias had nothing to say.

When God gives a promise, it's best to believe Him instantly. His word is infallible, and His promises never fail. They are to be taken at face value, or else our faith is silenced.

We are to abide in Him by an entire consecration, and to let Him abide in us by an appropriating faith. We are to give ourselves to Christ, and to take in return the Christ who gives himself to us—in other words, we are to believe Christ's promises and to act upon them.

AUGUSTUS STRONG

> See to it that no one takes you captive through hollow and
> deceptive philosophy, which depends on human tradition and
> the basic principles of this world rather than on Christ.
>
> COLOSSIANS 2:8, NIV

Centuries ago, when Egyptian troops first conquered Nubia, a regiment of recruits was crossing the desert. The heat was oppressive. Their supply of water was nearly exhausted. On the horizon they seemed to see a lake bordered with palm trees. The experienced Arab commander told his men that there was no lake in the distance and that what the soldiers saw was only a mirage. But the thirsty men trusted their sight more than the words of their commander. The men ran toward what they believed to be the cool waters of an oasis. Weeks later, authorities found the soldiers, all dead, far out in the desert, where they had fallen in their vain search to find water where none existed.

We are so easily deceived—particularly when we do not have a trustworthy guidebook to direct our way. Fortunately, God has provided such a guidebook in His flawless written Word, the Bible. The Scriptures truthfully reveal who God is, humankind's greatest need, and the loving lengths to which God goes to meet that need. Our task is to read the Word and then do what it says.

Jesus loves me—this I know, for the Bible tells me so.
ANNA BARTLETT WARNER

July 11

GOOD OUT OF EVIL

> The Scripture says to the pharaoh, "For this very purpose
> I have raised you up, that I may show My power in you,
> and that My name may be declared in all the earth."

ROMANS 9:17

Critics of God say the existence of evil proves His imperfection: "If God were all-powerful, He would stamp out evil in the world. If He were all-loving, He would rescue those who suffer as the result of evil deeds. Either God is not all-powerful or He's not all-loving. Either way, He is an imperfect God."

A righteous God and the existence of evil in His world do raise questions. But the Bible answers them: evil is a manifestation of sin, and because "God is light and in Him is no darkness at all" (1 John 1:5), He is not the cause of evil. But God *uses* evil to demonstrate His power and accomplish His purposes. When Samson chose in disobedience to marry a Philistine woman, God used it as a means to bring judgment upon that evil nation. When Joseph's brothers sold him into slavery, God used that betrayal to provide a safe haven for Joseph's family in a time of famine. With God, evil never has the upper hand. If you are feeling the effects of an evil action, know that God is able to cause good to come from it.

The ultimate goal of all creation is God's glory—and that includes the evil that temporarily lurks within it.

God is so powerful that He can direct any evil to a good end.

ST. THOMAS AQUINAS

July 12

WHAT GOOD WOULD I BE?

As God has distributed to each one … so let him walk.

1 CORINTHIANS 7:17

Until the mid-1990s, Argentina required every young man to spend two years in military service. One fellow who showed up at the induction center objected, "What good would I be? I have no arms!" Allegedly they put him in the army anyway. At basic-training camp, so the story goes, his commanding officer said, "See that fellow up there on the hill pumping water? Go tell him when the pail is full. He's blind."

Sometimes we can get caught up in wondering, *What good would I be?* and believing we have nothing to offer in service to God. As it turns out, we are all functioning parts of the whole body of Christ, and though we may not see the value of the gifts and abilities God has given us, He has a plan to use them in union with the talents of other believers to achieve a particular goal. In fact, He handpicked His workers and personally assigned their different abilities, knowing that's where they would thrive and serve Him best.

Dear Christian, do not wish for another believer's talents, for yours were given to you by your Creator, the One who knew your name even as He created the universe. Take joy in knowing that He has given you exactly what you're supposed to have.

You are the only person on earth who can use your ability.

ZIG ZIGLAR

The sign of the Son of Man will appear in heaven, and then all
the tribes of the earth will mourn, and they will see the Son of
Man coming on the clouds of heaven with power and great glory.

MATTHEW 24:30

As far back as 3500 BC, a touchstone was used to measure the quality of gold or silver. A nugget of supposedly pure gold or silver would be scratched on a touchstone of either slate or basalt. Then a mark from a known pure sample would be scratched next to the original, and the two scratches were compared. From that beginning, the word *touchstone* can now refer to anything that is used as a test of genuineness.

In that sense, the second coming of Jesus Christ is a touchstone for New Testament theology. Any doctrine about Christ that does not allow for His imminent, bodily return to earth must be held suspect as to its biblical foundation. So central was Christ's return in His own teaching (Matthew 24; John 14:1-4) that it must be considered necessary and non-optional. Any Christian not living with a moment-by-moment awareness of the possibility of Christ's return is living with a marginal view of who He was and is. Does your understanding of Christ keep you looking and listening for His glorious appearing?

The prospect of seeing a dearly loved one in the future keeps hope alive in the present.

---

*I wish [Jesus] would come in my lifetime so that I
could take off my crown and lay it at His feet.*

QUEEN VICTORIA

All these were the children of Asher, heads of their fathers'
houses, choice men, mighty men of valor, chief leaders.
And they were recorded by genealogies among the army
fit for battle; their number was twenty-six thousand.

1 CHRONICLES 7:40

A "last will and testament" has been used for centuries in the West
to mark the orderly transition of property from one generation
to the next. But there are some things that cannot be bequeathed by
a legal document.

Several generations after Asher (son of Jacob) died, it was said of
his thousands of descendants that they were the heads of their homes,
"choice men, mighty men of valor, chief leaders." But in the latter history of Asher's descendants comes the warning that character is not
a birthright—it must be developed and maintained. Asher's descendants ultimately failed to drive the Canaanites out of their assigned
tribal land, and by David's time they were not even mentioned in the
list of his chief rulers (1 Chronicles 27:16-22). That omission is an
indication that a godly heritage can vanish if it is not preserved.

As for the legacy you leave, make sure it influences as many generations as possible in both substance and example.

---

*This is all the inheritance I can give to my dear
family. The religion of Christ can give them
one which will make them rich indeed.*
PATRICK HENRY

CERTAINTY IN UNCERTAINTY

God is faithful, who will not allow you to be tempted beyond
what you are able, but with the temptation will also make
the way of escape, that you may be able to bear it.

1 CORINTHIANS 10:13

How many things in life (besides death and taxes) are absolutely certain? Even things like the rising and setting of the sun have a condition attached to them (Jeremiah 31:35-36). When we stop and analyze life's contingencies, it quickly becomes apparent that outside of God's promises, very little in life is certain.

It's ironic that one of God's certain promises concerns an area in which we feel *very* uncertain: our ability to escape temptation. When tempted, we suddenly feel unstable, insecure, and uncertain about the outcome. But here is the twofold certainty God has provided concerning temptation: you will never be tempted beyond your ability—that is, beyond your spiritual maturity level. And there will always—*always*—be a way to escape the temptation. By trusting in God's provision, you will be able to "bear" the temptation and ultimately escape it. God has said it, and that makes it certain.

Whatever tempts you is covered by this twofold provision. Ask God to reveal to you the "way of escape" He has promised to provide, and you will be able to bear any temptation.

---

*Most people who fly from temptation
usually leave a forwarding address.*

UNKNOWN

> Disguise yourself, that they may not recognize
> you as the wife of Jeroboam.
>
> 1 KINGS 14:2

Israel's King Jeroboam was worried. He wanted a dynasty, and his son—his heir—was sick. Despite his own hardened heart, Jeroboam knew that the Lord God had the answers of life and death, and he desperately wanted to consult a prophet of Jehovah. Evidently, however, he didn't want his subjects to know he'd been reduced to seeking help from God, so he told his wife to disguise herself and visit the prophet.

The Lord's man was not fooled, however. "Come in, wife of Jeroboam," he boomed. "Why do you pretend to be another person?" (14:6). The prophet then issued a message of judgment on her household for their evil ways.

How easy to practice secret sins and then attend church on Sunday without anyone suspecting. We can display humble faces and appear to be injured victims when, in reality, we're trying to manipulate the opinions of others. We can act with innocence toward our spouses while flirting with coworkers at the office.

But the Lord sees.

That should truly be both a great comfort to us and a great stimulus for purity.

Lord, remind me that You know every thought, test every heart, know every motive, and love every soul!

THE FORGIVABLE SIN

I acknowledged my sin to You, and my iniquity I have
not hidden. I said, "I will confess my transgressions to
the LORD," and You forgave the iniquity of my sin.

PSALM 32:5

There is an "unforgivable sin" mentioned in the Bible by Christ
Himself (Mark 3:29). It seems to have involved the Pharisees'
attributing Jesus' miracle power to Satan rather than to the Holy
Spirit (Mark 3:22). Indeed, that is a serious infraction. Could it be
committed today? Possibly—but I hope it's not a sin that a Christian
needs to worry about.

Strangely, Christians often think they have committed an "unforgivable sin." Not the one Christ referred to but one of their own making. Even though the New Testament epistles mention no sin that is
unforgivable, many believers live in a permanent state of guilt and
shame over something they have done: "What I did was awful. I'm so
embarrassed and ashamed. I don't see how God could ever forgive
me." They're convinced they will spend the rest of their lives on earth
being forgiven for everything except *that*. But the New Testament
says the only sins we haven't been forgiven are the ones we haven't
confessed (1 John 1:9).

Transforming your sin from unforgivable to forgiven is simply a
matter of asking and receiving.

Forgiveness works like oil in relationships.

JOSH McDOWELL

> To [His saints] God willed to make known what are
> the riches of the glory of this mystery among the
> Gentiles: which is Christ in you, the hope of glory.
>
> COLOSSIANS 1:27

A Greek professor told his class, "You have studied Christ himself, the whole Christ, all of Christ. When you study the Bible, you are studying the Lord himself. For all we know of the Lord is encompassed in these sacred pages."

It is true that the pages of the Bible contain everything we desire to know about Jesus, with one limitation: experiencing Him. Head knowledge of Jesus can never replace the experiential knowledge you will have of Him when you let those words penetrate your heart. To be sure, one would be hard pressed to find a genuine reader of the Bible who was not moved to a Jesus experience by way of those very words, for they are alive and at work. However, knowing all there is to know *about* Jesus pales in comparison to seeing a prayer answered in your life or experiencing God's grace and Christ's salvation firsthand. It is this intimate knowledge of Him that allows us not only to be witnesses *for* Jesus but witnesses *of* Jesus.

As believers, we must always be asking God to work in fresh ways in our lives through Scripture, prayer, and personal experience so that we may be able to personally share Christ with others.

Knowing the Bible is one thing; knowing the Author is another!

UNKNOWN

FAITHFUL LAST WORDS

It is God who arms me with strength, and makes my way perfect.

PSALM 18:32

A person's last words speak volumes. Whether they are the final words spoken on a deathbed, the words of an epitaph on a gravestone, the last thoughts we have before sleep, or what we say when parting from a loved one, last words reveal our first thoughts. Last words reveal priorities, hopes, and that which, left unsaid, would reveal a gap in who we are and what we believe.

While much of Samson's life left room for improvement, in his last words we find what, or rather Who, was at the core of his belief system: God. Samson had been captured, blinded, and enslaved by the Philistines. In a dying effort to bring defeat upon this enemy nation, Samson called out to God: "O Lord GOD, remember me, I pray! Strengthen me, I pray, just this once, O God" (Judges 16:28). And with his God-given strength, he pulled down the Philistine temple where he had been put on display. His dying words remind us of the thief crucified with Jesus who asked to be remembered by God (Luke 23:42-43). Both Samson's and the thief's final requests revealed what they hoped in most.

When it feels as if you're taking your last breath, upon whom do you call? Whether you are living in or leaving this world, make sure your last words are faithful ones.

Whatever we trust most, that is our God.

MARK DEVER

July 20
NO EARLS IN HEAVEN

> He chose us in Him before the foundation of the world ... having
> predestined us to adoption as sons by Jesus Christ to Himself.

EPHESIANS 1:4-5

Warwick Castle sits in the center of England, northwest of London. The first Earl of Warwick, Henry de Newburgh, occupied the castle from 1088 to 1119, and the current earl, Guy Greville, was born in 1957. Mr. Greville received the title Earl of Warwick after more than nine hundred years of careful succession.

The English are famous for their lords, earls, and barons and the idea of nobility as a birthright. That might work in the United Kingdom, but it doesn't work in the Kingdom of God: spiritual legitimacy is a personal decision, not a birthright. People aren't saved because their parents or grandparents were saved. In fact, Jesus told a parable about five foolish virgins who failed to provide oil for their lamps. When they sought to borrow oil from others, they were refused. Oil represents the Holy Spirit, who is given to individuals only by God. Are you resting in a spiritual pedigree or in your own personal relationship with Jesus?

Regardless of who your parents are or were, you are not a Christian until you are adopted by God the Father.

The tragedy of my life is that although I've led thousands
of people to Jesus Christ, my own sons are not saved.
BILLY SUNDAY

> Let us pursue the things which make for peace and
> the things by which one may edify another.
>
> ROMANS 14:19

One of the best ways to edify your church is to build up your pastor. Church members tend to expect perfection from their pastors, but they aren't likely to get it. They need to realize that pastors are imperfect human beings serving other imperfect human beings in an imperfect environment. Along the way, they'll make some blunders. Blessed are those pastors who have supportive, patient, encouraging members to build them up.

Have you been a little critical of your church staff? Your deacons or elders? Your Sunday school class? Your fellow members? Have you spoken critically of your church? The Bible says, "Let no corrupt word proceed out of your mouth, but what is good for necessary edification, that it may impart grace to the hearers" (Ephesians 4:29).

A builder needs to have the correct tools in order to construct a sturdy building. Our tongues should be trowels of love spreading the cement of graciousness, not wrecking balls shattering the nerves of others. If you've had a sharp tongue, replace it with love, joy, peace, patience, kindness, goodness, faithfulness, gentleness, and self-control (Galatians 5:22-23). Edify one another until Jesus comes.

*Knowledge, in itself, does not edify. It is love
that edifies; it is love that builds up.*
W. A. CRISWELL

GREATER WORKS? GREATER PRAYER!

If you abide in Me, and My words abide in you, you will
ask what you desire, and it shall be done for you.

JOHN 15:7

"If a little's good, a lot's got to be better." You've probably applied that principle at times in your life and found it's not always true. For example, a small amount of pie is good, but a lot is fattening. A small dose of fertilizer helps a plant to grow, but a big dose will kill it. A little ingredient in a recipe makes it perfect, but a lot makes it a disaster. But there are some areas of life where a lot is always better: prayer, for example.

Jesus once told His disciples something that no doubt amazed them: they would do greater works than He had done. He was leaving the earth and returning to heaven and was commissioning them to continue His words and works—but on a grander scale! While they were pondering that revelation, He told them how it would be possible: through prayer. The works (John 14:12) can be accomplished only through prayer (John 14:13). Imagine the kinds of works we could do if we prayed more than we do! Prayer is an area of the spiritual life where a lot is always better.

If you would like to accomplish greater works for Christ in your life, try starting with prayer. The greater the prayer *to* God, the greater the works *for* God.

The average church knows more about promotion than prayer.
LEONARD RAVENHILL

July 23

THE DIFFICULT SKILL

The fruit of the Spirit is . . . self-control.

GALATIANS 5:22-23

Self-control is not a popular virtue in our culture. We are an instant-gratification, act-on-impulse, if-it-feels-good-do-it society. In stark contrast, a popular parenting book encourages new parents to teach the lost skill of self-control to their children very early. The authors emphasize the importance of self-control by stating, "Self-control is a foundational virtue on which other virtues depend; such as kindness, gentleness . . . and many other behaviors essential for learning."[9] God must also view self-control to be of extreme importance, for it is listed in His Word as a fruit of the Spirit.

By himself, a child cannot understand the need to be self-controlled; thus God delegates the responsibility of teaching this virtue to parents. As Christian adults, we can fully grasp why it is so important to have control over our bodies, our energies, our motives, and our purposes; it is the only way we can truly be useful servants to God. And yet, it is still such a difficult skill to master.

Today, if you see the need for self-control in your life, ask God to teach you this vital skill. As your heavenly parent, He will be delighted to do so.

Man cannot live without self-control.

ISAAC BASHEVIS SINGER

---

9 Gary Ezzo and Robert Bucknam, *On Becoming Baby Wise: Book Two: Parenting Your Pre-Toddler from Five to Fifteen Months* (Sisters: Multnomah Publishers, 1995), 30.

July 24

ONE WHO GOES BEFORE

The Spirit also helps in our weaknesses. For we do not know what
we should pray for as we ought, but the Spirit himself makes
intercession for us with groanings which cannot be uttered.

ROMANS 8:26

The CEO of an American multinational corporation plans to travel to an Asian country to make an offer to purchase a small company in that country. The CEO doesn't know the language or customs of the foreign country, but one of his employees does. The CEO sends that employee ahead to set up the meeting and convey the purpose of the CEO's visit.

There are many times in life when we wish there were someone to go before us, to represent our interests or to intercede on our behalf. Unfortunately, that's not always possible. But there is one realm in which it is always possible to have one represent us, and that is in the realm of prayer. Sometimes we know we need God's help—or is it counsel or wisdom we need? Sometimes it's hard to tell. All we know is that we need God! In those times, the Holy Spirit goes before us to the Father and intercedes, telling Him what we need.

When you know you need to pray but don't know what to say, begin by thanking the Holy Spirit for going before you to the throne of grace.

---

*If thou couldst pray the best prayer in the world, without
the Spirit, God would have nothing to do with it.*
CHARLES HADDON SPURGEON

IS IT WORTH IT?

Your Father who sees in secret will reward you.

MATTHEW 6:18

One day the great Italian Renaissance artist Michelangelo happened to overhear a group of people admiring his *Pietà*, a statue of Mary cradling her Son, Jesus, after His death on the cross. One man attributed the work to another sculptor, much to the chagrin of Michelangelo, who took particular pride in the *Pietà*. Returning to the sculpture after dark that evening, Michelangelo carved his name on it so that no similar mistake would occur in the future.

Sometimes it's hard not to want the recognition and admiration of those around us. Whether our gift is preaching or teaching, writing or singing, evangelism or leading, we must keep a godly perspective and motivation in everything we do. During Jesus' earthly ministry, He certainly knew how to keep Himself from becoming entangled in the praises of men: He gave all the credit to His Father, for He knew His reward was waiting on the other side of the Cross.

If we fall into the trap of working or performing for the rewards of men, we are bound to miss out on our rewards in heaven. Is it worth losing eternal praise from God Himself to have but a moment of earthly glory?

He who merits praise he never receives is better off
than he who receives praise he never merits.

UNKNOWN

A MESSAGE TO SHARE

> Do the work of an evangelist.
>
> 2 TIMOTHY 4:5

World-famous violinist Fritz Kreisler (1875–1962) earned a fortune with his concerts and compositions, but he generously gave most of it away. So when he discovered an exquisite violin on one of his trips, he couldn't afford to buy it. Later, having raised enough money to meet the asking price, he returned to the seller, hoping to purchase that beautiful instrument. But to his great dismay, it had been sold to a collector. Kreisler made his way to the new owner's home and offered to buy the violin. The collector said it had become his prized possession and he would not sell it. Keenly disappointed, Kreisler was about to leave when he had an idea. "Could I play the instrument once more before it is consigned to silence?" he asked. Permission was granted, and the great virtuoso filled the room with such heart-moving music that the collector's emotions were deeply stirred. "I have no right to keep that to myself!" he exclaimed. "It's yours, Mr. Kreisler. Take it into the world, and let people hear it."

We have a message to share. Our heavenly Father created us as exquisite instruments, and the beautiful music we are to make is the good news of salvation through faith in Jesus Christ. We were made to be played.

The church has many tasks but only one mission.

ARTHUR PRESTON

THE HOPE OF THE PEOPLE

> Simon Peter answered Him, "Lord, to whom shall
> we go? You have the words of eternal life."
>
> JOHN 6:68

It was the German economist and philosopher Karl Marx who wrote, "Religion is the sigh of the oppressed creature, the heart of a heartless world, and the soul of soulless conditions. It is the opium of the people." Marx viewed religion (specifically, in his day, Christianity) as a sedative for people who lived without hope in anything else.

One wonders if Marx had considered the words of the apostle Peter. When some of Jesus' followers turned away from Him, He asked the Twelve, "Do you also want to go away?" And with unpredictable insight, Peter spoke for the group: "Lord, to whom shall we go? You have the words of eternal life." Peter was saying that even those who left Jesus would turn to something else. Everyone turns to something—even Karl Marx, who turned to the philosophy of man (but didn't live long enough to see it crumble as a system). Peter went on to say, "We . . . know that You are the Christ." Could you have taken Peter's place and spoken those words?

Jesus is the only person in history who provides hope beyond this life—hope in the resurrection from the dead and life in the world to come.

The word hope I take for faith; and indeed hope
is nothing else but the constancy of faith.

JOHN CALVIN

I have finished the race.

2 TIMOTHY 4:7

Sometimes there aren't enough minutes in a day—or days in a year—for all our work. Well, then, how would you like to have a 445-day year? It happened once. The early Romans established their calendar on a lunar model, and their year had only 355 days. In 46 BC, Julius Caesar mandated a new solar calendar, making the year 365 days long. To bring the new calendar on track, he added two extra months to that year, sticking them between November and December, and he also squeezed three extra weeks between February and March. The result was a one-time-only year of 445 days, which became known as the "Year of Confusion."

Sometimes every year seems like a year of confusion. But the secret to getting all your work done isn't adding days to the year; it's doing only what the heavenly Father has ordained for you. When Jesus ascended to heaven, there was still much work to be done, yet He said, "I have finished the work which You have given Me to do" (John 17:4).

Ask God for His agenda each day, and don't let the *urgent* usurp the *important*. Make sure to finish the work He gives you day by day.

Place all the hours of this day quite simply at
His disposal, and ask Him to make and keep you
ready to do just exactly what He appoints.

FRANCES RIDLEY HAVERGAL

July 29

BORN AGAIN

> Jesus answered and said to him, "Most assuredly, I say to you,
> unless one is born again, he cannot see the kingdom of God."
>
> JOHN 3:3

Suppose you were born in one country and learned its culture, language, traditions, and values as a child. Then your family moved to another country very different from your own. Suddenly, nothing was familiar—new words, new foods, new practices, new sights and sounds. You'd be overwhelmed! It would be like starting over—like being born again.

As imperfect as it is, such an analogy helps when thinking about the meaning of being born again into the Kingdom of God as an adult. Scripture says that before entering the Kingdom of God, human beings are subjects of Satan's kingdom, the kingdom of darkness (Colossians 1:13). In Satan's kingdom we learned to get something by grasping, but in God's Kingdom we get by giving. In Satan's kingdom we learned that the first shall be first, but in God's Kingdom the first shall be last. Everything is different; everything has to be relearned. That's one of the reasons Jesus said we must be born again.

If you're a follower of Jesus and you find yourself doing things differently from the ways of the world, rejoice! It's because you've been born again and are learning a new—and better—way to live.

---

*How momentous is the question, "Have I been born
again?" If not, and you die in your present state,
you will wish you had never been born at all.*

ARTHUR W. PINK

THE REAL ENEMY

We do not wrestle against flesh and blood, but
against principalities, against powers, against the
rulers of the darkness of this age, against spiritual
hosts of wickedness in the heavenly places.

EPHESIANS 6:12

For many years medical researchers thought that stomach ulcers were caused by stress and spicy foods. Then, in 1982, two Australian researchers discovered the *helicobacter pylori* bacterium and proved that it was the cause of some stomach ulcers. In 1994, the National Institutes of Health agreed and recommended treating ulcers with antibiotics instead of with milk.

In medicine, the enemy has to be identified before the proper defense can be used. And the same is true in the spiritual life. Many Christians, while believing in the devil *generally*, have not identified him as being the enemy of their *personal* lives. The apostle Paul wrote that the Christian's struggle in life is against spiritual powers under the control of Satan. To fail to identify one's true enemy is to fail to defeat him. It takes spiritual defenses to defeat a spiritual enemy.

When you find yourself in a soul-sick state, make sure you identify the cause. If it is spiritual in nature, only God's spiritual remedies will cure you.

---

*Jesus invited us not to a picnic, but to a
pilgrimage; not to a frolic, but to a fight.*
BILLY GRAHAM

THE ONENESS FACTOR

By one Spirit we were all baptized into one body—
whether Jews or Greeks, whether slaves or free—and
have all been made to drink into one Spirit.

1 CORINTHIANS 12:13

Not everyone has the privilege of attending a large family reunion. Many families are widely dispersed and have lost touch with one another. But when large families get together and meet distant cousins, they have no trouble bonding. Why? Because they share a common heritage.

Strangers in the body of Christ should be that way—distant spiritual cousins who bond immediately. After all, we have "one body and one Spirit . . . one hope . . . one Lord, one faith, one baptism; one God and Father of all" (Ephesians 4:4-6). Unfortunately, Christians too often stick to their own "families"—Baptist, Methodist, Presbyterian, and so on. The world looks at the body of Christ and wonders why we can't seem to get along better than we do. The early church, in its pre-denominational days, was known for its oneness and unity. They are characteristics every Christian should work hard to restore to Christ's body.

When you meet Christians who are strangers, give them the right hand of fellowship. There's nothing wrong with enjoying a taste of eternal unity right here on earth.

Unity is the essence of the body of Christ.

R. B. KUIPER

AUGUST

You are My flock, the flock of My pasture;
you are men, and I am your God.

EZEKIEL 34:31

Recently the Associated Press carried the story of a Maine couple whose dogs attacked a flock of sheep at a nearby farm, killing nine sheep and injuring ten others. The sheep in this area are famous for their prize-winning wool, but the dogs didn't care. They went for the throats and slaughtered the sheep indiscriminately. For days after the attack, the surviving sheep huddled in a group. Their flock instinct heightened; instead of scattering across the pasture as they normally did, they circled close to one another.

According to the Bible, God's people are sheep having a strong flock instinct. We need fellowship, and we often find safety and accountability in close relationships with other Christians. In dangerous days, we especially need to stay close to one another.

Are you in a small group in your church? Do you have a few close Christian friends who support you by their prayers and counsel? It's wonderful to pray regularly for a handful of people whom God places in our lives and to enjoy hearty, healthy fellowship.

Thank God for our Good Shepherd, and thank Him for placing us in flocks!

---

*Christians may not see eye to eye, but
they can walk arm in arm.*

UNKNOWN

ENERGIZED

May the God of hope fill you with all joy and peace in believing,
that you may abound in hope by the power of the Holy Spirit.

ROMANS 15:13

A man flying home from a mission project was weary. He worried that his overseas trip had been only partially productive, and he dreaded coming home to his desktop of work. He pulled out his Bible and began thumbing through it, and like a flash, certain verses about joy came to mind. He reached for a pen and paper and began writing them down: "In Your presence is fullness of joy". . . . "These things I have spoken to you, that . . . your joy may be full." . . . "The joy of the Lord is your strength." . . .

By the time he finished, he had a list of fifteen "joy verses" from the Bible, and those verses energized him like a divine tonic. He knew the Lord wanted him to return home and plunge into his work with joy.

We often need a jolt of energy to make it through the day, and the power of God's Word applied by God's Spirit gives us the strength we need. He energizes us. Perhaps that's what Paul had in mind when he spoke of "the energy Christ so powerfully works in me" (Colossians 1:29, NIV).

Do you need renewed strength today? Remember that spending time with Jesus energizes the soul.

God helping me, I will not rest until
endued with power from on high.

D. L. MOODY

WHAT EVERYONE NEEDS

> We all, with unveiled face, beholding as in a mirror the glory
> of the Lord, are being transformed into the same image
> from glory to glory, just as by the Spirit of the Lord.
>
> 2 CORINTHIANS 3:18

When it comes to radical spiritual transformations, it's easy for us to think of saints like the apostle Paul (from persecutor to protector of the church), John Newton (from slave trader to pastor), and Nicky Cruz (from street thug to street evangelist). But the truth is, every follower of Jesus has been transformed.

Before you met Jesus, you were something that needed radical transformation—what the Bible calls a "natural" man or woman (1 Corinthians 2:14). You may have been polite, friendly, generous, and well educated—hardly someone who appeared in need of transformation. But in God's eyes, the need was readily apparent. Only God can see the fallen human nature that does not know how to give glory to the Creator. If you think for a moment about your life before and since meeting Jesus, you'll see the transforming work only God could accomplish.

Whether the changes are subtle or significant, they are the work of the Holy Spirit within you, reproducing the life of Jesus (Romans 8:29). Don't forget today to thank God for the changes He has made.

Unless God changes a person's heart,
nothing lasting will be achieved.
WILL METZGER

A SIMPLE SONG

You shall surround me with songs of deliverance.

PSALM 32:7

Presbyterian minister A. B. Simpson, who founded the Christian and Missionary Alliance, was occasionally afflicted with depression. On one occasion while resting at Saratoga Springs, New York, he struggled with keeping joy in his heart. Strolling out to a religious meeting at a nearby campground, Simpson took his seat and listened for a word of encouragement. Nothing moved him until an African American quartet stood up and sang a simple spiritual. The refrain, repeated over and over, said, "My Jesus is the Lord of Lords: no man can work like Him."

Something about that simple song touched Simpson's troubled heart. "The truth of these words fell upon me like a spell," he later said. "It seemed like a voice from heaven. It possessed my whole being. . . . I went forth from that rude, old-fashioned service, remembering nothing else, but strangely lifted up."

Music is God's therapy for the heart, and the songs of Zion— whether old or new—have the ability to encourage us when little else will help. Are you listening to the right music? Are you saying, "Singing I go along life's road, praising the Lord, praising the Lord"?

For it to be a hymn, it is needful, therefore, for it to have three things: praise, praise of God, and these sung.

ST. AUGUSTINE

THE NEED FOR LIGHT

> The natural man does not receive the things of the
> Spirit of God, for they are foolishness to him; nor can he
> know them, because they are spiritually discerned.
>
> 1 CORINTHIANS 2:14

All spelunkers (cave explorers) know the true meaning of "I can't see a thing." Above ground, there is always a bit of light coming from somewhere to aid us. But in a cave, once you're far enough in, there is no light. None. *None at all.* It is the most complete experience of darkness we can have on earth.

Spiritual darkness is like that. The Bible says that before born again, we are "dead in trespasses and sins" (Ephesians 2:1). Spiritually dead means no spiritual life. None. *None at all.* That means we have no love for or understanding of the things of God "because they are spiritually discerned." We gain understanding only through the mysterious illuminating work of the Spirit. What believer hasn't had the "Oh, now I see!" experience in the spiritual life? All have, and will, as the Spirit opens our eyes to the truth of God for which the spiritually dead have no appreciation.

As you read God's Word today, pray with the psalmist, "Open my eyes, that I may see wondrous things from Your law" (Psalm 119:18).

---

*All of man's knowledge is based on God's
illuminating truth to the mind.*

W. ANDREW HOFFECKER

A LONG HAUL

> I beseech you therefore, brethren, by the mercies of God,
> that you present your bodies a living sacrifice, holy,
> acceptable to God, which is your reasonable service.
>
> ROMANS 12:1

When we've dedicated our bodies as living sacrifices to God, we don't just sit around and enjoy the experience. We constructively go out and serve.

One Sunday in Copenhagen, Corrie ten Boom, at eighty years of age, spoke from Romans 12:1, urging her audience to present their bodies to Christ as living sacrifices. After church, two nurses invited her to their apartment for coffee, and Corrie went with them—only to discover that they lived on the tenth floor of a building with no elevator. The task of climbing those stairs was almost more than she could stand, and she wondered if she might die en route. *Perhaps I am leaving earth to go to heaven,* she complained to herself.

Finally arriving in the apartment, Corrie found the parents of one of the girls waiting there, wanting to be saved, and both gloriously received Christ as their Savior.

On her way down the steps Corrie said, "Thank you, Lord, for making me walk up all these steps. And next time, Lord, help Corrie ten Boom listen to her own sermon about being willing to go anywhere You tell me to go—even up ten flights of stairs."[10]

Lord, make me willing, get me going, and take me higher!

---

[10] Corrie ten Boom, *Tramp for the Lord* (Fort Washington, PA: CLC Publications, 1974), 155.

Take heed to yourselves.

ACTS 20:28

A bank recently advertised its services with the words "Check your balances." Using online tools, customers can instantly check the balances on any and all of their accounts.

Perhaps you need to take a moment today to check your balances in another sense. There's the private you and the public you, and one of the secrets to good mental health is keeping the two in balance. Jesus ministered to the multitudes, and then He withdrew to the wilderness to be alone. Few of us want to be monks or nuns who retreat to desolate cells or adopt vows of silence. But if we're always surrounded by noise and people, we'll not have the necessary quiet to recharge our batteries and remain fresh and strong.

Our need for independence is balanced by our need for interaction, and our craving for solitude is matched by a need for society.

If you're too much alone, do something about it today. Volunteer. Make a phone call. Invite someone to tea. Get out and go to church. Knock on your neighbor's door with a plate of cookies.

If you're too rushed and busy, slow down a little. Take time for Bible reading. Take a little stroll through the park with your Bible in hand, and find a sunny bench where you can sit and read awhile. Take heed to yourself—and check your balances.

Lord, grant me the blessing of a balanced life!

IF THE LORD WILLS

> You ought to say, "If the Lord wills, we
> shall live and do this or that."
>
> JAMES 4:15

Experts are always predicting the future—how many hurricanes will strike this year, what will happen to the stock market, how the housing market will fare, which teams will end up in the World Series, and which products on store shelves will be hits.

It's risky business, because no one has the ability to see even five minutes into the future.

The writer of Ecclesiastes wrote, "A wise man's heart discerns both time and judgment, because for every matter there is a time and judgment.... For he does not know what will happen; so who can tell him when it will occur?" (8:5-7).

Wisdom is the ability to do God's will in God's timing; and though we do not know exactly what the future holds, we can always say, "If the Lord wills ..."

Make your plans prayerfully, and hold them loosely. And with every prayer request and every plan and project, give it to Him, saying, "Lord, if it be Your will ..."

---

*We don't know what the future holds, but
we know who holds the future.*

UNKNOWN

UNCOMFORTABLE WITH
THE CULTURE

Do not be conformed to this world, but be transformed
by the renewing of your mind, that you may prove what
is that good and acceptable and perfect will of God.

ROMANS 12:2

It has happened more than once. Missionaries leave the United States and, in time, become more comfortable in a foreign land than in their native country. They give various reasons: "It's quieter," "less materialism," "less peer pressure on our children," "the people are more receptive to the gospel." When they return to America to visit, they talk about "returning home" in a new way—they've exchanged their old home for a new one.

That's what it means to be a citizen of the Kingdom of God. Paul says our "citizenship is in heaven," not in this world (Philippians 3:20). That's why, over time, Christians begin to feel more and more out of place with the cultures of this world, why when they speak of "going home" they are referring to God's eternal Kingdom. *When* we exchange our earthly home for our Kingdom home is up to God. In the interim, our job is to so walk in the Spirit that we aren't "conformed to this world," that we aren't squeezed into the world's mold, as Bible translator J. B. Phillips put it.

When you leave home today, let it remind you of where your true home is—in Christ Jesus, now and for eternity.

If you stand on the Word, you do not stand in with the world.

VANCE HAVNER

Remember the words of the Lord Jesus, that He said,
"It is more blessed to give than to receive."

ACTS 20:35

This verse gives us an almost-forgotten beatitude. It was spoken by Jesus but not recorded by Matthew, Mark, Luke, or John. The apostle Paul knew of it, however, and recalled it in Acts 20, thus preserving it for us in Scripture.

This verse gives us a super-beatitude. There are many beatitudes in the Bible that begin with the words *Blessed is . . .* or *Blessed are. . . .* But only once in the Bible does the phrase "more blessed" occur. This verse tells us how to go beyond blessing to greater blessing.

This verse gives us a double blessing. First, there is the blessing of receiving, which is a very me-like thing. God created us as recipients. He is the Source, the Supply, the Endless Provider who gives universal blessings, daily blessings, and spiritual blessings.

But there is one blessing greater than receiving. It's the blessing of giving. Why is it more blessed to give than to receive? When we receive, we're acting like ourselves; but when we give, we're acting like God. Receiving is me-like. Giving is Christlike.

Have you experienced God's almost-forgotten, super, double blessing today?

Never forget that at the very heart of the
Gospel is the whole principle of giving.
DR. STEPHEN OLFORD

August 11

THE GIFT OF WEEDING

[The Lord] has filled them with skill to do all manner of work.

EXODUS 35:35

Jim didn't like teaching the boys' class at church, but he pressed on dutifully because he'd been asked and because he didn't want to disappoint his pastor. What he really liked, however, was using his day off to do yard work at the church. He devoted every other Tuesday to mulching, mowing, trimming, clearing, raking, planting, and weeding. He knew that the appearance of the church's lawn was important in attracting visitors to the Sunday services where they could hear the gospel. But truth be told, he was a poor Sunday school teacher.

One day after talking with his pastor, Jim realized he didn't have the gift of teaching. He had the gift of weeding—well, the gift of serving, of helping. When he began working more fully within his area of giftedness, he was happier, and so was everyone else.

The Lord has made each of us different, with different passions, abilities, and gifts. We're happier when we're doing what God has called and gifted us to do. Others will be blessed too, and the Lord will be honored.

Be good and true, be patient; be undaunted.
Leave your usefulness for God to estimate. He
will see to it that you do not live in vain.
GEORGE MORRISON

August 12

UNSEEN RIPPLES

Cast your bread upon the waters, for you
will find it after many days.

ECCLESIASTES 11:1

If you throw a stone into the middle of a lake on a starless night, will there be ripples? Will those ripples eventually reach the shoreline? Even if you can't see them in the darkness?

That's what we're doing when we share Christ with others and when we perform acts of compassion and kindness. We're tossing our words and actions into the lives of others, and we can be sure there'll be a ripple effect, even if we can't see it. When we serve Christ, we're doing more good than we know, for God has promised that His Word will not return to Him void (Isaiah 55:11).

Sometimes the Lord *does* let us see some of the fruit of our labors. Knowing we need encouragement, He allows us to see the partial results of our words or work for Him. The full results, however, can be seen only in heaven, and so we serve Him by faith, always abounding in the work, for we know that our labor in the Lord is not in vain.

You'll never be a failure if what you're doing
is ultimately for the glory of God.
RICK WARREN

August 13
EMPTY CUPS

> My people have committed two evils: they have forsaken
> Me, the fountain of living waters, and hewn themselves
> cisterns—broken cisterns that can hold no water.
>
> JEREMIAH 2:13

In his seventeenth-century devotional classic *A Serious Call to a Devout and Holy Life*, William Law describes a thirsty man who kept holding up one empty cup after another to his lips. No matter how beautiful the cups were, Law observes, and no matter how glittery and golden they seemed, the poor man only grew thirstier while lifting them to his mouth—for empty cups cannot quench thirst.

Many people today are seeking inner fulfillment and emotional peace by lifting one empty cup after another to their lips. But Jesus said, "If anyone thirsts, let him come to Me and drink. . . . Out of his heart will flow rivers of living water" (John 7:37-38).

Without the risen Christ in our homes and hearts, we're missing the kind of encouragement we need to keep going. He is the true source of encouragement, and as we partake of the living waters of His grace, we'll overflow with true encouragement into the lives of others.

Put down your empty cups, and drink richly of Christ!

---

*Awaken your soul into a zealous desire of that solid
happiness, which is only to be found in recourse to God.*
WILLIAM LAW

IT IS WELL. . . .

My brethren, count it all joy when you fall into various trials,
knowing that the testing of your faith produces patience.

JAMES 1:2-3

If there was ever a person who exemplified the right attitude during a time of trial, it was Horatio G. Spafford. Once a wealthy businessman, he was brought to financial ruin by the Great Chicago Fire of 1871 and shortly thereafter was crushed by the news that all four of his daughters had died while crossing the Atlantic. In light of these facts, it is astounding that he penned these words:

When peace, like a river, attendeth my way,
When sorrows like sea billows roll;
Whatever my lot, Thou has taught me to say,
"It is well, it is well, with my soul."

Spafford and his wife, who survived the shipwreck, went on to have two more daughters and then founded a group with a mission to serve the poor of Jerusalem.

When we experience trials of any kind, it can be tempting to get angry, demand justice, and act irrationally, crying out, "It's not fair!" But if we can catch a glimpse of Jesus' face as He unfairly hung on the cross, perhaps we will recall how He responded during the greatest trial of all time and will try to follow His example.

You cannot tailor-make the situations in life, but you
can tailor-make the attitudes to fit those situations.
ZIG ZIGLAR

BOILING EGGS

> Make a joyful shout to the LORD, all you lands! …
> Come before His presence with singing.
>
> PSALM 100:1-2

Years ago a pastor stayed the night in a young couple's home. When he awoke the next morning, he heard a beautiful voice singing "Nearer, My God to Thee," and he inquired about it at breakfast. He said he was pleased to hear the old hymn but remembered it being slower than he had heard it that morning. "Oh," replied the hostess, "that's because I wasn't paying too much attention to the words. It's a song my mom used to sing, and I've found it's a good one to boil eggs by: repeat the song five times rapidly for soft-boiled eggs and eight times for hard-boiled."

Some people believe that truly worshiping God in song means to sing without reservation, while others believe it is a private interaction. In reality, it doesn't matter how you sing during worship. What matters is that your heart and mind are focused on the words and that you are allowing the act of worship to draw you closer to the Lord.

If you feel something is lacking in your worship time, try paying close attention to the words and intentionally singing them to your Lord and Savior. Invest your whole heart in worshiping with song, and you will gain a deeper, more intimate relationship with God.

When I worship, I would rather my heart be without words than my words be without heart.

LAMAR BOSCHMAN

HUMILITY PLAYS THE
LEADING ROLE

Blessed are the meek, for they shall inherit the earth.

MATTHEW 5:5

If there was ever an example of true humility, it was in the life and ministry of Jesus Christ. He understood how important this virtue was to His heavenly Father. In fact, He became God's demonstration to believers of how humility is more important than ability. You see, God knew that in order for the sins of humanity to be forgiven once and for all, a sacrifice would have to be made. A life would have to be taken in order for our lives to be saved. Now here is where humility plays the leading role: Jesus humbled Himself and came down to humanity's level in order to permanently atone for all our sins, and it was precisely His humility that allowed God to use Him as the perfect sacrifice.

In the same way, if we desire to be used by God, all we have to do is be humble and allow Him to work through us. Our abilities—or lack thereof—are of little significance when God is looking for a humble spirit to use. Sometimes being of use to God is a matter of our attitude rather than our aptitude. So let humility play the leading role in your life, and watch as God uses you in ways you never dreamed.

*The sufficiency of my merit is to know
that my merit is not sufficient.*

ST. AUGUSTINE

Give to the LORD the glory due His name.

1 CHRONICLES 16:29

When Michelangelo finished painting the Sistine Chapel and received accolades from onlookers, he did not give credit to his paintbrush. Such a thing would be absurd. It was the artist who was responsible for the work; the brush was merely a tool used to carry out the creator's vision.

God's plan is like the ceiling of the Sistine Chapel, and we are but the paintbrushes in the hands of the Master Artist. Each one of us is used in a unique way to carry out a portion of God's plan, but we must remember to whom the glory belongs. For though we are called upon to be a part of God's grand scheme, when we stand back and view the masterpiece that emerges in the end, we will realize that only one as great as almighty God could have produced such beauty.

The Bible says, "Whatever you do, do all to the glory of God" (1 Corinthians 10:31). When we remove our "selves" from the picture, it becomes easier to achieve that goal. It also frees us from spiritual pride and allows us to be used to our fullest potential for the Lord. We can take joy in knowing God has chosen us to accomplish His goals; we must also take care to give Him the honor and glory that He so deserves.

To God be the glory, great things He hath done!

FANNY CROSBY

PERFECT SUBMISSION, PERFECT DELIGHT

> Obey those who rule over you, and be submissive, for they
> watch out for your souls, as those who must give account.

HEBREWS 13:17

The idea of submission isn't popular in our me-centered culture; we don't like others telling us what to do. We're wary of anything limiting our personal freedoms, and we equate submission with weakness. But the Bible teaches that while Christians are strong-willed, stout-hearted souls, the word *submit* should be in our vocabulary.

The Bible tells us to submit to one another in the fear of God (Ephesians 5:21). Wives are to submit to their husbands (Ephesians 5:22), and children to their parents (1 Timothy 3:4). Peter tells us to submit to the laws of the land for the Lord's sake (1 Peter 2:13). Younger people should have submissive attitudes toward older people, and servants toward their masters (1 Peter 5:5; 2:18). All of us are to submit to God (James 4:7).

The Lord has established lines of authority and responsibility for our welfare, and a healthy heart is one that knows when and how to defer his or her own wishes for the sake of godly obedience. After all, even our Lord Jesus submitted to the Father's will. Should we not do the same?

A heart resigned, submissive, meek, my great Redeemer's throne,
where only Christ is heard to speak, where Jesus reigns alone.

CHARLES WESLEY

CHERISHING THE WORD

> The grass withers, the flower fades, but the
> word of our God stands forever.
>
> ISAIAH 40:8

We occasionally read stories—perhaps it has happened to you—of people who find a box of letters in an attic, letters long forgotten or thought lost, that provide a window into the world of departed loved ones. The words immediately create memories and images of those precious to us—we can hear their laughter, feel their touch, even taste their tears. Once in hand, we vow never to let such treasured words escape us again.

When blessings are written down, they can be savored and enjoyed time after time. No wonder archaeologists and linguists treat ancient biblical manuscripts as if they are made of gold. Indeed, they are more precious than gold (Psalm 19:10)! The Bible has been called God's love letter to humankind. If we cherish letters from family members and friends, how much more ought we to cherish the love letter we've received from God? It's one thing keep the Bible in a place of honor, but it's an even better thing to read and commit its words to heart and mind.

The frequency with which we read and reread a letter from someone is an indication of its importance to us.

When you read God's Word, you must constantly be saying to yourself, "It is talking to me, and about me."

SØREN KIERKEGAARD

August 20

A CHILDREN'S CHEERLEADER

These words which I command you today shall be in your
heart. You shall teach them diligently to your children.

DEUTERONOMY 6:6-7

What expectant parents don't wrangle over baby names, discuss
nursery decor, haggle over finances, and prognosticate about
what the newborn will look like? Whose eyes will she have, Mom's or
Dad's? Whose chin? And will the little one be spared Grandpa's rather
protruding proboscis (large nose, to put it nicely)?

All parents want the best for their children. They want them to
grow up healthy, happy, and strong. More than anything, perhaps,
Christian parents want their children to grow up to love and serve
the Lord. And that requires deliberate, intentional moral schooling.

That training begins in the home. But it involves more than mere
instruction in the faith. It means encouraging your children when
they do right and when they succeed, and patting them on the back
for giving their best effort. Raising a godly, happy child in the negative
world in which we live today requires open and honest conversations,
laughter, and perhaps most important of all, modeling what a godly
marriage looks like with a mommy and daddy who love each other
and readily forgive each other's failings.

It is a truism that children learn more by our actions than by our
words, but it has never been truer than it is today.

*The best way to train up a child the way he should
go is to travel that road occasionally yourself.*
JOSH BILLINGS

THE LESSON BOOK

I have told him that I will judge his house forever for
the iniquity which he knows, because his sons made
themselves vile, and he did not restrain them.

1 SAMUEL 3:13

A boy stole a lesson book and took it home to his mother, who did not punish him, but encouraged the act. A little while later he stole a cloak and brought it to her, and again she praised him. As the boy grew into a man, he continued to steal things of greater value until one day, he was caught in the act and led away to a public execution. Just before his sentence was to be carried out, he noticed his mother in the crowd and shouted angrily to her, "Ah, if you had beaten me when I first stole and brought you that lesson book, I should not have come to this, nor have been led to a disgraceful death!"

Studies have shown that babies can thrive without sight, hearing, or smell but can die from lack of affection. In the same way, children can live without new toys, better clothes, and trips to Disneyland, but they will fail to thrive without boundaries.

Our Father in heaven gives us boundaries to live by because He knows what is best for us and He deeply loves us. As parents, let us follow His example and show our children love by giving them what they need: boundaries.

It is dangerous to confuse children with angels.
DAVID FYFE

"I LOVE MANKIND...."

Love your enemies.

MATTHEW 5:44

In the comic strip *Peanuts*, Linus once explained, "I love mankind; it's people I can't stand." English playwright W. Somerset Maugham similarly said, "I've always been interested in people, but I've never liked them."

Perhaps you can identify with those sentiments. People can be rude, obnoxious, selfish, foolish, trying, vexing, and vicious. Some of them even fall into the category of "enemies"—people who criticize us or try to take advantage of us. We naturally feel resentment, anger, fear, and even hatred.

Yet Jesus said, "Love your enemies, bless those who curse you, do good to those who hate you, and pray for those who spitefully use you."

We can do this only on our knees. The person we most dislike is still a soul for whom Christ died. We don't have to always agree with our critics or defer to our enemies, but loving unconditionally is simply letting the love of Christ flow through us like warm water through a pipe. The most unlovable person is the one who needs love the most. After all, if Christ loved us, He can help us love others.

So find someone you don't like, and pray for that person today!

Am I not destroying my enemies when I make friends of them?

ABRAHAM LINCOLN

> [Jonah] said: "I cried out to the LORD because of
> my affliction, and He answered me. Out of the belly
> of Sheol I cried, and You heard my voice."
>
> JONAH 2:2

Remember old Jonah? He had his personal plans made the day God approached him and asked him to go to Nineveh to preach to the Assyrians. Jonah thought better of that idea and jumped on a ship heading to Spain. Because this was not acceptable behavior for a prophet, the Lord allowed Jonah a few days of "R & R" (Rest and Regurgitation) to reconsider. After that, Jonah saw the light and also started to see things God's way.

The very fact that God would set Jonah aside in an uncomfortable place in order to get his attention ought to be a warning for us. This doesn't mean that every time we disobey God He's going to do the same to us. But it apparently is an option. After David had spent a number of months incapacitated because of sin, he said, "Do not be like the horse or like the mule ... which must be harnessed with bit and bridle" (Psalm 32:9). Instead, just do what you know you should. Don't give God a reason to consider setting you aside while you reconsider what He has asked you to do. Is there anything God has asked you to do to which you still haven't said yes?

Going where God wants you to go might not be nearly as unpleasant as the alternative.

It is much safer to obey than to rule.
THOMAS À KEMPIS

Behold, I am the LORD, the God of all flesh.
Is there anything too hard for Me?

JEREMIAH 32:27

"Rather than saying 'God, here is my problem,' we should put the problem into perspective by saying 'Problem, here is my God!'" Whoever wrote those words must have understood that there is no problem in our lives that God cannot handle.

When we make our problems the objects of our lives, it is easy to become discouraged and forget that we have a God who will sustain us during our trials. However, when we change our perspective and the order of the words, we see that God becomes the object and the focus of our lives. It doesn't seem as if such a small detail would matter much, but when you visualize introducing your problems to almighty God, suddenly they seem smaller, and you realize just how triumphant you can be with His help.

Often it is only a matter of changing our perspective in order to overcome adversity. No matter what troubles you are facing, always remember our God is big enough, strong enough, and powerful enough to take care of them. He is the answer to all of life's problems, and He is enough.

---

*He comes to us in the brokenness of our health, in
the shipwreck of our family lives, in the loss of all
possible peace of mind, even in the very thick of our
sins. He saves us in our disasters, not from them.*

ROBERT FARRAR CAPON

ALL DRESSED UP

> The lamp of the body is the eye. If therefore your eye
> is good, your whole body will be full of light.
>
> MATTHEW 6:22

John had done quite a bit of study over the last two years on the Christian's responsibility concerning the stewardship of creation. He had developed what he thought were some biblically based convictions and wanted to teach a small class of other interested believers to get some feedback on his ideas. But his church's leaders felt a course on "environmentalism" wasn't totally appropriate. John had been affirmed in his teaching gift on prior occasions and felt he had approached this new area of study carefully and prayerfully. He was all dressed up, spiritually speaking, but had nowhere to go.

What should John do? It can be confusing when we feel the Lord has equipped us to accomplish something for Him but it seems that no one else got the memo! Rather than be discouraged or angry, we should go back to the Lord and ask for further direction. Instead of forcing the issue, we need to ask God to create an understanding and willingness in the hearts of others to see the same need—and our ability to meet it. In the meantime, we must keep preparing for the work we believe we're called to do.

God's calling is for a purpose. Wait for His time to see it revealed.

Patience is the companion of wisdom.
ST. AUGUSTINE

ENTHUSIASM MAKES THE DIFFERENCE

Whatever you do, do it heartily, as to the Lord and not to men.

COLOSSIANS 3:23

Motivational speaker Jeffrey Gitomer points out, "At the beginning of any task, more than anything else, your attitude will affect its successful outcome." Whether you're calling on a customer, scrubbing the bathroom floor, writing an article, remodeling a bedroom, or running for political office, enthusiasm is vital.

A cheerful demeanor in the office is contagious, and a smile can transform a workplace. The Bible tells us to serve the Lord with joy and enthusiasm (Deuteronomy 28:47, NLT). Ephesians 6:7-8 says, "Work with enthusiasm, as though you were working for the Lord rather than for people. Remember that the Lord will reward each one of us for the good we do, whether we are slaves or free" (NLT).

Joy and enthusiasm don't necessarily come naturally; many people have to work at them. Let's all work on our joy and enthusiasm today. Whatever task you face, do it enthusiastically, and do it for the Lord!

People often say that motivation doesn't last. Well, neither does bathing—that's why we recommend it daily.

ZIG ZIGLAR

A JOURNEY NAMED MATURITY

These all died in faith, not having received the promises, but
having seen them afar off were assured of them, embraced them
and confessed that they were strangers and pilgrims on the earth.

HEBREWS 11:13

Most Christians are familiar with John Bunyan's *Pilgrim's Progress*. Benjamin Franklin said he supposed it to be "more generally read than any other book except, perhaps, the Bible." While most know the book, fewer are familiar with the complete title: *The Pilgrim's Progress from This World to That Which Is to Come.*

Pilgrim's Progress is about an "everyman" who makes his way from earth to heaven by varied and difficult paths. But it is on the path that he discovers salvation and grows to maturity. In other words, because God's goal for us is Christlikeness (Romans 8:29), the journey becomes the destination. It is on the journey toward heaven that we encounter the trials, tribulations, and blessings that conform our inner persons to the character of Christ. Heaven is our home, but being like Jesus is our goal.

The next time the journey seems difficult, remember: it's supposed to be! If Christ learned obedience through the things He suffered (Hebrews 5:8), it is likely we will learn it the same way.

---

*The Lord gets His best soldiers out of
the highlands of affliction.*
CHARLES HADDON SPURGEON

ALL THINGS

> [We are] predestined according to the purpose of Him who
> works all things according to the counsel of His will.
>
> EPHESIANS 1:11

In his overruling providence, our Lord not only works all things for our good (Romans 8:28) but also works all things according to the counsel of His will. His sovereign power can even transform our faults, failures, and mistakes into tapestries that bring Him glory. That doesn't give us the freedom to sin, but it does invite us to bring our "goofs" to Jesus, confident that they have been covered by His blood.

One evening just before an outreach service, evangelist D. L. Moody lost his temper with a man who had insulted him. Moody actually shoved the man. *This meeting is killed,* thought a friend. *The large number who have seen the whole thing will hardly be in a condition to be influenced by anything more Mr. Moody may say tonight.* But Moody rose with trembling voice, and his humble apology and tender confession so moved the crowd that the tide turned and the meeting was touched with divine power.

This doesn't give us an excuse for losing our tempers, but isn't it wonderful to know that our Lord works all things—even our faults—for our good and His glory? Encourage yourself with that today!

Slippings and strayings there will be, no doubt,
the everlasting arms are beneath us; we
shall be caught, rescued, restored.

J. I. PACKER

WORK AT IT EVERY DAY

Get wisdom!

PROVERBS 4:5

Have you ever noticed that people who are good at something work every day to get even better? Professional athletes hone their skills and build their bodies during the off-season; successful business owners keep working after everyone else has gone home; doctors attend seminars to stay up-to-date on the latest medical developments. The fact is, if you desire to be excellent at something, you must work at it every day.

The same is true for living a life surrendered to God. Christianity is a journey of growth and development through the gaining of wisdom on a daily basis. We must seek wisdom the way a runner seeks the physical ability to go ten more miles by doing a little more each time she runs. Proverbs tells us, "Those who seek me [wisdom] diligently will find me" (Proverbs 8:17). When we begin to seek wisdom, it will become a part of our everyday lives and guide us through each moment.

We are reminded countless times in God's Word that wisdom is worth more than all the riches we could ever dream of, but we must seek it and attentively work at becoming wise in the Lord, for wisdom is not a destination but a journey we must take part in every day.

As we trust God to give us wisdom for today's decisions, He will lead us a step at a time into what He wants us to be doing in the future.

THEODORE EPP

WAITING LIKE CALEB

> Joshua blessed him, and gave Hebron to Caleb
> the son of Jephunneh as an inheritance.
>
> JOSHUA 14:13

Do you know anyone who has had to wait a long time—a *really* long time—to do something he or she has always dreamed of? Maybe that person is you. Maybe you saved money for ten years to take a vacation to Europe. Maybe you waited thirty whole minutes for your child to get off the computer. Or maybe it took you five years to get up the nerve to go bungee jumping.

While waiting for anything in our hurry-up world is commendable, few people today wait as long as Caleb did. God had promised the children of Israel they would inherit Canaan, but they were too afraid to go in and take it—except for Joshua and Caleb. God made the rebellious generation wander in the wilderness for forty years until they died off. Then the new generation, along with Joshua and Caleb, got to go into the Promised Land. Forty-five years after being ready to make a home in Canaan, Caleb finally got to do it (Joshua 14:10). He didn't complain, didn't give up, and didn't blame God. He just waited until God said, "Now is the time."

If you are waiting for something, do it like Caleb did. Good things come to those who wait on the Lord.

Where there is patience and humility, there is neither anger nor vexation.

FRANCIS OF ASSISI

THE TRUTH, THE WHOLE TRUTH...

Has God indeed said, "You shall not eat
of every tree of the garden"?

GENESIS 3:1

A person's native language is the one he is most comfortable speaking, the one he reverts to impulsively, the one by which his values are most easily communicated. The Bible says that Satan's native language is lies (John 8:44). Whenever he opens his mouth—or motivates someone else to open his or her mouth—it will also be a distortion of the truth.

Twisting the truth is what Satan did with Eve in the Garden of Eden (Genesis 3). Distorting God's instructions is what Saul did when he was supposed to destroy the Amalekites (1 Samuel 15). When we find ourselves coloring the truth or distorting God's Word to serve our own interests, we know automatically the source of that motivation. Sometimes we try to treat the truth like notes in music. If the truth is A, but we tell it as if it's A-flat or A-sharp, we say, "But it's still an A!" That doesn't matter. It may be close to the truth, but it's not the truth. If you are ever tempted to embellish, exaggerate, distort, color, hide, or otherwise not tell the truth—stop!

The truth is the currency of the Kingdom. Lies are like counterfeit money—they render all transactions meaningless.

---

*A lie gets halfway around the world before the
truth has a chance to get its pants on.*
WINSTON CHURCHILL

SEPTEMBER

YOU'VE ALWAYS HAD THE POWER

The word of God is living and powerful.

HEBREWS 4:12

There is a famous scene at the end of *The Wizard of Oz* where Dorothy misses her opportunity to return to Kansas by hot air balloon and believes she will never be able to go home. All of a sudden, Glinda appears and says to her, "You've always had the power to go back to Kansas." Dorothy later recounts what she has learned: "If I ever go looking for my heart's desire again, I won't look any further than my own backyard."

If you own a Bible, then you need not look any further for guidance, instruction, healing, and inspiration. So often we search for the meaning of life and the solutions to our problems in the latest book, motivational CD, or support group. While there is nothing wrong with those things, they do not contain the living power that God's Word does.

When we start to wrap our minds around how powerful Scripture really is, a whole new world will open up to us as believers. And as we seek out direction in our lives, we'll begin to look no further than the Bible on our nightstand.

Hide God's Word in your heart, harness the power contained within its verses, and use it like the powerful resource it is!

Our lives are a manifestation of what we think about God.

ANONYMOUS

September 2

BE LIKE A TREE

He shall be like a tree planted by the rivers of water, that
brings forth its fruit in its season, whose leaf also shall
not wither; and whatever he does shall prosper.

PSALM 1:3

During the winter in the South, homeowners with lots of pine trees on their property dread a heavy snow or ice storm. These tall, thin trees are top heavy and have shallow root systems. When snow and ice build up on the upper branches, the trees can fall over easily and do great damage to a house. Oaks, on the other hand, have root systems that anchor them firmly to withstand weather, weight, and wind.

The author of Psalm 1 used a firmly established tree to represent a person who "meditates day and night" on God's Word (1:2). Because that tree has sunk its roots deeply to gain nourishment from the river, it "brings forth its fruit in its season." Referring to such a person, the psalmist says that "whatever he does shall prosper." When we sink our spiritual roots deep into God's Word, we will bear fruit. We will be blessed because our lives are based on truth—which affects not only our actions but our reactions to whatever life brings.

Meditating "day and night" is a discipline. It is the practice of taking in God's Word and then thinking about it all day, applying it to every situation, and capturing new insights as the day goes on. Try it!

The income of God's Word is the outcome of a changed life.

UNKNOWN

DAVID JEREMIAH | 257

STREET NOISE

The LORD gives wisdom; from His mouth
come knowledge and understanding.

PROVERBS 2:6

Some years ago, a retired missionary built a small garden with a trickling fountain in his backyard. When guests came by and sat with him in his garden, he would say to them, "You hear the traffic from the street, don't you? I hear the trickling of the fountain." He had trained his ears to tune out the noises from the street and to enjoy the tranquil splatter of the water.

Wisdom comes as we train our ears to tune out the world's noise and to hear the voice of God as He speaks to us with the wisdom of His Word in our hearts.

In his classic volume *Studies in Proverbs*, nineteenth-century expositor William Arnot wrote: "Those who hide the word within them, feeding on it as daily bread, acquire a habitual bent of mind towards things spiritual."

By meditating on Scripture, it's possible to become a wiser person, making better decisions, offering helpful counsel to others, and handling our emotions and reactions with maturity. "The LORD gives wisdom; from His mouth come knowledge and understanding."

---

*The Word of God is a vital seed, but it will not germinate
unless it be hidden in a softened receptive heart.*

WILLIAM ARNOT

NO STATUES FOR CRITICS

I have become the ridicule of all my people—
their taunting song all the day.

LAMENTATIONS 3:14

The story is told of a young musician whose concert was roundly criticized by the music critics of his day. The famous Finnish composer Jean Sibelius consoled him by patting him on the shoulder and saying, "Remember, there is no city in the world which has erected a statue to a critic."

Well, there might be such a statue somewhere. But there are surely more statues erected to remember champions and heroes than critics. Yet critics will always be the stone in the champion's shoe—and they may be found close to home. When the teenage David wanted to confront the Philistine giant Goliath, his own older brother Eliab was his biggest critic. David was accused of being prideful and insolent, of not taking the cost of war seriously. What happened to David can happen to anyone who wants to be a champion for Christ. Others who are fearful of stepping out in faith and obeying God will try to make themselves feel better by criticizing you. But if God is calling you to step out and trust Him, there is no safer place you can be.

Far better to be criticized by God's opponents than to disappoint God by not heeding His call.

Any fool can criticize, condemn, and complain, and most fools do.
BENJAMIN FRANKLIN

September 5

PORTABLE CAPSULES OF GRACE

There has not failed one word of all His good promise.

1 KINGS 8:56

A biblical promise is a tightly wrapped, power-packed, portable capsule of Scripture, written by God and designed to meet a specific need in our lives at a specific time and in a way that corresponds perfectly to His all-sufficient grace. The promises of God are His guarantees amid life's uncertainties. They're the basis of our lives of faith, and there are specific promises in the Bible to meet every condition and contingency in our lives.

Without God's infallible promises, we have no assurance about anything—no hope, no security, no safety, no encouragement, and no comfort. His promises provide all those things in an endless supply of grace for us each moment of every day.

As George Müller once put it, "Many times when I could have gone insane from worry, I was at peace because my soul believed the truth of God's promises."

We can trust God's promises. Not one word of them will fail, and we can both rest and rely on them for all our needs.

God's promises mark the parameters of His grace. Spoken with the authority of His Word, they define His goodness, for He does what He has promised, and no less.

DAVID JEREMIAH

September 6

STAND OUT IN THE CROWD

[Joseph's] master saw that the LORD was with him and
that the LORD made all he did to prosper in his hand.

GENESIS 39:3

In the food industry, separating the good from the bad is important. Workers watch as conveyor belts stream by, loaded with a harvest of fruit. Their trained eyes look for blemishes; their quick hands reach out and cull the unacceptable items. Because the vast majority of the fruit is good, when an imperfect sample appears, it stands out from the crowd.

"Standing out" works the opposite way as well, especially with regard to people. For instance, the Bible says Jesus of Nazareth was not noticeable for His outward appearance (Isaiah 53:2), yet He stood out in the crowd. Indeed, He stands out in the crowd of humanity as the most unusual person in history. Among His followers, those who are most like Him will stand out as well. The more of God's character that is revealed in us (the fruit of the Spirit, found in Galatians 5:22-23), the less like "the crowd" we will be. And people will notice. Has anyone ever told you there is something different about you? If they haven't, and if you continue to be conformed to Christ, they will.

Make it your goal in life to be so like Christ that people will be attracted to Him through you.

Preach the gospel every day; if necessary, use words.
FRANCIS OF ASSISI

DAVID JEREMIAH | 261

A MATTER OF PERSPECTIVE

Let a man examine himself, and so let him
eat of the bread and drink of the cup.

1 CORINTHIANS 11:28

Countries like England, with a king or queen, have a royal family through which the right to the throne passes. Children born into that family, especially the heir to the throne, live with a unique sense of responsibility. They are not their own persons—they belong, in a sense, to the people whom they serve. Being a member of a royal family creates a definite perspective by which life is viewed and lived.

Christians are members of a royal family—the household of God. We are brothers and sisters (Romans 8:29) of the coming King, Jesus Christ (Revelation 19:16), and thus have a unique perspective on life. That perspective is to be renewed, Scripture says, on a regular basis as we gather for a memorial meal at the Lord's Table. At the Communion celebration, we remember not only Christ's death for us but His return as King of kings. What He did and who He is create a perspective that should predict who we are and what we do.

As a member of a royal family, participating in the Lord's Table is not an option. Make sure you are there regularly to keep your perspective fresh.

---

*The heart preparing for communion should be
as a crystal vial filled with clear water in which
the least mote of uncleanness will be seen.*

ELIZABETH BAYLEY SETON

> We have no power against this great multitude that is coming
> against us; nor do we know what to do, but our eyes are upon You.

2 CHRONICLES 20:12

Cultural rebels have always waved the Me-against-the-World banner. It's one thing to choose to stand alone but another thing entirely to find yourself standing alone when it is none of your doing. That's what happened to one of the kings of Israel. His solution is worth imitating today. He stood before God and then stood against his enemy.

Jehoshaphat was a godly king of Judah. When word came to him that the armies of Moab, Ammon, and Edom were coming to attack Judah, he was humanly helpless. Judah had no military resources sufficient to repel such an invasion. He gathered the people of Judah and led them in prayer in the Temple, and he concluded with these famous words: "We [don't] know what to do, but our eyes are upon You." In answer to Jehoshaphat's prayer, a prophet of the Lord brought word from God (20:15): "Do not be afraid ... for the battle is not yours, but God's." The next day, God gave the people of Judah victory when the invading forces turned on one another. The next time you don't know what to do, pray Jehoshaphat's prayer to God: "My eyes are on You."

Your eyes have to be somewhere. Focus them on the Solution instead of on the problem.

———— ✦ ————

Faith isn't faith until it's all you're holding on to.
UNKNOWN

They worshiped Him, and returned to Jerusalem
with great joy, and were continually in the
temple praising and blessing God. Amen.

LUKE 24:52-53

Joy is the Christian's middle name. When Jesus ascended to heaven, the disciples returned to Jerusalem full of joy, and their joy was highly contagious. Shortly afterward, on the Day of Pentecost, Peter preached to the crowds and referred to Psalm 16: "You will make me full of joy in Your presence" (Acts 2:28). When the gospel reached Samaria, there was great joy in that city (Acts 8:8). Even when Paul and Barnabas were thrown out of Antioch, they were filled with joy and with the Holy Spirit (Acts 13:52).

The attitude of joy is one of our greatest witnessing tools. Sometimes we don't need to say a word; we just need a joyful spirit as we serve others and find ways of being useful for the Kingdom. Often the door of evangelism is opened on the hinges of joy, as others begin to want what we have.

Make up your mind that this will be a *joy*ful day!

In the pathways of sadness, sweetest lilies may grow;
Let us sow seeds of gladness—let the joy overflow.

ELIZA E. HEWITT

> Do not fear those who kill the body but cannot kill the soul. But
> rather fear Him who is able to destroy both soul and body in hell.
>
> MATTHEW 10:28

Hydrophobia is the fear of water. Nyctophobia is the fear of darkness. Acrophobia is the fear of high places. Xenophobia is the fear of strangers. Claustrophobia is the fear of confined places. According to the National Institute of Mental Health, approximately 6.3 million American adults have some type of specific phobia. That is a large number of people living in fear.

Without God, this world is a frightening place, but there is no need to lead a life of trepidation. We know the One who created the heavens and the earth and told the wind and the waves to obey Him.

If we call ourselves children of God, we do not have to fear the things of this world, because God tells us that He "has not given us a spirit of fear, but of power and of love and of a sound mind" (2 Timothy 1:7). The only fear we need to live in is the fear of the Lord, for He is awesome in might and perfect in holiness.

God is down in front. He is in the tomorrows.
It is tomorrow that fills men with dread. God is
there already. All the tomorrows of our life have
to pass Him before they can get to us.

F. B. MEYER

UPHILL CLIMB

> He led them on safely . . . and He brought them to His holy border.
>
> PSALM 78:53-54

Let's face it: the Christian life is not a walk in the park; in fact, most of the time it is an uphill climb on rugged terrain. It shouldn't surprise us, for Jesus told us that we would have tribulation in this world (John 16:33). Still, when trials come, we tend to question why this would happen to us. Fortunately, God's Word promises us a safe landing.

Joseph must have understood this at a young age when, after being betrayed by his own brothers, he faced so many trials that anyone else would have given up. He trusted the Lord with the outcome of his life; at the end of it all he was blessed beyond measure, and his family was preserved during a nationwide famine.

Billy Graham once said, "I've read the last page of the Bible. It's all going to turn out all right." It is precisely this perspective that will prevent us from becoming bogged down in the struggles that are inevitable in the lives of believers. It will also strengthen our resolve to press on until the return of our King.

Friend, if you are experiencing a trial, set your mind on the safety and blessing that lie at the end of your difficult journey, and trust the Lord with the outcome. He won't let you down.

God promises a safe landing, not a calm passage.

UNKNOWN

WHAT'S DONE IS DONE

It is good for me that I have been afflicted,
that I may learn Your statutes.

PSALM 119:71

The *Chicago Tribune* reported that on March 3, 1995, a thirty-eight-year-old man walking to his job decided to take a shortcut across eight lanes of the Tri-State Tollway. After he had made it across the four northbound lanes, the wind blew his hat back into the lanes he had just crossed. When he tried to retrieve his hat, he was struck by an eighteen-wheeler and died.

Life is strung together by choices. Like pearls on a thread, our choices are linked one to another until the strands of our lives are complete. Every time we come to a crossroads, the choice we make eliminates those we *could* have made, and the results are unchangeable. When we make the right choice, that's good. But when we make the wrong choice, what's done is done. It can be forgiven but not changed. When David was running from Saul, the people of a village that gave him assistance were later massacred by the king. David no doubt grieved the rest of his life over his choice to endanger those innocent people. If you have made a choice that led to sorrowful consequences, accept God's forgiveness and resolve to learn from your mistake.

What's done in life is done. But that doesn't mean it has to be done again.

Between two evils, choose neither;
between two goods, choose both.
TRYON EDWARDS

September 13

JUST AS YOU ARE

Know that the LORD, He is God; it is He who has made us, and not
we ourselves; we are His people and the sheep of His pasture.

PSALM 100:3

A proud grandmother was admiring the way her four-year-old
granddaughter had dressed herself—until she got to the feet.
"Why, honey," the grandmother said gently, "I think you've put your
shoes on the wrong feet."

The little girl looked down at her feet and then up at her grandmother. "But, Grandma, these are the only feet I've got!"

In her misunderstanding, the little girl made an important point,
one that modern, image-conscious people would do well to remember: the features God has given us are the only ones we've got! It's easy
today to become dissatisfied with who we are and what we have been
given: our looks, our intelligence, our skills and talents, our personalities, our physical build. But the Bible says we are the handiwork
of God—that He shaped us in our mothers' wombs. A large part of
becoming comfortable in our own skin is recognizing that we are
unique in God's sight. We are one-of-a-kind people, created to accomplish for Him what only we can.

Consider taking stock of who you are and thanking God for His
perfect wisdom in creating you to be one of a kind.

He who is not contented with what he has would not
be contented with what he would like to have.

UNKNOWN

THE CHOICE TO OBEY

> Though He was a Son, yet He learned obedience
> by the things which He suffered.
>
> HEBREWS 5:8

Bible students have debated a timeless question: was Jesus Christ *not able* to sin, or was He *able not* to sin? The first question suggests that because He is God, it was impossible for Jesus to sin. The second suggests that it was possible for Jesus to sin but that He was able *not* to sin because of His commitment to obedience. Regardless of how these questions are posed, this we know: Jesus is both God and man.

There is no better verse in the New Testament to illustrate Jesus' humanity than Hebrews 5:8, which says that Jesus "learned obedience by the things which He suffered." The very fact that Jesus had to learn to obey makes Him like us—a person with the choice to obey or not to obey. Jesus was the Son of God and learned to obey the Father. Christians are sons and daughters of God (Romans 8:15-16), and we must learn to obey the Father as well. It was through obedience that Jesus gained the Father's approval (Matthew 3:17) and fulfilled His Father's will for His life. And through obedience we will do the same.

Obedience to God is a choice for human beings. When we endure the suffering and choose to obey, life is the result (Deuteronomy 30:15-19).

---

*Joy is the natural outcome of the Christian's
obedience to the revealed will of God.*

JOHN BLANCHARD

September 15

GROUP EFFORT

> As the body is one and has many members, but all the members
> of that one body, being many, are one body, so also is Christ.
>
> 1 CORINTHIANS 12:12

As a group of amateur climbers scaled part of the Matterhorn near Zermatt, Switzerland, a vicious gust of wind came along the narrow ledge on which they were standing.

The guide quickly shouted, "Get down on your knees! You are safe only on your knees!" That's good advice for all of us: the ledges of life are narrow, and the winds are strong. Whenever storms come our way, we, too, need guides who will offer us solid counsel and encouragement.

When Paul was shackled by discouragement, God sent His special agent of encouragement. Barnabas—exhorting, encouraging, consoling—was the very embodiment of the ministry of the Spirit. He provided a model of bringing out the best in others. Our Creator has intentionally designed us for interdependence; no man is an island. Sooner or later life teaches us that we will not survive without many helping hands as well as the hand of God. This is the very meaning of the body of Christ, a collection of organs that are worthless individually but form a powerful organism when interconnected. Decide whether you will take the road of pride and self-sufficiency, which is a dead end, or the path of community and humility, which leads to life.

Dear Jesus, thank You for giving me the joy
of relationships with other Christians.

BROKEN VASES

> Whoever shall keep the whole law, and yet
> stumble in one point, he is guilty of all.

JAMES 2:10

Popular speaker Florence Littauer tells of being in a conference in Iowa in which an elderly preacher had asked the women in the church to bring their vases. He selected ten of them and displayed them on a table on the platform, saying they represented the Ten Commandments. He began to preach, and when he got to the first commandment and the sin of violating it, he drew a huge mallet from behind the pulpit and suddenly smashed the first vase with all his might. Everyone screamed in surprise. He proceeded to do the same with the remaining nine vases. The women were tremendously upset at the loss of their vases, but no one ever forgot the message about the breaking of the Ten Commandments.

It's strange that we're so unaffected now by our society's disregard for the Ten Commandments. It doesn't shock us anymore to hear God's name taken in vain or to hear a report that someone has cheated on his or her spouse. But we should be shocked, and we should be so aware of God's holiness that we ourselves will walk in daily obedience and faithfulness.

Let's look to God in His commandments, listen to what
He has to say, and try not to break the vases!

FLORENCE LITTAUER

OPEN DOOR, CLOSED DOOR

> When I came to Troas to preach Christ's gospel . . .
> a door was opened to me by the Lord.
>
> 2 CORINTHIANS 2:12

The largest bank vault door in the world is in the Federal Reserve Bank of Cleveland. It weighs more than ninety thousand pounds. It incorporates the largest door hinge ever built. When the atomic bomb was dropped on Hiroshima, Japan, in 1945, four vault doors in the Teikoku Bank, less than a hundred yards from the epicenter of the blast, survived, along with the contents of their vaults.

It may be possible to build doors to withstand man's most powerful assault, but Christ told the church in Philadelphia that God has doors no man can shut and doors that no man can open (Revelation 3:7-8). That means no one is able to delay or obstruct the plans and purposes of God. When God opens a door of service or opportunity, no one can shut it. And when He shuts a door, it is a waste of time to try to open it. Christians pray often for God to "open a door." When that door opens, there is only one way to go through it: by faith! God not only controls the door; He also controls what is on the other side.

If you have prayed for an open door, be ready to walk through when God opens it. And when an open door closes, be patient until it opens again.

---

*We are all faced with a series of great opportunities
brilliantly disguised as impossible situations.*
CHARLES SWINDOLL

TAKING REFUGE

The eternal God is your refuge, and
underneath are the everlasting arms.

DEUTERONOMY 33:27

John Elliott had trekked many miles through the deep snows of the mountain passes of the Rockies in southwestern Alberta, Canada. As dusk and exhaustion overcame him, he decided to rest. He made it wearily to his cabin but was so tired that it didn't cross his mind to light a fire or put on warm clothes. Outside, the blizzard continued to thrash the old cabin walls, but Elliott fell silent, paralyzed by the lure of sweet sleep.

Suddenly his dog, a St. Bernard, sprang into action and, with unrelenting whines, finally managed to rouse his near-comatose master. "If that dog hadn't been with me, I'd be dead today," Elliott said later. "When you're freezing to death, you actually feel warm all over and don't wake up because it feels too good."

This moving story illustrates the spiritual condition of many people today. They are cold spiritually and oblivious of their true condition. But God is close by to arouse such sleepers. He sends messengers to nudge them awake. If you're feeling sleepy, don't ignore God's prodding. Instead, thank Him for His loving disturbances which will save you from an eternal death.

Conscience tells us that we ought to do right, but it does not tell us what right is—that we are taught by God's word.

H. C. TRUMBULL

OLD CAMEL KNEES

The effective, fervent prayer of a righteous man avails much.

JAMES 5:16

The writer of the book of James is known in history as "Old Camel Knees." His knees were reportedly calloused because he spent so much time on them in prayer. His core belief about prayer is summed up in today's verse, which is rendered in the NIV as "The prayer of a righteous person is powerful and effective."

Yet James devotes a great deal of time to telling us how *not* to get our prayers answered. That is, he warns us against hindrances to prayer. In chapter 1, he cautions us not to ask with a doubtful, unbelieving heart. "That person should not think he will receive anything from the Lord" (James 1:7, NIV). In chapter 4, James warns that God will not answer unoffered prayers; "You do not have because you do not ask God," he writes in verse 2. And the Lord doesn't answer prayers offered for the wrong reasons: "When you ask, you do not receive, because you ask with wrong motives, that you may spend what you get on your pleasures" (James 4:3, NIV).

God longs to answer our prayers—in fact, He calls them *powerful* and *effective*—but it's important to pray with trusting hearts, specific requests, and godly motives.

*Faith in a prayer-hearing God will make
a prayer-loving Christian.*

ANDREW MURRAY

September 20

FREE GRACE

To each one of us grace was given according
to the measure of Christ's gift.

EPHESIANS 4:7

In *The Christian Reader*, Paul Francisco wrote about his experience as a child in church. On the first Sunday of every month, before Communion, a benevolence offering was taken. One Sunday, for the first time, his mother gave him a dime to put in the offering. That Sunday, he stood up to take the bread and cup along with everyone else, when his mother said, "You can't take Communion yet." "Why not?" Francisco asked. "I paid for it!"

We are amused by that young man's logic: we pay our money to God and get to partake of the privileges rightly ours. It's the American way! While we smile at a child's reasoning, how many adults view the grace of God the same way—something for which we must pay? Free grace takes a lifetime to contemplate—the idea that there is nothing we can do to earn God's love and forgiveness. Did anyone pay a price? Only Jesus, who resisted temptation, walked in holiness, and died as a sacrifice for our sin. Jesus paid for the gift that is freely given to us.

Few people would turn down a free gift, especially one of eternal value. Make sure you have embraced the gift that is yours.

---

*Mercy there was great, and grace was free;
pardon there was multiplied to me; there my
burdened soul found liberty, at Calvary.*
WILLIAM R. NEWELL

As each one has received a gift, minister it to one another,
as good stewards of the manifold grace of God.

1 PETER 4:10

Gifts come in all shapes and sizes. Some are wrapped in small boxes with fine paper and bows. Others are oversized and held together with strips of masking tape. Whatever the outward appearance, however, a gift's value is not truly appreciated until it is unwrapped and the contents revealed.

The same can be said of Christians. We have each been given a gift by God to equip the body of Christ and to do His work in the world (Romans 12:3-8). Just like fingerprints, our gifts are unique—given especially for us to use to minister in His name.

If we wonder what our God-given gifts are, we can ask God to help us unwrap them. Many times those around us can help us discern what our giftedness is. Once we understand our gifts, our potential to serve God and His church is limitless. God will empower us to minister to the people we come into contact with—according to our gifts. Remember today that your gift is meant to build up the body of Christ. If you don't know what your spiritual gift is, take steps to discover it.

---

*The Christian is strong or weak depending upon how
closely he has cultivated the knowledge of God.*

A. W. TOZER

THE POWER OF A PLAN

On the first day of the week let each one of you lay
something aside, storing up as he may prosper,
that there be no collections when I come.

1 CORINTHIANS 16:2

In the first century AD, persecution had driven the young Jerusalem church into hiding. Believers were ostracized by the Jewish community and could not buy or sell in the commercial markets. They were without food or money. The apostle Paul mounted a fundraising campaign among the churches in Achaia and Macedonia to raise money for the church in Jerusalem.

Paul proposed a plan to the Corinthians: every Lord's Day (Sunday) the believers would bring what funds they could and contribute them to a collection. When Paul arrived, the funds would be ready—there would be no panicky efforts to raise money. The plan worked, and Paul delivered the relief funds to Jerusalem (Romans 15:25-27). Whether we are giving time, talent, or treasure, a plan produces results. It's too easy for us to want to give, mean to give, and hope to give—and never get around to giving. A plan represents a commitment, a vow to the Lord, and gives us a track on which to run.

If your giving—whether time, talent, or treasure—has been sporadic, prayerfully consider committing to a plan. It won't be long before you'll never be without one again.

Failing to plan is planning to fail.

UNKNOWN

RESISTANCE TRAINING

> Submit to God. Resist the devil and he will flee from you.
>
> JAMES 4:7

A popular form of strength development has come to be known as resistance training. Instead of muscles pushing against gravity (as in weight lifting), they push against an opposing force generated by elastic resistance. There are two kinds of resistance training: *isotonic* if the body part is pushing against the force; *isometric* if the body part is resisting the force.

How would you describe a Christian's strength training: isotonic or isometric? That is, are we to push against the devil or stand firm against the devil? A clue is found in Ephesians 6:10-18. Paul described all the Christian's spiritual armor as defensive in nature (shield, helmet, and others) except for the sword of the Spirit (the Word of God). In fact, Paul actually says we are to "stand against" the schemes of the devil. The apostle Peter agrees: he says we are to resist, not attack, the devil. Therefore, the Christian gains strength *isometrically*, by standing firm against the strength of the devil.

Are your feet firmly planted? Are you growing stronger daily? Practice resistance training this week as you stand firm against the spiritual forces coming against you.

The Christian life is not a playground; it is a battleground.

WARREN WIERSBE

PANIC OR PEACE?

> From the end of the earth I will cry to You, when my heart
> is overwhelmed; lead me to the rock that is higher than I.
>
> PSALM 61:2

Rumors of financial disaster flew through the YMCA convention in Carlisle, Pennsylvania, and a sense of foreboding gripped the delegates. Telegrams began arriving with alarming reports of banks and financial institutions failing across the country. Many of those attending the conference were businessmen, and their fears were soon confirmed—it was the beginning of the financial panic of 1871.

One of the delegates, Erastus Johnson, was deeply troubled and looked to his Bible for comfort. He bathed his heart in the words of Psalm 61:2 and turned them into this hymn, which was sung repeatedly by the YMCA delegates in their sessions. It soon spread across the nation. Titled "The Rock That Is Higher Than I," the chorus is a simple prayer: "O then to the Rock let me fly, to the Rock that is higher than I!"

Perhaps you're in a state of panic yourself, overwhelmed by family concerns, financial needs, or failure. When your heart is overwhelmed, flee to the Rock that is higher than you are—the Rock of Ages.

O then to the Rock let me fly, to the Rock that is higher than I!
ERASTUS JOHNSON

PRAISE VERSUS THANKS

Our Father in heaven, hallowed be Your name.

LUKE 11:2

Many people mistake thanking the Lord for praising Him. Oftentimes we rattle off a list of things we are thankful for and move right to our requests, believing we have spent time giving glory to God. But there is a clear distinction between thankfulness and praise.

According to Merriam-Webster, to be "thankful" means to be "conscious of benefit received." In contrast, the definition of *praise* is "to glorify, especially by the attribution of perfections." The primary difference is that when we give thanks, our focus is on what God has done for us, whereas during praise, the focus is solely on Him.

The Bible lists a myriad of God's attributes for which we can glorify Him. It tells us that He is holy (Leviticus 19:2), just, perfect, and righteous (Deuteronomy 32:4), merciful (Psalm 116:5), mighty and infinite (Psalm 147:5), and sovereign (Psalm 47:8), to name just a few.

So let's remember to take a few moments at the beginning of each prayer to tell the Lord how much we love Him just for being the King of kings and Lord of lords.

When I give thanks, my thoughts still circle about myself to some extent. But in praise my soul ascends to self-forgetting adoration, seeing and praising only the majesty and power of God, His grace and redemption.

OLE HALLESBY

September 26

KNOWN BUT TO GOD

The fruit of the Spirit is . . . goodness.

GALATIANS 5:22

At Arlington National Cemetery there is a memorial tomb that contains the remains of unknown soldiers from various wars—primarily World Wars I and II—called the Tomb of the Unknowns. The inscription on the tomb reads: "Here Rests in Honored Glory an American Soldier Known but to God."

If you are ever in doubt about what makes a person great, do not look to the Hollywood elite or the upper crust of society. Greatness is not found in possessions, power, or prestige. Rather, it is found in goodness, humility, service, and character, all of which can be found in the majority of military men and women. They don't sign up to defend their country with the goal of being honored and glorified. They simply believe they are called to carry out this awesome responsibility.

What are you are pursuing in life? More things and more status? Or do you desire to carry out God's will and see Him glorified? If you truly wish to be great, follow the example of selfless, humble American soldiers and be a devoted Christian "known but to God."

The supreme test of goodness is not in the greater but in the smaller incidents of our character and practice.

F. B. MEYER

POINTING TO JESUS

> By this all will know that you are My disciples,
> if you have love for one another.

JOHN 13:35

You're sitting in your car, stuck in traffic on a freeway or busy thoroughfare. Looking around, you notice an exceptionally bright billboard rising high above the traffic on the side of the road. You look away for a moment and then look back—and the sign is showing a different advertisement! These digital billboards are like a Jumbotron screen at a sports stadium—full of images that change constantly with their bright, electronic displays.

"Capturing eyeballs"—it's the new standard in advertising, especially on the Internet. Capture a person's attention, and your chances of educating them and making a sale increase. Signs are important in more than just advertising. Jesus said there was one primary sign by which the world will know that we are His followers: the way we love one another. Sometimes a simple act of love will be a sign to others that there is something different about a person. And a conversation about Christ may follow.

Look for an opportunity today to be a sign that points to Jesus—by demonstrating His love to others.

Love is the queen of all the Christian graces.

ARTHUR W. PINK

GOOD PLANS

When you pass through the waters, I will be with you; and through
the rivers, they shall not overflow you. When you walk through
the fire, you shall not be burned, nor shall the flame scorch you.

ISAIAH 43:2

A reporter in Alaska, working on an article about caregivers, inter-viewed a woman who was caring for her husband as he battled chronic obstructive pulmonary disease. She was afraid to leave his side, but the strain was wearing her down. "It's sort of a helpless and hopeless feeling," she said. "You quickly become exhausted."

Perhaps you're a caregiver who can relate to those feelings. Or perhaps other factors in your life are producing feelings of helpless-ness, hopelessness, and exhaustion. Sometimes it's easy to forget that God knows the plans He has for those who love Him—and that they are good plans. He'll give you needed strength for each day, and His purposes will prevail in your life.

Take a moment right now to remind yourself that although you may not understand it all, God is working out His plan for you in Christ Jesus, working all things together according to the good coun-sel of His will (Ephesians 1:11). You can trust His guidance.

In heavenly love abiding, no change my heart shall fear.
And safe in such confiding, for nothing changes here.
The storm may roar without me, my heart may low be laid,
But God is round about me, and can I be dismayed?

ANNA WARING

THE ART OF (NO) COMPROMISE

Stand fast and hold the traditions which you were
taff taught, whether by word or our epistle.

2 THESSALONIANS 2:15

Some time ago I went to the "books" section of Amazon.com and entered the word *compromise* in the search field. My search returned more than 273,000 results. Fortunately, the first book on the list was by noted evangelical theologian Norman Geisler and author Ron Rhodes: *Conviction without Compromise: Standing Strong in the Core Beliefs of the Christian Faith.*

Is it possible to be a Christian without compromising? One has only to read the New Testament to see that neither Jesus nor Paul ever compromised on matters of theological truth. And when Peter did, he received a stinging rebuke from Paul (Galatians 2:11-12). Yes, there is room for concession at times on practical matters. But when it comes to giving in to critics of Christianity in order to spare their feelings, the Bible knows no such strategy. Christ and His gospel are a "stone of stumbling and a rock of offense" (1 Peter 2:8) to those who choose to disagree.

When your faith or your stand for Christ is challenged, ask yourself whose disappointment you would regret most: Christ's critics or Christ's?

It is better to die for a conviction than
to live with a compromise.
VANCE HAVNER

September 30
FIGHTING FROM THE TRENCHES

With him is an arm of flesh; but with us is the LORD
our God, to help us and to fight our battles.

2 CHRONICLES 32:8

During World War I, soldiers did most of their fighting from the trenches. It was the safest and most effective way to try to gain victory over the enemy. Just one peek over the parapet of the trench during daylight hours almost certainly meant death for the curious soldier, and thus the trench walls played guardian to thousands of heroic young men from 1914 to 1918.

Every day, Christians are fighting life's battles, spiritual or otherwise, from the trenches of prayer. But there are those who mistakenly believe they can stand up, face off with the enemy, and win with sheer determination. They are like the soldiers who do not heed the advice to keep their heads down.

Sometimes it feels as if the more we struggle, the more effective we are in the fight, but the Bible tells us that "the effective, fervent prayer of a righteous man avails much" (James 5:16). So the next time you find yourself braving the battlefield of life on your own, remember that there is safety within the trench walls of prayer. Victory can be yours when you bring your battle before the Lord.

Christ's soldiers fight best on their knees.

D. L. MOODY

OCTOBER

ANOTHER DAY TO SERVE JESUS

Light is sweet; how pleasant to see a new day dawning.

ECCLESIASTES 11:7, NLT

Put a finger to your pulse. Are you alive? Then be thankful! God has given you another day on this earth, and you can see the clouds floating in the sky, hear the birds in the trees, smell the roses, and tell others you love them. We have earthly service to attend to and tasks on earth to do for Jesus.

We don't know if we'll be able to do those things tomorrow, for we might be in heaven. Yes, in many ways, that would be better, but it would mean a ceasing of our earthly service. Paul told the Philippians that while he was eager to go on to heaven, he also desired to stay awhile longer on earth to serve them (Philippians 1:23-24).

So we have another day. Don't waste it in sin, self-pity, or laziness. Live to the fullest, for this is the day the Lord has made.

Rejoice and be glad in it!

Draw me day by day nearer to Thyself, until I be wholly filled with Thy love, and fitted to behold Thee, face to face.

EDWARD B. PUSEY

October 2

WINDOW ON THE WORLD

> The day of the Lord will come as a thief in the night,
> in which the heavens will pass away with a great noise,
> and the elements will melt with fervent heat; both the
> earth and the works that are in it will be burned up.
>
> 2 PETER 3:10

While astronaut John Glenn was preparing to orbit the earth, he learned that his space capsule, *Friendship 7*, would not have a window—the experts couldn't figure out how to design it. Glenn talked to NASA executives, worked with the engineers, and succeeded in getting a window installed. He couldn't imagine orbiting the earth and being unable to see it.

All of us would love a view from space, but there's a greater way of looking at our world—by studying it through the window of biblical prophecy. Most earthlings are shortsighted and are lost in the whirlwind of the present. But as Christians, we understand that world events are hurtling toward their preordained end as predicted in Scripture. At any moment, the trumpet may sound, and the curtain will fall on history.

We still have time to make a difference, but only if we view the world as God does and understand that history is His-story.

The advent of our Lord . . . is the foundation of our certainty and the secret of our patience.

G. CAMPBELL MORGAN

SHALL I GO?

You are my rock and my fortress; therefore, for
Your name's sake, lead me and guide me.

PSALM 31:3

Think of all the places you have to go on an average day—literally. You arise in the morning and go to the shower, then to the kitchen, then to the closet to get dressed, then to work, then to lunch, then to errands, then home . . . and those are only after you decided where to get married, where to go to school, where to live, where to work, and where to go to church.

Now—think about how many of those "wheres" you consulted God about before setting out. Where in your spiritual life do you draw the line between those things that you don't inquire of the Lord about and those you do? That line falls somewhere between what to eat for breakfast and whom to marry—and it's probably different for every person. Think of it a different way: is anything too trivial to ask the Lord about? Perhaps the key lies in developing what Paul called "the mind of Christ" (1 Corinthians 2:16)—a combination of asking God about some things and developing wisdom from Him about most other things, knowing how God would answer before we ask.

Do you live in an ongoing conversation with God about your next steps? Talk to God this week as if He is right beside you (He is) and cares about every decision you need to make (He does).

Man proposes, God disposes.
TRADITIONAL PROVERB

SPIRITUAL EXERCISE

Take heed to yourself and to the doctrine. Continue in them, for
in doing this you will save both yourself and those who hear you.

1 TIMOTHY 4:16

There are countless theories about the correct way to exercise. Some say you need high intensity for short periods of time, while others believe low intensity for long stretches is the key to being healthy and staying fit. Regardless of their different opinions, fitness professionals all agree on one thing: consistency is the most important factor in any exercise regimen. No matter what philosophy you subscribe to, the only way you will see results is with regular activity.

Football legend Dan Marino once said, "I just want to be consistent over a long period of time. That's what the great players do." Marino understood that the way players become great is through consistency, which fuels continual growth in their sport. What they do on a regular basis affects them as individual players and their ability to play on a team.

In the same way, the time we spend strengthening our relationship with God will directly affect our relationships with those around us in a positive way. When we have a healthy spiritual life, God will be able to use us in fresh, new ways to affect the lives of others.

---

*Lord, teach me the importance of consistently spending
time with You; that in order to be effective for You,
I must be affected by You on a regular basis.*

UNKNOWN

October 5

MEANS AND ENDS

Better is the poor who walks in his integrity than
one who is perverse in his lips, and is a fool.

PROVERBS 19:1

Throughout the ages, ethicists have debated the connection between means and ends: can immoral actions be justified in order to achieve moral outcomes? For example, would a prisoner be justified in paying a bribe to a dishonest jailer in order to get out of jail to save the life of his dying child? Does saving the life of the child justify dishonesty?

Fortunately, the Bible offers insight into this difficult question. When David, the new king of Israel, wanted to return the Ark of the Covenant to Jerusalem, God took a man's life for not handling the Ark in the prescribed manner. Then in 1 Samuel 6:19, "He struck down some of the men of Beth-Shemesh, because they had looked into the ark of the LORD." Why the harsh treatment? Specifically, because Israel needed to regain a lost fear (awe) and respect for God's holiness. Generally, because God is as interested in how we do things as in what we do. From God's perspective, the end doesn't justify the means: wanting to do something good doesn't excuse doing something bad.

If you are planning an action, look as closely at the "how" as you do at the "what." Make sure both bring honor to God.

---

*Mine honor is my life; both grow in one. Take
honor from me, and my life is done.*
WILLIAM SHAKESPEARE

WHAT IS THAT IN YOUR HAND?

The LORD said to [Moses], "What is that in your hand?"

EXODUS 4:2

Moses didn't have much—a handful of sheep on the slopes of a blistered mountain. He also had eighty years of memories, some of them sad and regretful. He had some clothes, a family, a wise father-in-law, a tent in the desert. That's about it.

Oh yes, he had a staff.

He'd probably found a branch broken from some sturdy tree, maybe six or seven feet long and reasonably straight. He'd seasoned and smoothed it to become his walking stick; plus, it was useful in herding sheep and warding off predators. But it was quite ordinary—just a rod.

On rugged Mount Horeb that day, as Moses argued with the Lord about his inadequacies for the mission being assigned him, God asked a simple question: "What is that in your hand?" It was a broken branch, a piece of dead wood, a rod. But the Lord wanted it, and the Lord touched it, and the Lord used it to baffle the magicians of Egypt, to turn the Nile to blood, to part the waters of the Red Sea, to create streams in the desert, and to deliver His people again and again.

What's that in your hand?

Little is much if God is in it.
BARBARA FAIRCHILD

DRAWN TO THE DIFFERENCE

As He who called you is holy, you also be holy in all your
conduct, because it is written, "Be holy, for I am holy."

1 PETER 1:15-16

People are often surprised when they meet a genuine, down-to-
earth Christian, someone they can relate to. They don't expect
someone with such high morals to be so real and likable. This percep-
tion is no doubt the result of a gross misinterpretation of the Christian's call to holiness, and it is why we must change our perspective
on how to live according to Jesus.

Christ never commanded us to be "holier than thou," which by
definition means "excessively or hypocritically pious." On the contrary, when He tells us to "be holy, for I am holy," He is referring to
His ability to connect with sinners and yet keep His character and
integrity intact.

That is the key to being effective witnesses, and when we learn to
accept people where they are while standing firm in our convictions,
they will be drawn to what it is that makes the difference in our lives.

*Few things are more infectious than a godly lifestyle. The
people you rub shoulders with every day need that kind of
challenge. Not prudish. Not preachy. Just spot-on clean living.
Honest to goodness, bone-deep, nonhypocritical integrity.*

CHARLES SWINDOLL

October 8

BRIGHT STARS

Those who are wise shall shine like the
brightness of the firmament.

DANIEL 12:3

Many city dwellers who visit the countryside comment on how bright the stars are compared to where they live. In reality, though, the stars have not gotten brighter. Rather, the darkness surrounding them has gotten darker, making them stand out.

Being a Christian in the world today can be discouraging at times when we look at how dark our surroundings are becoming. But just as stars shine brightest when enveloped by a pitch-black night sky, the light of Christ should be most radiant in our lives when we are surrounded by the darkness of this day and age.

Jesus said, "Let your light so shine before men, that they may see your good works and glorify your Father in heaven" (Matthew 5:16). Christian, do not be disheartened by the increase of evil in the world; it is simply our cue to take center stage and shine with all our might for the glory of our Savior.

Remember a small light will do a good deal when it is in
a very dark place. You put one little tallow candle in the
middle of a large hall, and it will give a good deal of light.

D. L. MOODY

CHOOSING AND USING TIME

See then that you walk circumspectly, not as fools but as
wise, redeeming the time, because the days are evil.

EPHESIANS 5:15-16

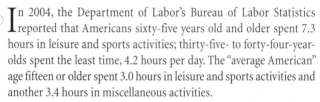

In 2004, the Department of Labor's Bureau of Labor Statistics reported that Americans sixty-five years old and older spent 7.3 hours in leisure and sports activities; thirty-five- to forty-four-year-olds spent the least time, 4.2 hours per day. The "average American" age fifteen or older spent 3.0 hours in leisure and sports activities and another 3.4 hours in miscellaneous activities.

In spite of how rushed and stressed everyone claims to be, it seems Americans have quite a bit of discretionary time on their hands each day. The question is, what do we choose to do with it? Once when King David was not occupied with kingly duties, he was found hanging out with Nathan the prophet—spending time in godly pursuits (2 Samuel 7:1-2). Later in his reign, when he had time on his hands, he ended up being guilty of adultery and murder (2 Samuel 11).

Time, once it passes or is used in ungodly pursuits, can never be regained. Why not keep track of your time this week and see how much of it is spent with the Lord?

Everyone has the same amount of time. The difference is that some choose to use it more wisely than others.

I am a shadow, so art thou; I mark the time, dost thou?

INSCRIPTION ON A SUNDIAL

FIRST LINE OF DEFENSE

[The Bereans] received the word with all readiness, and searched
the Scriptures daily to find out whether these things were so.

ACTS 17:11

For years, Bible teachers and preachers have used the following illustration: "The U.S. Treasury uses only one method when training new agents to detect counterfeit currency: trainees study the appearance of actual currency so long that they can immediately detect a counterfeit when they see it." Though the illustration makes for good preaching, it is not actually true.

But consider the premise generally: the more intimately we know the details of the truth, the more readily we can detect error. Such preparation would apply to theological truth as well. When false doctrines are presented to us, how will we know they are false unless we know what is true? If someone says he knows the date of Christ's second coming, we might believe him if we don't know what Jesus said in Mark 13:32. We should be like the Jews in Berea when they heard Paul preach—they studied the Old Testament daily to verify what Paul was preaching about the Messiah.

Make sure your first line of defense against theological error is a thorough knowledge of the truth.

Truth is always strong, no matter how weak it looks; and falsehood is always weak, no matter how strong it looks.

PHILLIPS BROOKS

NOT GOOD IF DETACHED

Abide in Me, and I in you. As the branch cannot
bear fruit of itself, unless it abides in the vine,
neither can you, unless you abide in Me.

JOHN 15:4

After her horrendous experiences in a Nazi concentration camp
during World War II, Corrie ten Boom became a roving evangelist, taking the message of Christ to the world. In bringing her story
to the United States, she frequently traveled by rail. She noticed that
the train tickets were perforated in the middle. The whole ticket had
to be presented to the attendant, who then separated the two halves.
In prominent letters on each ticket were the words "Not Good If
Detached."

That became the title of Corrie's book about John 15 and the reality of abiding in Christ. A branch must be connected to the vine for
the sap to flow uninterrupted and for the fruit to appear. If it's severed
from the vine, it withers and dies. It cannot bear fruit on its own.

Our daily connection with Christ allows the Holy Spirit to flow
through us, producing the fruit of the Spirit (Galatians 5:22-23).
Christlike qualities come as a result of our relationship with Christ,
and we become more like Him by spending time with Him in fellowship in His Word and by abiding in simple trust.

Are you "attached"?

───── ❧ ─────

*Without Him, I am nothing. Like some railway
tickets in America, I am "not good if detached."*

CORRIE TEN BOOM

Nathan said to David, "You are the man!"

2 SAMUEL 12:7

Jonathan Edwards, the great theologian and preacher of the First Great Awakening in New England, described what happened in his work *A Faithful Narrative of the Surprising Work of God in the Conversion of Many Hundred Souls in Northampton* (1736): "Many that came to Town, on one occasion or other, had their Consciences smitten, and awakened; and went home with wounded Hearts."

Having a guilty conscience in the presence of the holiness of God is not a happy situation for the guilty one. The mere presence of purity, joy, honesty, and love is enough to stir conviction. Part of the ministry of the Holy Spirit is to convict the world of sin, righteousness, and judgment (John 16:8). It can happen without a word being spoken, or it can happen when God uses a righteous person to confront the sinner—as Nathan the prophet confronted King David after the king had concealed his sin for almost a year. Either way, nothing makes a guilty sinner more miserable than the presence of the righteousness of God.

If you are harboring sin in your heart, you no doubt feel guilty whether you are a Christian or not. The only solution to such misery is to confess that sin to God and receive His forgiveness.

Guilt is the gift that keeps on giving.
ATTRIBUTED TO GARRISON KEILLOR

IT COULD BE TODAY

[Andrew] first found his own brother Simon, and said to him,
"We have found the Messiah" (which is translated, the Christ).

JOHN 1:41

Country music artist Tim McGraw's hit single "Live Like You Were Dying" was a number one hit in 2004. It tells the story of a man faced with a terminal disease and how he chooses to spend his final days on earth: skydiving, bull riding, fishing, and mountain climbing. At a deeper level, the man also begins to read the Bible and to forgive everyone who has ever wronged him.

All of us are faced with the terminal disease called death, which should keep us motivated to use our time wisely. But the Christian has an even more urgent deadline approaching: the Rapture of the church, when Jesus Christ returns to call those who are His to meet Him in the sky. The Bible says that event could happen today. If you lived today as if it were your last day on earth, what would you do differently? Most important, who would you tell about Jesus? Who would you urge to repent of their sins and receive God's forgiveness if you knew that Jesus' return was just a few hours away?

The truth is, His return is nearer now than it was yesterday—and it could be today. Who is waiting for you to share the Good News of the gospel before it is too late?

---

*Your greatest danger is letting the urgent
things crowd out the important.*

CHARLES E. HUMMEL

LIFE IN A TRIANGLE

As each one has received a gift, minister it to one another,
as good stewards of the manifold grace of God.

1 PETER 4:10

When you stand between the rails of a long, straight railroad track, the two rails seem to converge in the distance—as if you are standing on the base of a long, thin triangle looking toward the point. The rails don't really converge, of course, but they appear to.

For most people, life takes on the shape of a long triangle receding into the future. As infants, we stand on a broad base with a life's worth of possibilities before us. But fast forward to life's later years, and we should be standing somewhere near the point—a life well defined and well spent. A child doesn't know what he will become—doesn't know his gifts and strengths and abilities. But we hope that adults have allowed the sides of the triangle to gradually narrow until they have found their niche. Discovering the spiritual gifts God has given us is part of the process of learning about ourselves. Spiritual gifts are God's way of saying, "This is who you are and what you should do."

If you feel as if you're living in a rectangle rather than a triangle, ask God to sharpen your focus—to make you the best possible steward of the grace He has revealed in your life.

Stewardship is what a man does after he says, "I believe."
W. H. GREAVES

PRAYING ALWAYS

We give thanks to the God and Father of our
Lord Jesus Christ, praying always for you.

COLOSSIANS 1:3

The most gifted writer about prayer in American Christian history was the Civil War–era pastor E. M. Bounds, who practiced what he preached and exemplified what he taught in his writings. In describing prayer in the Pauline epistles, Bounds wrote, "To seek God as Paul did by prayer, to commune with God as Paul did ... this makes a saint, an apostle, and a leader for God. This kind of a life engages, absorbs, enriches, and empowers.... This kind of praying brings ... Pauline gifts. Pauline praying costs much.... Pauline praying is worth all it costs. Prayer which costs nothing gets nothing. It is beggarly business at best."

Then Reverend Bounds continued with a simple but insightful comment: "Paul was in the habit of praying, but he prayed not by mere force of habit."

It's important to establish habits of prayer, but prayer is more than a habit. It is grappling with the issues of life in the presence of God before the throne of grace. How important to be in the habit of praying, but how vital that our prayers be offered by more than just force of habit!

Let's learn to pray like Paul!

All things are opened by prayer. They could shut up Paul from preaching, but this could not shut him up from praying.

E. M. BOUNDS

NO FEAR OF BAD NEWS

He will not be afraid of evil tidings; his heart
is steadfast, trusting in the LORD.

PSALM 112:7

At first reading, Psalm 112 seems too good to be true; but on further study, we realize it's so good it *must* be true. This psalm
explains how God blesses us when we praise Him, fear Him, and
delight in His commandments (112:1).

Our children will be blessed by our faithfulness (112:2); our needs
will be met (112:3); we'll become more gracious, compassionate, and
righteous (112:4); and more generous and discreet (112:5). Best of all,
we'll be secure in our hearts, unafraid of bad news (112:6-8).

This isn't a promise that bad news will never come, for we all
read the headlines every day and sometimes face that dreaded call
in the night or those difficult conversations with a friend. But faith
turns the bad news into topics of prayer and objects of trust, for we
know God works all things together for those who love Him (Romans
8:28). Because of God's sovereignty and Christ's resurrection, we have
a peace the world can never understand. Our hearts are "steadfast,
trusting in the LORD."

---

*[The] peace of God . . . is an unspeakable calmness
and serenity of spirit, a tranquility in the blood of
Christ, which keeps the souls of believers, in their
latest hour, even as a garrison keeps a city.*

JOHN WESLEY

MARS?

Many, O LORD my God, are Your wonderful works which
You have done; and Your thoughts toward us cannot be
recounted.... They are more than can be numbered.

PSALM 40:5

Astrophysicist Stephen Hawking said recently at a conference that human beings must quickly establish a base on the moon and colonize Mars, otherwise global warming or another catastrophe may drive the human race to extinction. "Life on earth is at the ever-increasing risk of being wiped out by a disaster such as sudden global warming, nuclear war, a genetically engineered virus, or other dangers we have not thought of yet," he said.

The Bible teaches that earth's days *are* numbered, but the Bible also says that God has not abandoned us, nor has He forgotten His children. Psalm 139:17 says, "How precious also are Your thoughts to me, O God! How great is the sum of them!" Jeremiah 29:11 says, "I know the thoughts that I think toward you, says the LORD, thoughts of peace ... to give you a future and a hope."

We can forget the Lord, but He can never forget us. He loves and knows and cares, and we should think about *that*. When your world is threatened, it isn't Mars you need, but the Master.

God's thoughts of love are very many, very wonderful,
very practical! Muse on them ... no sweeter subject ever
occupied your mind. God's thoughts of you are many.
CHARLES HADDON SPURGEON

KING OF KINGS

He has on His robe and on His thigh a name written:
KING OF KINGS AND LORD OF LORDS.

REVELATION 19:16

The pages of history record the names of men who, at various times, "ruled the world." There were the Egyptian pharaohs and the kings of Assyria, Babylon, and Persia. Then came Alexander the Great, the Roman caesars, and Eastern lords like Genghis Khan. In the modern era, Hitler and Stalin come to mind. Because none of these ruthless leaders ever ruled the *entire* world, we're inclined to think it can't be done.

Yet the Bible says that one man, the God-Man, will rule over the entire world: Jesus Christ will be King of kings. But before He comes, another will attempt to wrest the world from God's control. His biblical name is the Antichrist (1 John 2:18; 4:3)—one who is the opposite of the true Christ (Greek *anti*, or "in place of"). He will convince the whole world to follow his lead in persecuting the nation of Israel and warring against Christ when He returns. But his rule will be short lived. After seven years of his tyranny, Christ will return and vanquish his armies.

Christians should never live in fear of rulers who accumulate power. Jesus Christ is waiting in the wings of heaven to assume His throne as King of kings over all the earth.

*He who is the King of the kingdom of heaven is
at the same time the Father of its citizens.*
WILLIAM HENDRIKSEN

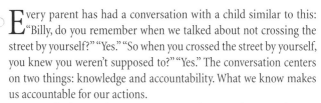

October 19

ACCOUNTABLE LIVING

> Everyone to whom much is given, from him much
> will be required; and to whom much has been
> committed, of him they will ask the more.

LUKE 12:48

Every parent has had a conversation with a child similar to this: "Billy, do you remember when we talked about not crossing the street by yourself?" "Yes." "So when you crossed the street by yourself, you knew you weren't supposed to?" "Yes." The conversation centers on two things: knowledge and accountability. What we know makes us accountable for our actions.

Jesus had a similar conversation with a Jewish man who was interested in inheriting eternal life. He knew the Law said to love God and one's neighbor, but he wasn't sure he wanted to love *all* his neighbors. So Jesus told him a story about a Samaritan who did love his neighbor unconditionally—and told the Jewish man he ought to imitate the Samaritan's way of showing sacrificial love for others. Jesus' point was this: since you know the Law says to love your neighbor (Leviticus 19:18), you are responsible to do it. Our knowledge makes us accountable for what we know we should do but choose not to do.

Knowing the will of God is a weighty responsibility. We are accountable for everything before God (Luke 12:42-48), but especially for what we know.

Knowledge therefore is vain and fruitless,
which is not reduced to practice.
MATTHEW HENRY

AMBASSADORS, NOT CITIZENS

Our citizenship is in heaven, from which we also
eagerly wait for the Savior, the Lord Jesus Christ.

PHILIPPIANS 3:20

Diplomats are protected from prosecution and harm while repre-
senting their country in another nation. Even a nation's embassy
is considered the sovereign territory of the visiting nation. In other
words, diplomats are subject to the laws of their own nation, not the
laws of the nation to which they have been appointed.

Likewise, Christians should think of themselves as diplomats,
or "ambassadors for Christ" (2 Corinthians 5:20) during their stay
in this world. While we are subject to the civil laws of the governments under which we live (Romans 13:1-7), we operate under the
spiritual laws of our home nation: the Kingdom of Heaven. We live
under Christ's law of love (John 13:34) and the "law of the Spirit of
life in Christ Jesus" (Romans 8:2). The "fruit of the Spirit" marks our
behavior, and "against such there is no law" (Galatians 5:22-23). If you
feel constrained to obey the laws of this world, you need to be set free
from "the law of sin and death" (Romans 8:2).

We are ambassadors to, not citizens of, this world—and should
live accordingly.

*Christians are not citizens of earth trying to get to heaven,
but citizens of heaven making their way through this world.*
VANCE HAVNER

October 21

EARLY WARNINGS

> I myself always strive to have a conscience
> without offense toward God and men.
>
> ACTS 24:16

In Ewa Beach, Hawaii, sits a rather plain-looking, white-block building with a small ramp leading to the front door. It is unimposing, but what happens there could save thousands of lives. It's the Pacific Tsunami Warning Center, established in 1949. Its purpose is to continually monitor the Pacific Basin for seismic activity and provide early warning flashes for possible tsunamis.

The human heart also has an early warning system, established in the soul, which continually monitors the seismic activities of sin in our lives. It's called the conscience. The apostle Paul's desire was to serve Christ with a pure conscience (2 Timothy 1:3).

One man quipped, "Conscience is that still, small voice that is sometimes too loud for comfort."

Are you listening to your conscience? The Bible warns that if we don't heed this still, small inner voice, it may become seared and defiled (1 Timothy 4:2; Titus 1:15). When that happens, it's like disconnecting the sirens and signals from the Pacific Tsunami Warning Center.

If your conscience is speaking to you about some matter, hear it and heed it!

There is no pillow as soft as a clear conscience.

FRENCH PROVERB

THERMOMETER OR THERMOSTAT?

Do not be deceived: "Evil company corrupts good habits."

1 CORINTHIANS 15:33

In a letter from the Birmingham jail, Dr. Martin Luther King Jr. wrote these words: "In those days the church was not merely a thermometer that recorded the ideas and principles of popular opinion; it was a thermostat that transformed the mores of society."

Although those words were written more than fifty years ago, they still speak a poignant truth today. Are we, as Christians, acting as thermometers or as thermostats? Are we merely rising and falling to the spiritual degree of those around us, or do we set the standard for our environment? The Bible says to "put away from yourselves the evil person" (1 Corinthians 5:13). This does not mean we are to ostracize those who do not yet know the Lord; it simply means that if Christian brothers or sisters are living in sin and we find ourselves being influenced rather than being an influence, we should separate ourselves from them.

Perhaps a gentler way of saying it is this: care for your spiritual environment. Cultivate relationships that are mutually encouraging in the Lord, and as much as possible, be the thermostat that sets the spiritual temperature so that others may see Christ reflected in your life and rise to His degree.

Thermostats are change agents and affect others around them.

CLINT PASCAL

October 23

RIPPLES

A posterity shall serve Him. It will be recounted
of the Lord to the next generation.

PSALM 22:30

Just as tossing a stone into a lake creates ripples to the shoreline, so
our simple acts of witness produce results that extend to the return
of Christ.

Early one Sunday, a young man dragged himself home from a
night of partying. As an instructor at Tampa's Arthur Murray dance
studio, he was single, popular, and unhindered by morality. He collapsed into bed, setting his radio alarm for midafternoon. When
the radio came on, he was jolted awake by the preaching of Donald
Barnhouse, who was asking, "Suppose you were to die today and stand
before God, and He asked you, 'What right do you have to enter into
my heaven?'—what would you say?"

That's the moment the Holy Spirit touched D. James Kennedy,
who became one of America's eminent pastors and is now with the
Lord. At the time, however, no one knew the results of that broadcast.
It was unknown to Dr. Barnhouse, to the producers of the show, to
the supporters who had given their gifts to put it on the air, or to the
workers in the studio. Only heaven could tabulate the results.

You're doing more good than you know. Don't ever underestimate
the handful of stones you're throwing into the pond whenever you say
a word for Christ.

Do all the good you can by all the means you can.
JOHN WESLEY

October 24

HEAVENLY HOSPITALITY

Be hospitable to one another without grumbling.

1 PETER 4:9

In AD 600, Pope Gregory the Great commissioned a hospital to be built in Jerusalem to care for Christian pilgrims. The English word *hospital* was derived from German *hospes*, or "host," and became the foundation for words like *hotel*, *hostel*, and *hospitality*. The idea of hospitality is best pictured as it was in AD 600—refreshment and repose for the needs of those who journey to your door.

One of the most interesting verses in the New Testament deals with hospitality. Hebrews 13:2 warns believers to welcome and entertain strangers generously, because the strangers might be angelic beings instead of human beings! Is that possible? It happened to Abraham when the Lord Himself and two angels paid him a visit (Genesis 18:1-3; 19:1). Abraham's hospitality was exemplary—he set them under a shade tree, gave them water to wash their feet, and prepared a sumptuous meal for them. The principle to draw from Hebrews 13:2 is that since we don't know which strangers are angels and which aren't, we should treat every stranger the way we'd treat a heavenly visitor.

Be prepared for the Lord to interrupt your plans with a knock on the door. You never know who might be on the other side.

Hospitality should have no other nature than love.

HENRIETTA MEARS

DAVID JEREMIAH | 311

October 25

SPIRITUAL CEDAR

> The righteous shall flourish like a palm tree,
> he shall grow like a cedar in Lebanon.
>
> PSALM 92:12

Sadly, the majestic cedar trees of Lebanon are few and far between today compared to how they covered the mountains in biblical times. They did not grow in Israel, but only in the higher elevations to the north. They grew straight and strong, up to ninety feet tall, and could live for three thousand years. And they were highly prized for building. King David lived in a cedar palace, and Solomon contracted with Tyre to bring great rafts of cedar logs, with which to build the Temple, down the Mediterranean coast.

Lebanon cedars are a perfect analogy for the growth of the righteous. First, they must have the right conditions. And when they do, they grow slowly, stand up straight against the elements of the world, and become highly prized for their usefulness. Such are the elements of spiritual growth. If you are growing spiritually, it is because you have put yourself in the right environment, you are strong enough to resist the world, and you are being used by God. If not, it may be time for a change.

Like a cedar, growth for a Christian is normal and is to be expected, with the ultimate result of being valuable in service.

All growth that is not towards God is growing to decay.

GEORGE MACDONALD

AS GENEROUS AS CHILDREN

In a great trial of affliction the abundance of their joy and
their deep poverty abounded in the riches of their liberality.

2 CORINTHIANS 8:2

Did you hear about the mother who asked her children to give some of their allowance to support orphaned children? "These children have no mother or father, not even an aunt or uncle," the mother explained. "Would you like to give some of your money to help them?" The children thought for a moment and then announced their decision: "Let's give them Aunt Martha!"

Fortunately, that reply is not typical of children when it comes to money. They are usually incredibly generous about donating their own money and raising funds from others for worthy causes. We could learn a lot by imitating their behavior. Or, we could imitate the Macedonian Christians about whom the apostle Paul wrote so eloquently (2 Corinthians 8:1-5). When they heard that the believers in Jerusalem were suffering and needed food, they gave generously—above and beyond their own ability. They did what we should do—believe that God gives to us not only for our needs but also to meet the needs of others.

The next time you have the opportunity to give, do so with the innocence and generosity of a child who never worries about supply.

———— ⋘◉◈◉⋙ ————

It is more blessed to give than to receive.
JESUS OF NAZARETH

October 27

THE LIGHT OF OBEDIENCE

By faith Abraham obeyed when he was called to go out
to the place which he would receive as an inheritance.
And he went out, not knowing where he was going.

HEBREWS 11:8

Go into any of the big-box hardware/home center stores and you'll find an entire section devoted to flashlights. Some of them are huge! They advertise millions of candlepower in brightness and can light up objects a quarter mile away. These lights are a far cry from the tiny, handheld oil lamps in biblical times—only one candlepower in strength, lighting up objects perhaps five feet away!

The psalmist writes that God's Word is "a lamp to [his] feet and a light to [his] path" (Psalm 119:105). And in the mind of the Israelite, God's Word was something to be obeyed. As I obey God's Word where I stand today, it will give direction for the next move I should make. In other words, there is no need to see a quarter mile down life's path if I am not going to obey and take the one step God has made clear from where I stand. If you are seeking direction for your life, obey what God has shown you today. Do that one day at a time and, looking back, you'll realize the entire way has been illuminated.

Obedience is not a matter of seeing the whole path, only the next step. Obedience increases seeing.

The way to the knowledge of God is by obedience.
WILLIAM TEMPLE

THE WORLD IS YOUR NEIGHBORHOOD

The entire law is summed up in a single command:
"Love your neighbor as yourself."

GALATIANS 5:14, NIV

If our English word *neighbor* had stuck to its etymological roots, determining who our neighbor is might have been a bit easier. *Neighbor* is derived from a German word that was a compound made up of "near" and "dweller, especially a farmer." In other words, in centuries-ago Germany, a *nahgabur* was someone, likely another farmer, whom you knew because he lived near you.

But when Jesus told the story of the Good Samaritan, He established a definition that predated Europe's Middle Ages. Your neighbor is not necessarily someone who lives near you, nor does it have to be someone with whom you are acquainted. According to Jesus in Luke 10:25-37, your neighbor is any person who has a need that you are able to meet. Jesus made the point in His parable that the man the Good Samaritan helped was a stranger—not a "near-dweller." Yet the Samaritan assumed the responsibility for doing everything he could to help.

Today we think of neighbors as those who live on our street or in our neighborhood. Yet, using Jesus' definition, we have many more neighbors than those. We need to broaden the boundaries of our neighborhood to include the whole world.

If my heart is right with God, every human being is my neighbor.

OSWALD CHAMBERS

THY FATHER CALLETH THEE

> God so loved the world, that he gave his only
> begotten Son, that whosoever believeth in him
> should not perish, but have everlasting life.
>
> JOHN 3:16, KJV

An aged Quaker named Hartman had a son in the army. When he received news that a dreadful battle had taken place, he went to the scene of the conflict to find him. The officer said the army believed the boy was dead, because he had not answered to his name. This did not satisfy the father, however, and he set out across the battlefield to call for his beloved son, who was dearer to him than life. Night set in, and Hartman continued searching by lantern until a gust of wind extinguished the light. In desperation, he began shouting, "John Hartman, thy father calleth thee!" Finally, in the dark distance, Hartman heard his boy's voice crying, "Here, Father!" The old man then took his son in his arms, carried him to headquarters, and nursed him back to health.

God loves us more than life itself, and as His beloved Son hung on the cross and died for our sins, He shouted to us in a dark world, "(*Your name here*), thy Father calleth thee!" Have you cried, "Here, Father"?

---

*So long as we imagine it is we who have to look
for God, we must often lose heart. But it is the
other way about—He is looking for us.*
SIMON TUGWELL

OSMOSIS AND INERTIA

I press toward the goal for the prize of the
upward call of God in Christ Jesus.

PHILIPPIANS 3:14

Consider a couple of concepts from the world of science: osmosis is the gradual transfer of fluid from one side of a membrane to the other until there are equal amounts on both sides. Inertia is the tendency of a body at rest to remain at rest, to resist acceleration, to remain in the same line of movement unless acted on by a stronger force.

In layman's terms, osmosis is the gradual, unconscious, hit-or-miss process of absorption—like learning to speak French by living in France for twenty years. Inertia is resistance to movement or change—like preferring the status quo. Spiritually speaking, too many people try to grow spiritually through osmosis without overcoming inertia. Over a lifetime you might grow a little spiritually by attending church services on Sunday—assuming you overcome inertia by getting out of bed. But true spiritual growth only happens intentionally—by planning and moving. If you don't make a conscious effort to grow spiritually, the likelihood is that you won't. But you can grow spiritually if you will set goals in important areas and then achieve them.

No one grows spiritually by osmosis or without overcoming the resistance to change.

*You cannot propel yourself forward by
patting yourself on the back.*

UNKNOWN

October 31

THE COST OF COMPASSION

When he was still a great way off, his father saw him and had
compassion, and ran and fell on his neck and kissed him.

LUKE 15:20

The word *sacrifice* is the costliest word in the biblical lexicon, especially when it comes to the price God paid—allowing His Son to be sacrificed for our sins. Sacrifice means to offer up something of one's own—to relinquish ownership, to give it up for a higher purpose or calling. But there is another word that has a high price attached to it, one that gets less attention than *sacrifice*.

The cost of *compassion*, while perhaps not as high as that of sacrifice, is nonetheless high—as all compassionate people can attest. Take the father of the prodigal son in Jesus' parable, for instance (Luke 15:11-32). When the rebellious son returned home after a period of profligate living, the father welcomed him home with compassion. What price did he pay for his compassion? How about the sleepless nights he had spent agonizing over the fate of his son? Or the forgiveness he extended? Or the large sum of money that the son had wasted in riotous living?

Compassion's price is the loss of whatever we could be doing for ourselves instead of spending ourselves on another. Keep your compassion account balanced, ready to spend when needed.

Compassion will cure more sins than condemnation.

HENRY WARD BEECHER

NOVEMBER

THE HOUSE HE'S BUILDING

> Unless the LORD builds the house, they labor in vain who build it.
>
> PSALM 127:1

Years ago, before Josh McDowell was the well-known speaker and author he is today, he joined the staff of Campus Crusade for Christ. He was sent to the ministry headquarters at Arrowhead Springs in California and received his first assignment: washing the floors in the lobby of the former resort hotel. He thought he was going to be working with the ministry's leaders, and instead he was relegated to watching them walk by as he scrubbed the floors they walked on. Later, he said it was one of the most important lessons he ever learned: it takes preparation to be used by God.

Moses learned that lesson, spending forty years in the Midian wilderness as a shepherd before leading his countrymen out of Egypt. Jesus spent forty days in the Judean wilderness before beginning his public ministry. Difficult periods of preparation are God's way of saying, "Only I know what you need to know to be successful. Trust Me." The psalmist said, "Unless the LORD builds the house, they labor in vain who build it."

If you're going through a difficult time right now, trust the Lord. The house He is building (you) needs whatever you're learning as you wait on Him.

A season of suffering is a small price to pay for a clear view of God.

MAX LUCADO

If we love one another, God abides in us, and
His love has been perfected in us.

1 JOHN 4:12

In the mid-1930s, a German Protestant pastor was abducted from his church. Suspected of aiding and abetting Jews, he was thrown into prison without a hearing, a trial, or even a phone call to his family. The prison guard outside his cell hated everyone associated with Jews. He purposely skipped the pastor's cell when meals were handed out, made him go weeks without a shower, and gave him the most difficult jobs on the labor gang. The pastor, on the other hand, prayed that he would be able to love this guard with God's love. As the months went by, the pastor smiled at the guard, thanked him for the few meals he did receive, and even talked to him about agape love. The guard never said anything, but he heard it all, and one night he cracked a smile. The next day the pastor received two meals and was able to shower for as long as he wanted. Finally, one afternoon the guard personally made the long-awaited call to the pastor's family, and a few months later, he was released.

It is against our human nature to love someone like that prison guard, but through His power, God can give us the ability to love the unlovable.

---

*The love, even for your enemies, which Jesus
commands, is not our work but His work in us.*

THOMAS GREEN

BEARING HIS NAME

In the Name of our God we will set up our banners!

PSALM 20:5

A judge in New Mexico ruled against the wishes of a man wanting to legally change his name. The man wanted to call himself by an obscene term. The man claimed that he had a right to call himself by whatever name he wished, and the name he wanted was a word that wouldn't be printed in most newspapers in America, let alone a book like this! Thankfully the judge refused his request.

How wonderful to know that as Christians, we are called by God's name, which is high and holy. The word *Christian* means "Christ's Ones." Acts 15:14 says that God is choosing a people for Himself to bear His name. When we become His children, we bear His name and should reflect His character.

Like the Psalmist, let's rejoice that God has given us the heritage of those who fear His name (Psalm 61:5). And we can pray, "Look upon me and be merciful to me, as Your custom is toward those who love Your name" (Psalm 119:132).

I find letters from God dropped in the street—
and every one is signed by God's name.

WALT WHITMAN

THE WOODEN BOWL

Receive one another, just as Christ also received us.

ROMANS 15:7

A frail, old man went to live with his son, daughter-in-law, and young grandson. Every night, the family ate dinner together, but because of the old man's shaky hands and blurred vision, he had difficulty eating. Peas would roll off of his spoon, and he almost always spilled milk on the table as he tried to take a drink. His son and daughter-in-law became very frustrated and decided to have him sit at his own table in the corner where they wouldn't have to deal with the mess. Because the old man had broken a dish or two, they gave him a wooden bowl to eat out of. One night, the old man's son noticed his boy playing with some wood scraps, and he asked him what he was doing. The boy answered, "I am making a wooden bowl for you and Mommy to eat from when I grow up." The boy's parents were speechless and in tears. From that moment on, the grandfather ate at the table with the rest of the family, and somehow, the messes he made never bothered them again.

Impatience can be the result when expectations are not met. No one is perfect, and expecting perfection from someone will be frustrating and unproductive. Choose to love people for who they are, as they are. That's how God loves us, and He asks us to do the same for others.

Deal with the faults of others as gently as with your own.

UNKNOWN

THE HUMAN TOUCH OF KINDNESS

He who despises his neighbor sins; but he who
has mercy on the poor, happy is he.

PROVERBS 14:21

Mamie Adams always went to a branch post office in her town because the postal employees there were friendly. When she went there to buy stamps just before Christmas one year, the lines were particularly long. Someone pointed out that there was no need to wait in line because there was a stamp machine in the lobby. "I know," said Mamie, "but the machine won't ask me about my arthritis."[11]

The human touch of kindness is our specie's distinguishing mark and something many go without, due to all of the world's technological advances. Just like Mamie, many people would rather sacrifice the modern-day convenience of a machine in order to receive a friendly greeting from another living, breathing human being. Jesus understood the importance of kindness and took great care in being kind to everyone, especially the downtrodden and unsaved. He knew this was the key to opening the hearts of those who otherwise might never respond to His love.

Make it your goal to be kind to everyone; you never know who might be in need of the human touch of kindness.

It is the duty of every Christian to be Christ to his neighbor.

MARTIN LUTHER

---

[11] *Bits and Pieces* (December 1989), 2.

SERVE WITH JOY

We are His workmanship, created in Christ Jesus for good works.

EPHESIANS 2:10

Recently a young man wrote to a noted business magazine, seeking advice about his job. He said he had fallen into the position because there were no other options for him, but it was a job he hated. He detested arriving at the office every morning, was bored out of his mind all day, and left as early as possible every afternoon. He so disliked his work that it was affecting his sleep and his relationships with his girlfriend and his parents. He described his clients as "boorish," his position as "worthless," and his work as "mindless, menial, miserable drudgery."

Perhaps we all face an unpleasant job situation at one time or another, but our work for the Lord is a different matter. As Christians, we're each given a personal ministry, a work that only we can do for the Kingdom. Every day we have the obligation of fulfilling the Lord's agenda for our lives, and every day there are some good works for us to do. These aren't burdensome or boring; they are enriching, fruitful, and pleasing to the Lord.

How wonderful that the Divine Employer has a task for us today! Serve Him with joy, and always abound in the work of the Lord, "knowing that your labor is not in vain in the Lord" (1 Corinthians 15:58).

Joy is the holy fire that keeps our purpose
warm and our intelligence aglow.

HELEN KELLER

A sound heart is life to the body, but envy
is rottenness to the bones.

PROVERBS 14:30

Today's society is obsessed with steering clear of things that are harmful to the body. It seems that just about every product is fat-free, sugar-free, caffeine-free, or hormone-free. We spend millions of dollars every year on sunscreen, anti-aging products, organic food, and antioxidant-rich vitamins in order to prevent sun damage, wrinkles, and cancer. In essence, we do our bodies good by staying away from those things that are bad for us.

While we know that eating right and taking care of our bodies in general is important, the Bible tells us that "bodily exercise profits a little, but godliness is profitable for all things" (1 Timothy 4:8). As much as we take care to avoid unhealthy things for our bodies, we should be even more concerned about staying away from ungodly things in our lives, such as envy.

Nothing good or profitable ever comes from envy. It only creates misery for the envious person. So, if you desire to lead a long and healthy life, remember to do your body good by living an envy-free lifestyle.

*The man who keeps busy helping the man below him
won't have time to envy the man above him.*

HENRIETTA MEARS

STAYING FOCUSED

> Do not turn from [the law] to the right hand or to
> the left, that you may prosper wherever you go.
>
> JOSHUA 1:7

In the early centuries of the Christian church, a movement of ascetics developed. These individuals became hermits, living in caves and other isolated places as a way to remove themselves from the impurities of the world and enhance their own holiness. One of the most famous was Symeon the Stylite, who lived atop a fifty-foot stone pillar for thirty-six years, until his death in AD 459.

It would be spiritually safe, though thoroughly impractical, for us to retreat to a cave or climb atop a pillar to live. There is much in life to distract us as we journey through this world, but no physical protection can guard the thoughts and intents of the heart. We need a way to keep our priorities, values, and decisions focused only on the will of God for our lives. The Bible refers to such choices as obedience—the outworking of the believer's committed faith. When Joshua was heading into the spiritually dangerous, pagan land of Canaan, God cautioned him to obey *all* the Word of God, staying focused—turning neither to the right nor to the left.

A daily prayer for obedience is how we keep our eyes focused on Christ. But it's up to us to pray the prayer.

The best measure of spiritual life is not ecstasies but obedience.

OSWALD CHAMBERS

BE A FRUIT INSPECTOR

Every tree is known by its own fruit. For men do not gather figs
from thorns, nor do they gather grapes from a bramble bush.

LUKE 6:44

Grafting merges the fruiting portion of one plant or tree with the rooting portion of another. The trunk of an apple tree of one variety, for instance, called the rootstock, will have grafted to it the flowering or fruiting portion of a different apple tree, called the scion. When the tree matures, it bears fruit that the rootstock tree would never have borne otherwise.

That may work in the world of horticulture, but it does not work in the spiritual world: the fruit cannot be different from the root. Or, as Jesus put it, "Every tree is known by its own fruit." Jesus spoke these words when warning against false prophets: test a prophet's fruit and you will know that prophet's root. But the principle applies across the board—even to Christians. Galatians 5:22-23 describes the fruit of the Spirit—the character traits of a true follower of Jesus. Anyone bearing fruit unlike the character of Jesus calls his own spiritual rootstock into question.

Fruit inspection is always in order—not others' fruit, but our own. Make sure there is no discrepancy between fruit and root in your life.

---

*It is no use to anybody for a tree to bud and blossom
if the blossom does not develop into fruit.*

MARTIN LUTHER

In His law he meditates day and night.

PSALM 1:2

Laura Wilkinson, a radiant Christian, is a diver from Texas who practiced hard for the 2000 Olympics in Sydney. But during preparation, she broke three bones in her foot. Unable to work out, she did the next best thing. Several times a day, Laura used mental imagery to practice her dive. She visualized herself climbing up to the ten-meter platform and walking through the motions of her complex high dives. She would see each split second of her approach, posture, position, dive, entry into the water, and swim to the side of the pool. Her cast came off just before the Sydney Games, and she went on to compete and to win the first gold medal for a female American platform diver in nearly forty years.

Our minds are powerful tools for adjusting our attitudes and actions. As we meditate on God's Word, mulling it over day and night, our thoughts are transformed. And our thoughts become the basis of all we are and all we do. A bit of hurried "devotion" in the morning isn't enough. Meditation happens all throughout the day. Through meditation, we digest the wonders of God's Word and translate them into everyday victory.

A deep knowledge of spiritual things can only come by the way of unhurried reflection upon God's truth and by prayer.

MERRILL UNGER

THE SECRET COMPARTMENT

The LORD lives! . . . Therefore I will give thanks to You, O LORD,
among the Gentiles, and sing praises to Your name.

2 SAMUEL 22:47, 50

In 1794, James Monroe, who later became America's fifth president, purchased a Louis XVI desk containing a secret compartment that no one but the owner knew about. In 1906, one of Monroe's descendants, a child, damaged the desk. The family took the desk to a cabinetmaker, and the cabinetmaker discovered the secret compartment. It contained priceless documents, including letters from Thomas Jefferson and James Madison. In one of the letters, Jefferson had written, "How little do my countrymen know what precious blessing they are in possession of, and which no other people on earth enjoy."

That's a secret that also resides in the secret compartment of the Christian's heart. Every day our cups overflow. Every day we're recipients of one blessing after another. Every morning we see new mercies and rediscover God's great faithfulness.

Don't keep thanksgiving a secret. Find opportunities today to be grateful. Take the most optimistic view of things. Look up with a smile and trust almighty God and His Word. Praise God from whom all blessings flow.

For these blessings we owe Almighty God, from whom
we derive them, and with profound reverence, our
most grateful and unceasing acknowledgements.

JAMES MONROE

Though the LORD is on high, yet He regards the
lowly; but the proud He knows from afar.

PSALM 138:6

Paul Graves was sworn in as mayor of Sandpoint, Idaho, in January 2000. In a 2007 article in Spokane's *Spokesman Review* newspaper, Graves said this about public service: "While hubris seems more in style these days, it is humility that serves us all much better." He cited Albert Einstein: "The significant problems we have cannot be solved at the same level of thinking with which we created them." And he paired those words with Paul's in Romans 12:3: "Do not think of yourself more highly than you should. Instead, be modest in your thinking" (GNT).

Humility. Modesty. What a concept! If many of our problems are caused by a lack of humility (that is, by pride), then we will need to think differently to solve them. The most different way is abject humility before God—the fall-down-on-your-face kind of humility that says, "God, I can't figure this out. I'm dependent on You alone. Please grant me wisdom and help. I humble myself before You."

The thinking that got us into trouble cannot get us out. When you are in trouble, humble yourself before God and receive His grace to help in time of need.

———— ∽◦∾ ————

Humility is the only certain defense against humiliation.

UNKNOWN

God resists the proud, but gives grace to the humble.

JAMES 4:6

Few people would dare write a book on the subject of humility—
we feel innately disqualified. But one man did write a wonderful
book on this subject—the South African pastor Andrew Murray. In
all, Murray wrote 240 books, many of them about holiness. In his
midfifties, he contracted a mysterious throat ailment that took him
from the pulpit for two years. Many years later, recalling the life lessons of that period, he preached twelve sermons on the subject of
humility, and they were published when he was nearly eighty.

"There is nothing so divine and heavenly," wrote Murray, "as
being the servant and helper of all. The faithful servant who recog-
nizes his position finds a real pleasure in supplying the wants of the
master and his guests. When we realize that humility is something
infinitely deeper than contrition, and accept it as our participation in
the life of Jesus, we will begin to learn that it is our true nobility. . . .
When I look back upon my own Christian experience, or at the church
of Christ as a whole, I am amazed at how little humility is seen as the
distinguishing feature of discipleship."

His humility became our salvation.
His salvation is our humility.
ANDREW MURRAY

November 14

GRACIOUS WORDS

All bore witness to Him, and marveled at the
gracious words which proceeded out of His mouth.
And they said, "Is this not Joseph's son?"

LUKE 4:22

Everyone knows the value of a snack as an energy booster. Half an apple or a tangerine or a handful of grapes, all natural sources of sugar (carbohydrates), can be the fuel our internal engines need to allow us to shift into a higher gear when we feel tired. The ancients didn't know the science, but they knew the value of "carbs" as a source of energy: Jonathan's "countenance brightened" (1 Samuel 14:27) when he ate the honey from a honeycomb.

Did you know there is something else that can refresh a tired and weary soul as quickly as honey? Proverbs 16:24 says, "Pleasant words are like a honeycomb, sweetness to the soul and health to the bones." How many souls, even "bones," are sick and downcast because it has been so long since they've heard a pleasant word? One of the reasons Jesus Christ was so loved was because of the "gracious words which proceeded out of His mouth" (Luke 4:22). People couldn't believe that an ordinary person ("Joseph's son") could speak so graciously and with such a healing effect.

The next time you encounter a tired soul or sick body, speak some pleasant and gracious words. It may be just what the Doctor ordered.

Words, those precious cups of meaning . . .

ST. AUGUSTINE

REASONS TO PRAISE GOD

I will praise You, for I am fearfully and wonderfully made;
marvelous are Your works, and that my soul knows very well.

PSALM 139:14

Instead of trying to catch their children doing something wrong, conscientious parents try to catch them doing something *right*—and praise them for it: "Your drawing is amazing!" "I appreciate the way you let your sister go first." "You always seem ready to help. That's a great quality." "Thank you for saying please and thank you so often."

The point is, there are myriad reasons to praise our children. And there are even more reasons to praise our heavenly Father, if we will be attentive to Him. We may not say, "I praise you, Lord . . ." every time—but a word of thanks serves the same purpose. As an exercise, keep a slip of paper tucked in your Bible, and make a growing list of the reasons you have to praise God when they come to mind. Chances are, keeping such a list will increase your attentiveness to, and awareness of, all that God does on a regular basis in your life.

Such a list will also keep you from resting on your spiritual laurels. ("Thank You for saving me twenty years ago.") You will discover fresh new reasons to praise Him every day.

O for a heart to praise my God, a heart from sin set free;
A heart that always feels Thy blood so freely shed for me.

CHARLES WESLEY

Let your eyes look straight ahead.

PROVERBS 4:25

Horses are high-strung animals, and easily spooked. That's partly because their marginal vision is limited. They can see what's in front of them, but anything coming from the left or right startles them, and they're easily distracted by peripheral objects. That's why you often see blinders on horses. Blinders keep horses focused on what's immediately before them, which prevents them from being scared by movement along a parade route or race course.

Christians, too, need blinders. Job says, "I have made a covenant with my eyes; why then should I look upon a young woman?" (Job 31:1). The psalmist says, "I will set nothing wicked before my eyes" (Psalm 101:3) and "Turn away my eyes from looking at worthless things" (Psalm 119:37).

Much of today's evil comes in a visual form—on television and in movies, and on the screens of our computers and portable electronic devices. Make a covenant with your eyes not to look at unholy images, and ask God to turn your eyes away from worthless things.

"Let your eyes look straight ahead."

To keep the heart in a good estate . . . first, [make a] careful study of the senses, specially of the eyes.
CHARLES HADDON SPURGEON

November 17

MAKE IT HAPPEN

I will walk in Your truth. . . . I will praise You, O Lord my
God. . . . And I will glorify Your name forevermore.

PSALM 86:11-12

A commercial for the Royal Bank of Scotland Group depicts four
businesspeople eating lunch, when suddenly one of them starts
to choke on his bite of food. His colleagues begin discussing the situation, noting that he is in fact choking and that they know exactly
what to do—the Heimlich maneuver. They then go into detail about
how to properly perform the maneuver but never once get up to help
their coworker in any way. During their conversation, a man from
another table comes over and saves the choking man's life by performing the Heimlich and then quietly walks away. The tagline at the
end of the commercial is "Make it happen."

It is easy to utter words of gratitude to the Lord during prayer and
worship, but it is quite another thing to make those words come alive
day in and day out. While expressing our thankfulness through worship is important, our aim should be productive gratitude, actively
living in praise and thanksgiving. Today, when you stop to consider
the many blessings God has given, don't let your gratitude end with
words; rather, "make it happen" with a grateful heart and joyful spirit.

---

*As we express our gratitude, we must never forget that the
highest appreciation is not to utter words but to live by them.*

JOHN F. KENNEDY

We will bless the LORD from this time forth and forevermore.

PSALM 115:18

In the movie *Pay It Forward*, the concept of paying someone back for a good deed is replaced with the idea of passing the blessing on to another person instead, creating an endless chain of giving to others what has been given to you. The thought is that, in time, people everywhere will look for ways to "pay it forward" and the world will become a better place.

As Christians, we have the opportunity every day to pay it forward to those who are lost in this world by giving them a glimpse of Christ through our kindness. We were each given a gift when Jesus hung on the cross and died for our sins; every time we demonstrate His love to someone, we bless not only them but also our Lord and Savior.

The Bible tells us that when we stand before our Maker to account for our time on earth, what we have done for "the least of these" will be as if we did it unto God Himself. So let's eagerly search for ways to bless those whom God places in our path, with the ultimate aim of glorifying our heavenly Father.

All the blessings we enjoy are Divine deposits, committed to our trust on this condition, that they should be dispensed for the benefit of our neighbors.

JOHN CALVIN

SWIFT TO HEAR

Love ... is not provoked.

1 CORINTHIANS 13:4-5

If you're in a hotel room and you can hear the people talking next door, you might turn on a radio to drown out the intruding noise. The radio provides a type of "white noise"—competing sound frequencies designed to make it harder for your brain to pick out the intruding voices. White noise generators—machines that produce a low sound made up of thousands of frequencies at once—are used wherever an intruding sound needs to be quieted.

Without knowing it, we live in a world filled with white noise. There are seemingly thousands of voices and sounds competing for our brain's attention. The problem is that they do their job too well: they keep us from hearing the one voice we truly need to focus on— the voice trying to break through all the white noise. That voice might be our spouse, our child, a friend in need, a counselor with a word of reproof—or it might be the voice of God. Think how much misunderstanding and resulting anger could be avoided if we could tune out all the voices except the one we really need to hear. The apostle James called it being "swift to hear" (James 1:19).

Whose voice is competing for your attention? Make it a point this week to isolate the important voices and give them your full attention.

---

*When he brings out his own sheep, he goes before them;
and the sheep follow him, for they know his voice.*

JOHN 10:4

HEAVY BACKPACKS

Praise be to the Lord, to God our Savior,
who daily bears our burdens.

PSALM 68:19, NIV

Pediatricians are concerned that many children are carrying too much weight in their school backpacks. Lugging too heavy a burden around all day can trigger chronic back, neck, and shoulder pain, and some doctors think it can lead to scoliosis. As a rule of thumb, a child's backpack shouldn't be heavier than 10 to 20 percent of his or her body weight.

Many of us carry around burdens that are too heavy. Here are some of the Bible's best "burden" verses:

- I am the LORD your God who brings you out from under the burdens. (Exodus 6:7)
- Cast your burden on the LORD, and He shall sustain you. (Psalm 55:22)
- When I was burdened with worries, you comforted me and made me feel secure. (Psalm 94:19, CEV)
- My yoke is easy and My burden is light. (Matthew 11:30)

Is your backpack too heavy? Cast your cares on Him by faith, and say with the psalmist, "Praise be to the Lord, . . . who daily bears our burdens"!

If you want rest, O weary souls, ye can find it nowhere until ye come and lay your burdens down at His dear pierced feet.

CHARLES HADDON SPURGEON

Yes, I will sing aloud of Your mercy in the morning.

PSALM 59:16

Experts in the health and fitness field state that there are many benefits to exercising in the early morning before your day gets into full swing. These benefits include increased mental sharpness, more energy, and regulated appetite. If you are a morning exerciser, you no doubt have your own list of positive results from starting your day with a workout.

The same is true for those who begin each day with praise; they feel more focused on the Lord throughout the day and more content with what God has given them, and they exude joy that comes from setting their minds on God's goodness before their day begins.

Scripture tells us to "set your heart and your soul to seek the LORD your God" (1 Chronicles 22:19), and it stands to reason that if we spend a few moments praising God each morning, our day will have a firm foundation in Christ and we can meet whatever comes our way with His wisdom, strength, patience, and joy.

Before we engage ourselves in His work, let's meet
Him in His Word . . . in prayer . . . in worship.

CHARLES SWINDOLL

RESTART YOUR COMPUTER

Love . . . keeps no record of wrongs.

1 CORINTHIANS 13:4-5, NIV

The modern computer dates back to the 1930s and 1940s, and the personal computer to the 1970s. But the most powerful computer in the world was created thousands of years ago: the human brain (and its spiritual manifestation, the human mind). One of the most powerful applications today for computers is financial record keeping—keeping track of every last penny. And the human mind has the same capacity.

One fault of the human brain is that it has to be refreshed frequently to hold on to facts and figures lest they fade from memory. But that's not a problem for people who have been hurt by others—they replay the hurt daily until it gets seared into their cortex. Years later they can tell you when and how the offense occurred and how much it hurt. The Greek language of the New Testament had a word for such record keeping: *logizomai*. And Paul says in 1 Corinthians 13:5 that love doesn't *logizomai*. Love keeps no records of wrongs suffered; love forgives and forgets. God casts our sins into the depths of the sea (Micah 7:19), and we should do the same with the sins of others.

Restart your mental computer today. Erase the old files, and forgive.

"I can forgive, but I cannot forget" is only another way of saying, "I will not forgive."

HENRY WARD BEECHER

BDF (BEST DIVINE FRIEND)

No longer do I call you servants, for a servant does not know
what his master is doing; but I have called you friends.

JOHN 15:15

In the Old Testament, *friend* is a covenant term: Abraham was the friend of God (Isaiah 41:8); Jonathan and David were covenant friends (1 Samuel 18:1-4). Proverbs 18:24 says there is a friend "who sticks closer than a brother"—someone to whom you go to reveal the depths of your heart when needed. You've been hurt and need advice on what to do—so you go to your best friend.

Problem: best human friends are fallible. You rehearse your hurts to them, and you bring another person into an already complicated situation. You ask for advice that may or may not be helpful. You're troubled when you arrive and are likely still troubled when you leave. Fortunately, for life's most challenging situations, every Christian has a best divine Friend: Jesus Christ. Picture yourself as one of His original twelve disciples and what it would have been like to say, "Jesus, I've got this problem. Can You help?" You have that same opportunity today, since Jesus calls you His friend and invites you to find "help in time of need" from Him (Hebrews 4:16).

Best human friends are great. But a best divine Friend is, well, divine!

---

*I have a great need for Christ; I have
a great Christ for my need.*
CHARLES HADDON SPURGEON

> Oh come, let us worship ... before the LORD our Maker.
>
> PSALM 95:6

What is worship? A. W. Tozer describes it this way: "Worship is to feel in your heart and express in some appropriate manner a humbling but delightful sense of admiring awe and astonished wonder and overpowering love in the presence of that most ancient Mystery ... which we call Our Father Which Art in Heaven."[12]

For some, the word *worship* conjures up awkward feelings of being uncomfortable while singing in a church setting, but notice that Tozer never mentions singing, raising hands, or even being with others. Rather, he states it is expressing "in some appropriate manner" that which you feel in your heart toward God. In fact, the most commonly used word for worship in the New Testament, the Greek word *proskuneo*, has more to do with an intimate reverence toward God, being still and quiet before Him in awe and adoration.

The beauty of worship is that it is not limited to what anyone believes it should be. Whether you prefer raising your hands in public or falling prostrate in the privacy of your own home, the most important thing is for your worship to be personal, selfless, intimate, and from the heart.

In the end, worship can never be a performance.
. . . It's got to be an overflow of your heart.

MATT REDMAN

---

[12] A. W. Tozer, quoted in D. J. Fant, *A. W. Tozer: A Twentieth Century Prophet* (Camp Hill, PA: Christian Publications, 1964), 90.

November 25

LEMONADE

> Indeed it was for my own peace that I had great bitterness.
>
> ISAIAH 38:17

The financial panic of 1907 started with a run on the Knicker-bocker Trust Company of New York that exhausted the bank's reserves in a day and a half. In a matter of weeks, the panic had spread across the country, and banks everywhere closed. According to legend, one family was especially hard hit. Their investments and business enterprises foundered, and their dreams for the future evaporated. But they were resourceful, for they had two assets they could still use. The first was the mother's cooking skills, and the second was an old adobe building near the train station.

And so, the Hilton family opened their first hotel.

There's an old saying that if life hands you a lemon, make lemonade. Problems bring possibilities to us that would not have otherwise occurred, and it's important to prayerfully consider how we can turn liabilities into assets.

In Isaiah 38, King Hezekiah suffered a debilitating illness, but by the end of the story, much good had come from it, including an extension of his life and a song of praise. If you're suffering through bitterness and pain now, remember that God has promised to work all things together for good to those who love Him (Romans 8:28). Look ahead in hope, and look around in resourcefulness. Make some lemonade.

Our greatest lessons come out of pain.

RICK WARREN

> One of [the lepers], when he saw that he was healed, returned . . .
> and fell down on his face at His feet. . . . So Jesus answered and
> said, "Were there not ten cleansed? But where are the nine?"
>
> LUKE 17:15-17

Edward Spencer, a seminary student, was part of a lifesaving squad when a ship ran aground on the shore of Lake Michigan in 1860. Spencer waded into the freezing water again and again, rescuing a total of seventeen passengers and permanently damaging his health. Years later at his funeral, it was mentioned that not one of the people he rescued ever thanked him.

Those in attendance at Spencer's funeral must have been thinking, *How could you not thank the person who saved your life?* In all fairness, those who were rescued most likely thought about thanking him but didn't know where to find him or just became so busy with life that they forgot.

As Christians, we have so many reasons to thank and praise our heavenly Father. He not only saved us from the clutches of sin, but He also continually provides for us, loves us, blesses us, and guides us. With everything He is and everything He does, how could we *not* praise Him? We may often think of thanking our Lord and Savior, but we also need to act upon those thoughts, taking time each day to intentionally express our gratitude with praise.

Feeling gratitude and not expressing it is like
wrapping a present and not giving it.
WILLIAM ARTHUR WARD

Let the peace of God rule in your hearts, to which
also you were called ... and be thankful.

COLOSSIANS 3:15

A newspaper article once read, "Abie Nathan is leading a new children's crusade! Nathan, who operates a pirate radio station aboard his 'Peace Ship' in the Mediterranean, has promised to give a scroll with the biblical quotation from Isaiah, 'And they shall not learn war any more . . .,' to any child who smashes his military toys. He has also offered to buy the complete stock of war toys from any store which agrees not to sell them in the future."

While people may disagree about the best way to bring about world peace, most would agree that this man's idea, though optimistic, is not the way to go. In the same way, the world's ideas about finding peace, such as generating more income or exploring various religions, simply do not work.

The Bible tells us that the key to peace is a thankful heart in the midst of trials: being thankful that we have a loving and caring God, thankful that He will never leave us nor forsake us, thankful that God is in control. So instead of trying to create peace ourselves, let us come before the Lord with a thankful heart and have "the peace of God, which surpasses all understanding" (Philippians 4:7) bestowed upon us.

*Our confident trust in the Lord will allow us to
thank Him in the midst of trials because we have
God's peace on duty to protect our hearts.*

JOHN MacARTHUR

GOD CENTERED

> Of Him and through Him and to Him are all
> things, to whom be glory forever. Amen.
>
> ROMANS 11:36

We have centers for everything: ministry centers, childcare centers, convention centers, medical centers, and shopping centers. There's the Lincoln Center in New York, the Centers for Disease Control in Atlanta, the National Hurricane Center in Miami, and the Kennedy Center in Washington. The word *center* comes from a Greek term meaning a prick or sharp point, specifically the exact point marking the middle of a geometric circle.

If something is the center, everything else revolves around it. Just as the planets orbit around the sun, our habits, hearts, affections, and thoughts must revolve around the Lord Jesus, who is the ultimate center of all reality (Colossians 1:17).

The French writer François Fénelon advises us to become so committed to God's glory that all other motives pale in comparison, saying, "It is then that God becomes … the center of the soul, to which all its affections tend."

When we're self-centered, we're self-deceived. When God is central, we can have confidence that He is in control and that our worlds are aligned correctly.

Stars and angels sing around Thee, center of unbroken praise.
HENRY VAN DYKE

November 29

FIVE SIMPLE RULES

I am a companion of all who fear You, and
of those who keep Your precepts.

PSALM 119:63

The best way to have friends is to be one, and we can all do that. Fortunately, the rules for being a friend are simple enough for anyone to master.

First, work on your relationship with the Lord every day. The love we need for others comes from Him, and if we walk in the light as He is in the light, we'll have fellowship with one another. And with His love come His joy, peace, and patience.

Second, avoid the use of the word *I*. When you're with others, ask about *their* day, *their* hobbies, *their* health, *their* families, and *their* burdens.

Third, don't be easily offended. "The prudent overlook an insult" (Proverbs 12:16, NIV). Good friends have thick skins and aren't touchy or easily hurt.

Fourth, be cheerful. No one wants to be around a grumpy, irritable, or depressed spirit. Your mood can lift many hearts during the course of a day. Be *friendly*!

Fifth, drop everything to help your friend in a time of crisis. After all, you never know when you'll be on the receiving end.

Cultivate your friendships, and they will come back to bless you.

---

*A friend knows when you have a need and comes
to strengthen you in the hand of God.*

DAVID JEREMIAH

I thank God, whom I serve with a pure conscience,
as my forefathers did, as without ceasing I
remember you in my prayers night and day,

2 TIMOTHY 1:3

Fourteen-year-old Tony Hicks shot and killed twenty-year-old Tariq Khamisa. Tariq's father forgave Tony's family, forgave Tony himself, and then started the Tariq Khamisa Foundation, through which he has spoken to over half a million young people about the true costs of violence. He is also trying to get Tony, who never had a father, released from his life-sentence conviction so he can come to work at the foundation named for the young man he killed—something Tony is eager to do. Tony says, "I had a man forgive me for taking the life of his son."

Willing to serve as a result of being forgiven is not a strange scenario to Christians. The apostle Paul is our prime example: "I thank God, whom I serve." He never got over the fact that the One he persecuted called him to be His chief apostle. Every Christian is in the same place: forgiven by God and called into His service. Our willingness to serve is a good indication of how much we value our forgiveness.

If you see an opportunity to serve, try looking at it as Paul did: as a grateful response to the God who has forgiven all your sins.

---

*The most holy service that we can render to God
is to be employed in praising His name.*

JOHN CALVIN

DECEMBER

WRONG AGAIN

Eye has not seen, nor ear heard, nor have entered into the heart of
man the things which God has prepared for those who love him.

1 CORINTHIANS 2:9

A Gallup poll was conducted before the 1948 presidential election,
and it wrongly predicted that Thomas E. Dewey would become
the next president. Shortly after Harry Truman's victory, a police
officer stopped George Gallup for driving the wrong direction on a
one-way street. After reading the name on Gallup's driver's license,
the officer smiled and said, "Wrong again!"

Trying to guess the outcome of any election is part and parcel of
politics, but this practice cannot be applied to the life of a Christian.
So often we try to out-plan God, falsely believing we know what is
best for ourselves, when all we have is a limited view of our lives. God,
however, has a limitless view and sees every minute detail, knowing
exactly how to give us the very best of what He has to offer.

The Bible tells us that "a man's heart plans his way, but the LORD
directs his steps" (Proverbs 16:9). The key is letting go of control and
allowing God to direct our steps so that we may ultimately end up where
He wants us, right in the middle of an amazing life. If we will just allow
Him to lead, He will unfold a plan that is too wonderful to comprehend.

*Lift up your eyes. Your heavenly Father waits to
bless you in inconceivable ways to make your
life what you never dreamed it could be.*

ANNE ORTLUND

December 2

RUDY

Humble yourselves under the mighty hand of
God, that He may exalt you in due time.

1 PETER 5:6

Expected to work in the refinery and live a blue-collar life just like his father, five-foot-six Daniel "Rudy" Ruettiger had a dream to play for the Fighting Irish of Notre Dame and make something more of his life. It took him two years of junior college and three rejections before he was finally accepted at Notre Dame and placed on a practice squad. Grateful just to be among the best collegiate players of the game and living his dream, Rudy got the surprise of his life when, in the last game of his senior year, Rudy's coach put him in the game. He sacked the opposing quarterback and was carried off the field on the shoulders of his teammates. To this day, no other Notre Dame player has had that honor.

So often, we have an attitude of entitlement instead of humility, wishing to be more, do more, and have more right away. But just as Rudy rose to his place of honor through humility and contentment, Christ says that "he who humbles himself will be exalted" (Luke 14:11). As you go through your day, strive not for greatness or honor; rather, aim to be humble, and believe that God will exalt you in due time.

Humility is a paradox; the moment you think you've finally found it, you've lost it. And yet, God expects (and rewards) an attitude of servant-like humility in His followers.
YOUR DAILY WALK

DAVID JEREMIAH | 353

December 3

NIP AND TUCK

A man's wisdom makes his face shine, and
the sternness of his face is changed.

ECCLESIASTES 8:1

Television's *Nip/Tuck* program about cosmetic surgery is on to
something. Americans spent more than twelve billion dollars in
2013 on cosmetic procedures, and that number is rising. The most
common surgical option was liposuction, with 403,000 procedures
performed. Botox was the most common nonsurgical remedy, performed on 3.1 million people.

Think what you will about cosmetic surgery, the simplest way to
improve your appearance is to smile. The Bible has much to say about
the appearance of the human face. Solomon writes in Ecclesiastes 8:1
that a person's wisdom makes his face shine, and in Proverbs 15:13,
he says that "a merry heart makes a cheerful countenance."

Improving inward character should take priority over outward
appearance so that when people look at us, they see the real us instead
of a facade. That kind of beauty can't be bought for twelve billion
dollars. It's priceless.

A smile is a curve that sets a lot of things straight.

ANONYMOUS

December 4

UNCONDITIONAL LOVE

> Husbands, love your wives, just as Christ also
> loved the church and gave Himself for her.
>
> EPHESIANS 5:25

Counselors of all persuasions agree that nothing can drive a wedge between married couples faster than connecting love to performance, especially when husbands communicate to their wives, "Perform or else." "Keep a perfect house, raise great kids, support my career, and provide meaningful intimacy—and do it happily—and I'll love you," says the husband who treats his marriage like a business deal.

The Bible puts Christ in the place of the husband and the church in the place of the wife and says husbands should love their wives as Christ loves the church. That means husbands are to love their wives unconditionally—no strings attached. God's kind of love is unconditional, and it is His complete love that makes us feel accepted and embraced by Him. With conditions comes failure, with failure comes separation, and with separation comes loneliness. Wives who are lonely in their marriages today are most likely married to husbands who practice conditional love.

Husband, if you need a model for how to love your wife, study the way Jesus Christ loves you.

---

*Every Christian family ought to be, as it were, a
little church, consecrated to Christ, and wholly
influenced and governed by his rules.*

JONATHAN EDWARDS

NEVER SURRENDER

Why are you cast down, O my soul? And why are you
disquieted within me? Hope in God; for I shall yet praise
Him, the help of my countenance and my God.

PSALM 42:11

Christian theologian Richard John Neuhaus was being driven from the airport to a speaking engagement. During the drive, one of his hosts went on and on about the disintegration of the American social fabric and the disappearance of Christian values and virtues from the culture. After what was a tedious drive listening to the man talk, Neuhaus finally was able to offer this response: "The times may be bad, but they are the only times we are given. Remember, hope is still a Christian virtue, and despair is a mortal sin."

It may be true that Christian values and virtues are disappearing, but there is one virtue that should remain as long as a single Christian survives: the virtue of hope. Regardless of how bleak the circumstances are, hope can continue. Hope cannot be taken from the Christian—it can only be surrendered. And as long as God exists, there is reason for the Christian to hope. After all, it is God who is in charge of the present and the future, not society or culture.

Whether your concerns are cultural or personal, as long as you refuse to surrender your hope in God, you will live to praise Him another day.

What oxygen is to the lungs, such is
hope for the meaning of life.
EMIL BRUNNER

December 6

THE BEST PLACE TO BE

*Peace I leave with you, My peace I give to you; not
as the world gives do I give to you. Let not your
heart be troubled, neither let it be afraid.*

JOHN 14:27

A quick survey of Internet dating sites—as well as brick-and-mortar "speed dating" businesses in major cities—would lead one to think being single is a disease that needs to be cured. First there were websites devoted to matching up singles—and they took the Internet by storm, quickly becoming the most popular new category of websites. But now dating websites are specializing into sub-sites that help singles find each other more quickly on the basis of religion, age, location, and most recently, lifestyle preferences such as cooking and fine foods.

But that's a sign of the times, not a sign of what's right. In God's eyes, singleness is a season of life like any other—no better and no worse. By activating their singleness for the Lord, singles are able to experience the joy of service. They are able to live with peace and thanksgiving, not in a state of anxiety. If you are single, be thankful for the time and ability you have to walk uninterrupted with Christ (1 Corinthians 7:33-34).

It has been well said that the best place in the world to be is the place to which God has led you today.

---

*Next to faith this is the highest art—to be content
with the calling in which God has placed you.*

MARTIN LUTHER

THE PRECIPICE

Great is Your mercy toward me, and You have
delivered my soul from the depths of Sheol.

PSALM 86:13

Eminent geologist Professor Louis Agassiz used to conduct research by being lowered over a precipice in a basket. The men who lowered him would weigh the professor before every trip to make sure they had the strength to bring him back up. One day, however, they lowered him farther than he had ever gone before, until all the rope was let out. When it came time to pull him up, the men were unable to do so because they had failed to account for the length and weight of the rope itself. The professor had to wait on the precipice until additional help arrived.

Every time we refuse to submit to God, we lower ourselves further and further over the precipice of sin and rebellion, and it becomes more and more difficult to climb back up. Fortunately, the rope of God's mercy is long enough to reach us even in our deepest sin.

If you have bought into the lie that by submitting to God you will miss out on life, understand this: true blessing comes from total submission to the one and only person who desires to bless you beyond measure. Like the father waiting with open arms to receive his long-lost son, your heavenly Father waits for you with arms full of grace and a life full of blessing.

*The degree of blessing enjoyed by any man will correspond
exactly with the completeness of God's victory over him.*

A. W. TOZER

BAG OF CEMENT

Today, if you will hear His voice, do not harden your hearts.

HEBREWS 3:7-8

A man was driving down a bumpy country road when he spotted a bag of cement that had apparently fallen out of the back of a truck. Not wishing to see a perfectly good bag of cement go to waste, he stopped to pick it up, believing he could get some use out of it. But when he reached down to pick up the bag, it was surprisingly heavier than he expected, due to the fact that it had solidified into an immovable piece of concrete. The bag of cement was created for a specific purpose, but because it never reached its intended destination, it became a useless rock.

Just like that bag of cement, many people appear to be usable on the outside, but when God tries to draw near to them, they have hardened their hearts to His love and purpose.

Fortunately for us, it is never too late to listen to the voice of God. If you have made no room in your life for almighty God and you wish to have a relationship with Him, pray and ask Him to soften your heart through His saving grace. You will then become a person with a purpose and a destination.

Of all the pursuits open to men, the search for wisdom is most perfect, more sublime, more profitable, and more full of joy.

THOMAS AQUINAS

PRAISE AND HOPE

> I will hope continually, and will praise You yet more and more.
>
> PSALM 71:14

See if you can find one Christian, just one, who is filled with praise for the Lord—but is hopeless. Or see if you can find one who is hopeful about the present and future but never praises the Lord. Hope and praise seem to go together in the Christian life—and why shouldn't they? For the Christian, to have hope is consistent with having faith in a gracious God, meaning He is worthy of praise. One flows naturally from the other.

The psalmist combines these two elements when he finds himself in the hand of "the wicked . . . the unrighteous and cruel man" (Psalm 71:4). In spite of his dire situation, he says he will continue to hope and will praise the Lord "more and more" (71:14). The more the psalmist hopes, the more he praises; and the more he praises, the more he hopes! It is a self-perpetuating cycle, with each virtue stimulating the other. What about you? If you find yourself hopeful but lacking praise, check the object of your hope. If you're praising but lacking hope, check the object of your praise.

Praise keeps hope alive while hope becomes a reason for praise.

Be not afraid of saying too much in the praises of God. . . . All the danger is of saying too little.

MATTHEW HENRY

GOD WILL APPEAR

Nebuchadnezzar spoke, saying, "Blessed be the God of
Shadrach, Meshach, and Abed-Nego, who sent His angel
and delivered His servants who trusted in Him."

DANIEL 3:28

How would you have felt if you were Peter? King Herod had begun a persecution of the church in Jerusalem, highlighting it with the murder of the apostle James, the brother of John. When he saw that this pleased the Jewish leaders, he seized Peter also and put him in jail. If you had been Peter, wouldn't you have thought that Herod planned to murder you as well? How alone would you have felt?

The church prayed diligently that night for Peter. He was chained to two Roman soldiers, and there were guards at the doors of the jail. Talk about lonely—bound in chains through the night, with the prospect of meeting a sword in the morning! But suddenly the church's prayers were answered as an angel appeared to Peter and set him free. When Peter realized that God had appeared, he said, "Now I know for certain that the Lord . . . has delivered me" (Acts 12:11). You might never find yourself chained and condemned to die for Jesus. (Or you might.) But whatever your predicament, if you will wait, God will come to you with peace, protection, or a promise.

It is not a question of whether God will appear when you are in trouble, but how.

When Jesus is present, all is well, and nothing seems difficult.
THOMAS À KEMPIS

GOD LOVES NOBODIES

Behold, an angel of the Lord stood before [the shepherds], and the glory of the Lord shone around them, and they were greatly afraid.

LUKE 2:9

A gospel group called The Williams Brothers had a hit with their song "I'm Just a Nobody." It was about a down-and-out man who lived on the streets and spent his days telling people about Jesus. He was laughed at and harassed by passersby, but that didn't stop him. The chorus of the song was his life message: "I'm just a nobody trying to tell everybody about Somebody who can save anybody."

The shepherds in the fields outside Bethlehem might have felt the same way when the angels from heaven appeared to them: "Why did God choose us, a bunch of nobodies, to be the first to hear of the birth of the Messiah in Bethlehem?" They were just a bunch of nobodies who probably later told everybody about the Somebody in Bethlehem who could save anybody. Why did God reveal Himself to shepherds instead of to important royal officials? Perhaps to signal the kind of King who was coming into the world: gentle and humble, a Servant-Shepherd who came to tend to God's flock.

If you sometimes feel like a nobody, rejoice! God seems to gravitate to the nobodies of this world when He wants them to meet Somebody who can save everybody.

God uses men who are weak and feeble enough to lean on Him.

HUDSON TAYLOR

I WROTE IT!

[Jesus said,] "These things I have spoken to you, that My
joy may remain in you, and that your joy may be full."

JOHN 15:11

A pastor was on a hospital visit when a nurse told him about a particular patient who was in need of some encouragement. "She is very deformed and her body has been twisted since childhood. She really needs someone to try to cheer her up." The pastor agreed to visit her, and upon entering the room, he told her he had something for her—a happy, uplifting, encouraging book that had helped many people with depression. The woman examined the book and responded, "I really ought not to take this book, sir." The pastor replied, "Why not? Have you already read it?" She said, "I have not only read it; I wrote it!"[13]

It is amazing to think that this woman, who was crippled from birth, knew and understood happiness so well that she was able to write a book on the subject. No matter what we know, however, discouragement can enter our hearts. We must choose to have definitive joy because of whom we follow.

If you find that you are living a joyless life, remember that you have a Savior who loves you, died for you, and is awaiting your arrival in heaven. That should surely fill your heart with inexpressible joy and gladness.

To be filled with God is to be filled with joy.

ANONYMOUS

[13] Nathan Johnson, "The Other Side of Sadness," www.sermoncentral.com.

CHANGE AGENTS

Because they do not change, therefore they do not fear God.

PSALM 55:19

We often grumble about change. We don't like the new songs at church, the new exits on the freeways, the new shows on television, or the new prices at Starbucks. President Woodrow Wilson once lamented, "If you want to make enemies, try to change something."

Some changes aren't for the better, but nothing improves without *some* change, and being flexible is the best way to keep from being bent out of shape. That said, the hardest change is the kind we determine to make in our own lives.

Let's suppose we could look at ourselves from the outside. Pretend you were a total stranger and you spent a day with yourself, objectively observing *you*. What changes would the "objective you" suggest to the "real you"?

Every once in a while, we have to take a look at ourselves and say, "I'm not going to live like this anymore. I'm going to change."

We can be our own change agents as we find areas of life needing improvement and start on them at once.

Without realizing it, you try to improve yourself at the start of each new day; of course, you achieve quite a lot in the course of time. Anyone can do this; it costs nothing and is certainly very helpful.

ANNE FRANK

FRIEND IN DEED

The Scripture was fulfilled which says, "Abraham
believed God, and it was accounted to him for
righteousness." And he was called the friend of God.

JAMES 2:23

Everyone has a circle of friends that gets more intimate as the circle gets smaller. Jesus had 120 in His largest circle after His ascension (Acts 1:15). Then there were seventy-two who were trained disciples (Luke 10:1), and then twelve who were with Him for the three years of His ministry (Matthew 10:1-4). Within that group were His three closest friends, Peter, James, and John (Mark 9:2), among whom John seems to have been the closest (John 13:23; 20:2).

In John 15:14, Jesus drew the lines of friendship a different way: anyone who keeps His commandments can be considered His friend. By "friend" Jesus meant someone with whom He would communicate and co-labor, someone He could trust to carry out His will when He left earth and returned to heaven. The question for today's believer is, Am I the kind of disciple that Jesus would see as a friend? Am I committed to obeying His commands? Can He count on me to fulfill His mission in His absence?

Those who would be friends of Jesus may have to forsake some earthly friends. It's one thing to be the friend of man, another to be the friend of God.

---

*The golden rule for understanding in spiritual
matters is not intellect, but obedience.*

OSWALD CHAMBERS

December 15

ANGRY PRAYERS

> Righteous are You, O LORD, when I plead with You;
> yet let me talk with You about Your judgments.

JEREMIAH 12:1

There are a lot of books on the subject of prayer, but few contain chapters on "angry prayers." The greatest book on prayer, however, is the Bible, and it records some angry prayers—when perplexed souls, confused by life, complained to God. The writer of Psalm 44:23-24, for example, writes, "Wake up, O Lord! Why do you sleep? . . . Why do you look the other way?" (NLT).

In Jeremiah 12, the "weeping prophet" complains to the Lord, saying, in effect, "Lord, I know You are righteous, but I don't understand why You're allowing these heartbreaks."

While we mustn't harbor bitterness toward God—after all, He is righteous, and He does do all things well—it is all right to express our frustrations and questions to Him. Even Jesus cried, "My God, My God, why . . . ?" (Matthew 27:46).

God knows all about us, and He's concerned about the details of our situations. We should never fear telling Him anything. It's by expressing our innermost feelings that we come to the point of confessing our sins and understanding His perspective, which heals our minds.

So be honest in prayer, even when you're angry. Tell Him all about it, and you'll find His grace is sufficient.

In spiritual work everything depends upon prayer.

ANDREW MURRAY

ALL THESE PEOPLE

The burden is too heavy for me.

NUMBERS 11:14

The pressures and problems bore down on Moses like burdens on a camel's back. The last straw came when the children of Israel grumbled and whined about their menu in the wilderness. Moses couldn't stand it any longer: "Moses said to the LORD, 'Why have You . . . laid the burden of all these people on me? Did I conceive all these people? . . . Where am I to get meat to give to all these people? . . . I am not able to bear all these people alone, because the burden is too heavy for me'" (Numbers 11:11-14).

For us, the problem may not be "all these people" but "all these problems," or "all this pain," or "all these pressures." We feel like the patriarch Jacob, who said, "All these things are against me" (Genesis 42:36). But the Bible says that all these things work together for good to those who love the Lord (Romans 8:28), and Romans 8:37 says, "In all these things we are more than conquerors through Him who loved us."

Like a camel with a heavy burden, we sometimes need to kneel in the desert place and let the Lord take care of things, down to the last straw.

Every time a Christian goes through the Valley of Trouble, there is always a door of hope.

HEART VS. HAND

> When [the Magi] had come into the house . . . they
> presented gifts to Him: gold, frankincense, and myrrh.
>
> MATTHEW 2:11

Frankincense was a clear, yellowish resin obtained from certain trees that grew in northern India and Arabia, treasured for its aroma and healing properties (Exodus 30:34). Myrrh was a spice valued as a medicine and cosmetic (Psalm 45:8; Mark 15:23). And gold was . . . well, it was gold, the most valuable commodity in human history. These were the three gifts presented by the magi to the baby Jesus in Bethlehem.

The magi's gifts were valuable indeed. But the impression given by Scripture is that the magi could afford the gifts they brought. They were scholars, perhaps astronomers, likely in the upper echelons of their own society. It would be a mistake to assume that only gifts of extreme value are appropriate to give to God. To the contrary, the Bible commends those who give out of their poverty—like the poor widow who gave two small coins, "her whole livelihood" (Mark 12:44), and the Corinthians who gave out of their "deep poverty" (2 Corinthians 8:2). It is not the size of the gift, but the size of the heart that matters most.

The next time you give to God, look first at what's in your heart before counting what's in your hand.

Give from the bottom of your heart, not the top of your purse.

UNKNOWN

SONGS OF THE SEASON

> Praise the LORD! For it is good to sing praises to our
> God; for it is pleasant, and praise is beautiful.
>
> PSALM 147:1

If anything characterizes the Christmas season, it is music—especially George Frideric Handel's *Messiah*. But in addition to formal choral presentations, there are the traditional Christmas hymns sung by choirs in churches and by carolers in neighborhoods.

How did Christmas become the season of glorious songs? Besides the fact that music is woven into the fabric of the Old Testament, beginning with the song of celebration following the Exodus from Egypt (Exodus 15), the first Christmas was marked by psalm singing and songs. Mary sang what is now called the Magnificat when she visited Elizabeth (Luke 1:46-56), and Zechariah lifted his voice in praise when John the Baptist was born (Luke 1:67-79). And when Jesus' parents presented him in the Temple, Simeon spoke a song of praise (Luke 2:29-32). Then there were the glorious words the angels declared to the shepherds (Luke 2:13-14).

This Christmas season, don't fail to lift your voice in song as you praise God for the indescribable gift of His Son, Jesus Christ.

---

*My ready tongue makes haste to sing the
glories of my heavenly King.*

CHARLES WESLEY

AS GOOD AS DONE

Before the mountains were brought forth, or ever
You had formed the earth and the world, even
from everlasting to everlasting, You are God.

PSALM 90:2

If you stretched a 2,700-mile-long piece of string from the East Coast to the West Coast, that would represent eternity. Then if you went to Kansas and put a pencil dot on the midpoint of the string, that would represent time as we know it on earth. Then if you went up in the space shuttle and looked down on the string with the little dot in the middle, you'd see time relative to eternity—the way God sees everything at once.

Our little pencil dot is small compared to the "everlasting to everlasting" that God sees, yet it's still significant to Him. But because He sees our dots all at once, He sees past, present, and future at the same time. So when God moved the prophets in the Old Testament to tell of the coming Messiah to be born in Bethlehem, the prophets had to wait for it to happen. But God saw the prophecy and its fulfillment all at once. Prophecy is important because it represents a completed event in God's sight. Jesus was born in time, but God saw it in eternity.

Don't ever doubt God's promises and prophecies. Once spoken, they're as good as done.

---

*Bethlehem and Golgotha, the Manger and the Cross, the
birth and the death, must always be seen together.*

J. SIDLOW BAXTER

GOD WITH US

Behold, the virgin shall conceive and bear a
Son, and shall call His name Immanuel.

ISAIAH 7:14

"I mmanuel" consists of two Hebrew words: *im* (the preposition *with* coupled with the plural *us*, yielding *immanu*), and *'el* (God). *Immanu* + *'el* = "God with us." Perhaps more than any other word in the Bible, *Immanuel* represents the essence of both the Christian and the Christmas message: God has invaded the domain of man and dwelt among us.

Immanuel was prophesied by Isaiah, and the Gospel writer Matthew declares Jesus of Nazareth to be the fulfillment of that prophecy (Matthew 1:22-23). The apostle John best captures the meaning of Immanuel in John 1:14: "The Word became flesh and dwelt among us, and we beheld His glory." Sadly, many who celebrate Christmas today have never understood the central point of the season: God with us. God entered the human race in the person of a baby who was the God-Man, Jesus Christ, Savior of the world. To fail to recognize Immanuel at Christmas is to miss the reason for the season.

Many who acknowledge "God with us" have never said, "God with me." Don't let this Christmas pass without making sure God is with you in the person of Jesus Christ in your heart.

―――――⸎―――――

There is a fountain filled with blood drawn from
Emmanuel's veins; and sinners plunged beneath
that flood lose all their guilty stains.

WILLIAM COWPER

AWKWARD GIFTS

> Every good gift and every perfect gift is from above,
> and comes down from the Father of lights.
>
> JAMES 1:17

The *Wall Street Journal* once ran an article on the awkwardness of exchanging gifts in the office or among business associates. "As if it's not hard enough to buy gifts for the family," said the paper, "consider having to get a colleague something that doesn't break the bank but seems thoughtful at the same time." The newspaper described one boss who gave his secretary a beautiful set of candles he found packed away in his home closet. Unfortunately, it was the same set she had given him the Christmas before, and the hurt feelings haven't quite healed yet.

God's gifts are never awkward, inappropriate, or thoughtless. He puts infinite care into His blessings, and every gift is good and perfect. John 1:16 says that from the fullness of His grace, we have all received one blessing after another. Psalm 68:19 says, "Blessed be the Lord, who daily loads us with benefits."

God's greatest gift is Jesus Himself, and it's up to us to receive or decline this blessing. As we give and receive gifts this Christmas, the theme of our hearts should be, "Thanks be to God for His indescribable gift!" (2 Corinthians 9:15).

What more could He give? God gave His all—He
gave Himself. Who can measure this love?

CHARLES HADDON SPURGEON

EMPTY THE CANTEEN

As it is written, "The just shall live by faith."

ROMANS 1:17

A man lost in the desert was near death for lack of water when he came upon a pump with a canteen hung on the handle along with a note. The note said, "Below you is all the fresh water you could ever need, and the canteen contains exactly enough water to prime the pump."

For a lot of us, it would be difficult to believe the note and empty the entire contents of the canteen for the promise of unlimited water. Such an act would require tremendous faith.

The Bethlehem shepherds exhibited this kind of faith when they were told of the birth of Jesus. If they had not trusted God's guidance to the manger, they might have missed the opportunity to meet and worship the Savior of the world!

Thankfully, when we are asked by God to step out in faith, we are not putting our trust in a note that may or may not be trustworthy. Instead, we are following the directives of the Lord, who "is a shield to all who trust in Him" (2 Samuel 22:31).

The next time God asks you to trust Him, remember the shepherds, for theirs is an amazing example of how we should exercise our faith.

You cannot see faith, but you can see the footprints of the faithful. We must leave behind "faithful footprints" for others to follow.

DENNIS ANDERSON

ORDINARY ENOUGH TO BE USED

> Behold, there was a man in Jerusalem whose name was
> Simeon, and this man was just and devout, waiting for the
> Consolation of Israel, and the Holy Spirit was upon him.
>
> LUKE 2:25

Among the wondrous lessons of the Christmas story is this one: we don't have to be famous, great, wealthy, talented, experienced, or extroverted to serve the Lord. The "stars" of the Nativity story are unknowns—a young working-class couple from Nazareth, an unknown resident of Bethlehem who loaned them a cave, a handful of smelly shepherds, a devout fellow named Simeon, and an aged widow named Anna.

They were ordinary enough to be used by God.

When we are reminded of this, it helps us overcome our fears of being unqualified to serve the Lord. It isn't highly trained specialists the Lord needs most, but devout people who, like Simeon, are faithful to the house of the Lord and who wait for God to work. Remember what Paul said: Not many great people are chosen. Not many wise or noble or famous (1 Corinthians 1:26-29). It is simple, humble, ordinary people that God uses most often so that the glory will be His alone.

Let's all be sons of Simeon—just and devout, touched by the Holy Spirit, and available at a moment's notice.

Too many are missionaries by proxy but not in
person. God's program begins where we live.
VANCE HAVNER

> By this we know that we know Him, if
> we keep His commandments.
>
> 1 JOHN 2:3

A time-honored saying warns us that "a chain is only as strong as its weakest link." There were more than six hundred legal links in the chain of the Old Testament law—so many that no one could keep them all. It took the sacrifice of an innocent animal to remove the guilt of those who failed to keep the law. The apostle James clarified in the New Testament what was implied in the Old: breaking even one of God's laws made a person guilty of breaking them all.

The yoke of the law weighed heavily on the minds of the Jews. Besides the laws given through Moses, the religious leaders added hundreds more traditions that made the yoke even heavier and harder to bear (Mark 7:1-5). But when Jesus came, He announced a different kind of yoke, one that is "easy and . . . light" (Matthew 11:30). It is not a yoke free from law, but a yoke that is easy to bear because we are given the Holy Spirit to help us glorify God and are offered forgiveness when we don't. Christmas is a time to celebrate the fact that Christ has come to show us how to keep God's laws.

The weakest link for us is our sinful human nature. But when we accept the Christ of Christmas, we are given His nature—a nature that wants to keep God's law.

When the law of God is written in our
hearts, our duty will be our delight.
MATTHEW HENRY

LASTING MEANING

Glory to God in the highest, and on earth
peace, goodwill toward men!

LUKE 2:14

A man by the name of A. F. Wells once stated, "Take Christ out of Christmas, and December becomes the bleakest and most colourless month of the year."

If you have ever celebrated Christmas without understanding its true meaning, that statement probably rings eerily true. Many people go through the motions of the holidays—buying gifts, baking cookies, and sending Christmas cards—but after it is all said and done, they are left with a longing in their hearts, a vast emptiness that was not filled by all the merriment of the season. December becomes a month in which credit cards and stress levels are maxed out. And though precious memories are made on Christmas morning, there is no lasting meaning for the celebration.

For Christians, however, Christmas is a time to celebrate and rejoice that Jesus came down in the form of a baby and brought salvation to an undeserving world. Today, focus your thoughts on the only true and lasting meaning of Christmas, that Christ came down from heaven to bring us gifts that remain even after the day is over: hope, peace, and love.

The birth of Jesus—Saviour, Messiah, Lord—
translates all that is shabby, despairing, and
dying into newness, joy, and life.
JENNIE C. OLBRYCH

> Nor is there salvation in any other, for there is no other name
> under heaven given among men by which we must be saved.
>
> ACTS 4:12

Christian leaders who appear on secular television talk shows are often asked whether they believe Jesus is the only way to heaven. If the answer is "Yes, Jesus is the only way," the interviewer often paints the Christian as intolerant, arrogant, narrow-minded, out-of-date, and fanatical.

But if the interviewer were talking to a physician who had made a medical breakthrough for a terrible disease, would he say, "Doctor, how intolerant to think this is the only cure for this disease"?

If he were talking to a mathematician about the multiplication table, would he say, "Professor, how can you be so arrogant as to believe that three times three always equals nine"?

By its very nature, truth is narrow, precise, and factual. Jesus said, "I am the way, the truth, and the life. No one comes to the Father except through Me" (John 14:6). In this day of pluralism and political correctness, it's important to know that Christ is still the only One who can save from sin. Do you think God would have given His own Son had there been some other way?

Trust in Christ alone, and trust Him today.

God help us if we preach anything else but
Jesus and Him alone for salvation.

PAIGE PATTERSON

A PROMISE A DAY

> You are God, and Your words are true, and You
> have promised . . . goodness to Your servant.
>
> 2 SAMUEL 7:28

As we shift gears for a new year, remember that God has a promise for every day, a reassurance for every crisis, and grace for every need. You can take the year one day at a time—and one promise at a time—praying for God's direction as you face the opportunities and challenges of the next twelve months.

E. M. Bounds writes, "Prayer is based directly and specifically upon God's revealed promises in Christ Jesus. It has no other ground upon which to base its plea. . . . Prayer goes by faith into the great fruit orchard of God's exceeding great and precious promises, and with hand and heart picks the ripest and richest fruit."

It's impossible to determine the specific number of promises in the Bible because they're scattered throughout Scripture in so many phrases and forms that it's often hard to say whether a verse is a command, a truth, a promise, or a prayer. It's like a vault full of precious jewels. But wherever we find them in the Bible, they are precious and true. A promise a day keeps the devil at bay. Get a jump on the New Year by committing yourself to a promise-anchored year.

Promises are God's golden fruit to be
plucked by the hand of prayer.

E. M. BOUNDS

ALL WE LIKE LIZARDS

Do not stray.

It isn't often that Canadians worry about crocodiles, but one summer, panic struck in Vancouver when reports surfaced of a crocodile on the loose. The reptile was finally captured and taken to an animal shelter. As it turned out, it wasn't a crocodile at all, but a large lizard named Turtle who had wandered away from home. "He must have gone through the wooden gate," his owners told the newspaper.

There's a wandering instinct inside all of us. The Bible says, "All we like sheep have gone astray; we have turned, every one, to his own way" (Isaiah 53:6). Perhaps the hymnist was remembering this as he wrote, "Prone to wander, Lord, I feel it; prone to leave the God I love."

While the path away from Jesus may be aimless, the path back to Him is a straight line. There's always a way back to the Savior, no matter where we've strayed. The week between Christmas and New Year's Day affords a prime opportunity to correct unhealthy patterns in life, to make new resolutions for Him, and to get back on the "straight and narrow."

Let's say with the psalmist, "The wicked have laid a snare for me, yet I have not strayed from Your precepts" (Psalm 119:110).

There is nothing trivial in this life. By the neglect of slight commands, a soul may speedily get out of the sunlit circle and lose the gracious plentitude of Spirit-power.

F. B. MEYER

December 29

EBENEZER

> Samuel took a stone and set it up between Mizpah
> and Shen, and called its name Ebenezer, saying,
> "Thus far the LORD has helped us."
>
> 1 SAMUEL 7:12

Dr. F. W. Boreham told of a scrap of paper that was framed and displayed in his parents' home. The words on it said: "Hitherto Hath the Lord Helped Us." One day he asked his mother about it, and she told him of a time when she and her husband faced a crisis. She had been distressed for weeks, but one day as she paced back and forth, she paused in front of an almanac hanging from the wall.

"The only thing I saw was the text in the corner," she said. "It was as if someone had spoken the words: 'Hitherto has the Lord helped us.' I was so overcome, I sat down and had a good cry; and then I began again with a fresh heart and trust."

What a great verse for the New Year! The same God who brought us this far will lead us on. He is "our help in ages past, our hope for years to come." If we live in the light of eternity knowing our times are in His hands, we can face each day "with a fresh heart and trust."

Hitherto has the Lord helped us.

Here I raise mine Ebenezer; hither by Thy help I'm come.
ROBERT ROBINSON

December 30

SUFFICIENT FOR THE FUTURE

> [The Lord] said to me, "My grace is sufficient for you,
> for My strength is made perfect in weakness."
>
> 2 CORINTHIANS 12:9

It's hard for us to imagine the apostle Paul in a state of weakness, but a perusal of 2 Corinthians chapters 6 and 11 shows us that he suffered terribly as an apostle for the sake of Christ. The most unique experience with weakness that Paul had was one we can learn the most from because it was unnamed. It is the sustaining principle, not the specific problem, that is important.

Paul was made weak by some affliction, and it no doubt concerned him because of its likely impact on his future ministry. How could he serve if he was sidelined by a serious problem? But God said, "Trust Me, Paul. I know *the* future and *your* future. I will give you grace to do all you need to do." And He did. Paul became thankful for his weakness because it highlighted God's strength. Just as God knew Paul's future, so He knows yours. If you are worried about your future, perhaps this coming year—especially if you see limitations on your horizon—trust God. The same grace He gave to Paul, He will give to you.

Your future is not bigger than God, nor are your limitations larger than His grace. Your faith in Him means your future is with Him.

Trust the past to God's mercy, the present to God's love, and the future to God's providence.
ST. AUGUSTINE

December 31

ONE RESOLUTION

> Have I not commanded you? Be strong and of good
> courage; do not be afraid, nor be dismayed, for the
> LORD your God is with you wherever you go.
>
> JOSHUA 1:9

Today is the day when most people make up a list of New Year's resolutions—and splurge in anticipation of the rigors of the coming year. If the goal is to lose weight, they enjoy a final dessert. If the goal is to stop buying on credit, they make one final purchase using their plastic. And if the goal is to begin having a morning quiet time, they sleep in one last day.

Research shows that most New Year's resolutions are broken, in spite of our best intentions. Perhaps a better way to approach the New Year would be to have one goal: to be filled with the Holy Spirit (Ephesians 5:18). That means keeping short accounts when it comes to sin and listening for the Spirit's guidance and appropriating His strength every day. It is likely that after a year of walking with the Spirit, much more change will have occurred than by trying to keep the most noble of human resolutions. Begin the New Year with the objective to live a Spirit-filled life—and see what will be accomplished in and through your life in the coming year.

One goal achieved by the power of the Spirit would be better than a multitude of unfulfilled good intentions.

He who has the Holy Spirit in his heart and the
Scriptures in his hands has all he needs.
ALEXANDER MACLAREN

DR. DAVID JEREMIAH serves as senior pastor of Shadow Mountain Community Church in El Cajon, California. He is the founder and host of Turning Point, a ministry committed to providing Christians with sound Bible teaching relevant to today's changing times through radio and television, the Internet, live events, and resource materials and books. A bestselling author, Dr. Jeremiah has written more than forty books, including *Captured by Grace, Living with Confidence in a Chaotic World, What in the World Is Going On?, The Coming Economic Armageddon, God Loves You: He Always Has—He Always Will,* and *What Are You Afraid Of?*

Dr. Jeremiah's commitment to teaching the complete Word of God continues to make him a sought-after speaker and writer. His passion for reaching the lost and encouraging believers in their faith is demonstrated through his faithful communication of biblical truths.

A dedicated family man, Dr. Jeremiah and his wife, Donna, have four grown children and eleven grandchildren.